Indian Social Structure and Change

Indian Social Structure and Change

K.L. Sharma

RAWAT PUBLICATIONS

Jaipur • New Delhi • Bangalore • Guwahati • Kolkata

ISBN 978-81-316-0083-2 (Hardback)

Reprinted, 2023

Published by
Prem Rawat for **Rawat Publications**
Satyam Apts., Sector 3, Jawahar Nagar, Jaipur 302 004 (India)
Phone: 0141 265 1748 / 265 1748
E-mail: info@rawatbooks.com
Website: www.rawatbooks.com

New Delhi Office
4858/24, Ansari Road, Daryaganj, New Delhi 110 002
Phone: 011-23263290

Also at *Bangalore*, *Guwahati* and *Kolkata*

Typeset by Rawat Computers, Jaipur

Printed Nice Printing Press, New Delhi

For my daughter *Rachna*,
son-in-law *Bhanu*, and
granddaughter *Annika*

Contents

Preface

Indian society is not simply a conglomeration of various ethnic, religious, linguistic, caste and regional collectivities. It is also quite complex in terms of differentiation in each one of the collectivities and their historical and socio-cultural specificities. A discussion on the patterns of unity and diversity focuses on continuity and change as well in the Indian society. Indian society is a panorama, to a large extent a unique one, which has absorbed diverse languages, cultures, religions and people of different social origins at different points of time in the past. These diversities are specific in patterns of life, styles of living, land tenure systems, occupational pursuits, inheritance and succession rules and *rites de passage*. The British rule in India accentuated some of these socio-cultural and economic differences. The idea of unity is inherent today in Indian Constitution which pronounces values of secularism, socialism and democracy as its main ideals.

Hierarchy and inequality are deeply rooted in India's tradition, and are also found in practice in the form of the inequally placed caste and class groups. These have resulted into persistence and equilibrium because of the organic linkages and interdependence of different socio-economic groups. However, Indian society witnessed change due to foreign invasions, migration, natural calamities, struggle for power, and policies of the Mughal and the British empires. Changes in the post-independent era have occurred mainly due to the Five-Year Plans and developmental schemes in the fields of industry and agriculture. Expansion of higher education has been on an enormous scale. Some of the educated people have been benefited, but some have found it difficult to get suitable employment. Recent revolutionary changes in the fields of technology and communication have opened up new channels of employment and mobility for the urban educated young men and women in particular.

New forms of social and economic disparities have emerged in the post-independent India due to lack of 'distributive justice'. The developmental programmes have helped the traditionally better off more than those who were downtrodden and who genuinely needed social and economic betterment. However, the Scheduled Castes, the Scheduled Tribes and the other weaker sections of society have been benefited a lot in the fields of education and employment. They are today socially more awakened than what they were before independence, but the more needy and the deserving have been much less benefited than the better off from among their ranks.

The effort in this book is to provide a comprehensive and analytical view of the Indian society and social change to the students at the apex level of schooling and at the level of undergraduate studies.

The scheme of chapters is indicative of the comprehensive coverage. It also speaks of our emphasis on the analysis of social structure, processes of social change and social problems. Though we have analysed the contemporary Indian social situation, yet our effort is to see it in terms of its historicity, particularly in the context of the caste system, weaker sections, women and social change. The book is a revised and edited version of my earlier book *Indian Society*, written for the NCERT, New Delhi, in 1987.

K.L. Sharma

Acknowledgements

Innumerable colleagues, friends and students have contributed to the initial shaping of this book and to its subsequent revisions and improvements. I wish to thank them all, particularly Prof. Dinesh Kumar Sharma and Prof. Manju Bhatt of the NCERT for their constant support and help. Prof. Dinesh Sharma was the main support in the first print of the book in 1987. In subsequent prints, Prof. Manju Bhatt was equally involved in organisation of discussions and workshops for improvements of the book. To several teachers from Delhi who actively participated in the discussions, I express my thanks to them. The late Prof. S.C. Dube and the late Prof. S.K. Lal guided workshops held at Srinagar and Jodhpur, respectively. At Udaipur, Prof. S.L. Doshi and his colleagues rendered valuable comments and suggestions. Prof. Yogendra Singh has always been available to offer advice and suggestions on relevance of such a text. I am sincerely grateful to all of them.

In updating of data on SCs, STs, OBCs, minorities, populations, crime, etc., I have received help from Prof. (Mrs.) Sudesh Nangia, Prof P.M. Kulkarni and Prof. Sachidanand Sinha of JNU, and I gratefully acknowledge the same for sparing their valuable time. The comfort of staying with my daughter Rachna and her husband Bhanu in the USA made it possible for me to revise the last reprint. I wish to record their affection and concern during my stay with them in 2006. Lastly, I am grateful to Mr. Kailash Rawat, proprietor of Rawat Publications, for showing keen interest in republication of the book.

1 Indian Society: Unity and Diversity

India is a plural society both in letter and spirit. It is rightly characterised by its unity and diversity. A grand synthesis of cultures, religions and languages of the people belonging to different castes and communities has upheld its unity and cohesiveness despite foreign invasions, and the Mughal and the British rule. National unity and integrity have been maintained even though sharp economic and social inequalities have obstructed the emergence of egalitarian social relations. It is this synthesis that has made India a unique mosaic of cultures. India fought against the British Raj as one unified entity. India is, in fact, a panorama of its own type, without a parallel in other continents. Foreign invasions, immigration from other parts of the world, and the existence of diverse languages, cultures and religions have made India's culture tolerant, on the one hand, and a unique continuing and living culture, with its specificity and historicity, on the other.

Hinduism, Jainism, Buddhism, Islam, Sikhism and Christianity are the major religions. There are 22 national languages, besides several hundred dialects. There is diversity not only in regard to racial compositions, religious and linguistic distinctions, but also in patterns of living, lifestyles, land tenure systems, occupational pursuits, inheritance and succession law, and practices and rites related to birth, marriage, death, etc.

Post-independence India is a nation united against several odds and obstacles. The idea of unity of India is inherent in all its historical and socio-cultural facts as well as in its cultural heritage. India is a secular state. It has one Constitution providing guarantees for people belonging to diverse regions, religions, cultures and languages. The country is inhabited by people belonging to all socio-economic strata. The Five-Year Plans and several other developmental schemes are geared to the upliftment of the poor and weaker sections of society.

Topography and Environment

The name 'India' is derived from 'Sindhu' (Indus) – the great river in the North-West. In traditional and legendary Hindu literature, India is called Bharatakhanda; and sometimes, it is also called Jambudvipa, one of the seven concentric legendary islands comprising the earth. India is a vast country which extends upto 3,200 km from south to north and 3,000 km from east to west. The entire area spans over 3.3 million sq. km. Its coastline extends for 7,600 km. In spite of its diverse geographical features India looks like a single natural geographical entity. Geographical unity of India is reinforced by religious centres spread all over the country. The Hindus, Muslims, Sikhs, Christians and people of other faiths with their respective places of worship are spread all over the country and they live together and greet each other on festivals, etc. They also participate together in political activities. The political unity of India has been maintained by a uniform administrative and constitutional set-up and law of the land.

N.K. Bose (1967), a renowned social anthropologist, has listed five geographical features which have had a direct or indirect bearing upon the history and civilization of India. These are: (i) the comparative isolation or protection afforded by the northern mountain ranges, (ii) the character of the two coasts of the peninsula, (iii) the tropical heat and rainfall, (iv) the character of the soil, and (v) the presence of extensive alluvial plains in the north, and of a plateau in the south.

The Himalayas and the Gangetic Plains

The Himalayas separate India from Sinkiang in the extreme south of China and from Tibet. The Himalayas are known as the abode of gods and sages. Mount Kailas and Mansarovar lake are considered the holiest of the pilgrimages for Hindus. The Ganga, the Sindhu and the Brahamputra originate from the Himalayas. The Himalayas have contributed to a large extent to the development of the Indo-Aryan civilization. The outer ranges of the Shivaliks, the first step upward from the plains, are significant for their geological wealth. Shimla and Darjeeling are two popular hill stations connecting the plains with the Himalayan mountains.

The Hindu Kush range consists of northern Afghanistan. This range has historical importance as the Aryans and Alexander entered India through this path. Several other groups including the Mongols also came to India through this way. Kashmir is famous for its scenic beauty. Kashmir was from early times an influential centre of Hindu culture; it was a home of Sanskrit scholars and poets; it helped in spreading Indian culture to central Asia and produced in Kalhana the only true Indian historian of antiquity. The Brahamputra valley is in the north-east. It has potential for the cultivation of tea, jute, rice and fruits. This part, surrounded by dense forests bordering Tibet and China, is inhabited by the sub-Himalayan tribes of the Daflas, Abhors, Moubas, Mushmis and others.

The Ganga plain, the central belt of hills and desert, and the peninsula are the main geographical and cultural parts of the subcontinent. At least five important battles were fought in this part of India. Delhi is in the south of this tract. In the basin of the Ganga have ever been founded the chief kingdoms of the plains, the most ancient cities, the earliest centres of Indo-Aryan civilisation, industry and wealth. The mighty river has flowed through the ages in an unceasing process of regeneration of the soil, spreading life and strength among the millions who venerate her as Mother Ganga and purify themselves in its sanctifying waters at the *tirthas* of Hardwar, Prayaga and Varanasi. The land in this basin is extraordinarily fertile with immense agricultural wealth. The Ganga, the Brahamputra and their tributaries have ensured fertility and wealth from the plains in the north up to the plains of West Bengal. The Yamuna, Chambal, Narmada and Son stretch across some parts of the central plains. The Mahanadi irrigates the fertile fields of Orissa. The Kaveri, Krishna, Godavari and Periyar flow through the southern states. All these rivers have contributed to agricultural prosperity.

The Aravalli Range

The Aravalli range is the oldest mountain range in western India. In the north-west, the Thar desert has protected the country from foreign infiltration. The Banas is the well-known river in this part of the state of Rajasthan. The famous salt lake of Sambhar is in the Jaipur district. Another range of mountains contains the Vindhyas, connecting the north with the south. A number of pre-Aryan tribes, with their distinct cultures and languages, have lived in this rugged mountainous range. The Narmada valley connects the Vindhyas on the north with the Satpura Mahadeo-Maikala range on the south. The Tapti flows parallel to the Narmada to the west and the Mahanadi to the Bay of Bengal in the east.

Peninsular India

Peninsular India consists of Kanyakumari, the Malabar and the Coromandel coasts. There are a few good, natural harbours along both coasts. Kochi, Goa and Mumbai are on the western side, offering safe anchorage for ships. Peninsular India developed and maintained a fairly brisk maritime trade with the rest of the world. Even the eastern lands, beyond the Bay of Bengal, were colonised by the rulers of the peninsula. Rulers such as the Satavahanas, Pallavas and Cholas maintained a strong navy.

Rocks, ranging from the Satmala-Ajanta ranges to the Nilgiris, are a special feature of this part of India. This is, in fact, a plateau bounded by the Western and the Eastern Ghats. The state of Karnataka lies on the Coromandel coast. Cotton, tea and coffee are produced in the Kerala-Karnataka region. The area has numerous elephants. The hill tribes – the Kadar, Muduvar and Pulayan – are found in this area.

Cotton is the main product of this fertile region. Mumbai to Agra and Mumbai to Pune are the two main road and rail links known as the Thalghat and the Bhorghat, respectively.

Important towns and cities have come up on the banks of rivers, on sea coasts and trade and pilgrim routes. This is true about the cities of Patna, Kolkata, Varanasi, Hardwar, Mumbai, Chennai, Surat, Bharuch, Allahabad, Pondicherry, Goa and many others. Trade and political factors contributed to the growth of the cities like Kolkata, Mumbai and Chennai.

Despite the variety of topographical and climatic features, India has remained a unified social formation. Peninsular India fostered cultural variety and variations among the communities who inhabited the area. The north, however, did not remain a closed and rigid social formation due to many external influences from the north-west.

SOCIO-CULTURAL UNITY AND DIVERSITY

Historicity of Unity in Diversity

The Indian cultural tradition is unique. The notions of *dharma* (normative order), *karma* (personal moral commitment) and *jati* (caste) as the hierarchical principles of social stratification are basic to Indian culture. A certain level of configuration of these elements and consensus have brought about persistence and equilibrium in Indian society, and hence no major breakdown has taken place in its culture. It is said that the change is *in* the cultural system and not *of* the system. In other words, basic cultural and social values and norms still continue with some modifications. The values of *dharma*, *karma* and *jati* continue to guide social and cultural activities to a large extent. Hence, change is *in* the system and not *of* the system. However, the contemporary India has witnessed basic structural changes in economic and political fields. The traditional value system has lost its ground to a considerable extent as the *jati* has acquired a new form, and it is no more an effective mechanism of division of labour and status determination.

The uniqueness of the Indian culture does not simply refer to its esoteric nature. It requires a thorough study in terms of its history. Absorption and assimilation characterised social and cultural change. Aryans and Dravidians lived together. Hindus and Muslims lived in close proximity – socially and culturally. Later on, Christians joined them. Today, Hindus, Jains, Muslims, Sikhs, Christians and people of other faiths participate together in the government, industry, commerce and other sectors of public life. Thus, there has been a continuous unity even in the situation of stark diversity. Diversity is reflected in thousands of caste groups, each having its own rituals, rites, rules and customs. It can be seen in terms of linguistic, religious and other ethnic variations. The styles of life differ from region to region and vary even between different castes and religious groups within the same village. Some rulers made conscious efforts to ensure unity in diversity.

The emperor Ashoka worked for the unity of India by achieving cultural and religious harmony and administrative efficiency. Akbar, one of the most powerful Mughal emperors, projected the concept of a state religion called *Din-e-Illahi*, a synthesis of Hinduism and Islam. The majority of Muslims in villages transformed their social life beyond recognition. They mingled with Hindus freely in almost all walks of life. The Hindu *rajas* and Muslim kings recognized literary and artistic abilities in individuals from both the communities. Kabir and Nanak were greatly influenced by the teachings of Islam. Conversion to Islam, and later on to Christianity, and today to Buddhism, has resulted in a 'mixed' culture. The Father of the Nation, Mahatma Gandhi, worked throughout his life to achieve national unity and integrity through communal harmony, upliftment of the poor and downtrodden and propagation of a just social order.

The colonial India has two histories. One is of colonialism produced by the colonisers, and the other is of India's culture and civilization perpetrated through its intellectual and philosophical fervour. India's history, its architectural treasures, its literature, philosophy, music, drama, dance, and its other fine arts, all contributed to its social life, and could not be destroyed by alien rule. It is this history which remained neglected during British Raj.

Mahatma Gandhi desired radical changes. However, he wished to associate such changes with India's tradition and cultural heritage. Jawaharlal Nehru, the architect of modern India, with a modern and secular outlook, upheld India's past with reverence and a sense of pride. He (1956) writes: "Yet the past is ever with us and all that we are and that we have come from the past. We are its products and we live immersed in it. Not to understand it and feel it as something living within us is not to understand the present. To combine it with the present and extend it to the future. to break from it where it cannot be so united, to make all this the pulsating and vibrating material for thought and action – that is life."

In another passage, Nehru highlights India's cultural heritage. He (ibid) writes: "The rising middle classes ... wanted some cultural roots to cling on to, something that gave them assurance of their own worth, something that would reduce the sense of frustration and humiliation that foreign conquest and rule had produced... The past of India, with all its cultural variety and greatness, was a common heritage of all the Indian people, Hindu, Moslem, Christian and others; and their ancestors had helped to build it." But Nehru never wanted the deadwood of the past to dominate the present. He was, in fact, a man with a democratic spirit and modern outlook.

Forces of Unity in Modern India

M.N. Srinivas (1952), a noted sociologist, writes: "The concept of unity is inherent in Hinduism. There are sacred centres of Hindu pilgrimage in every corner of the land. Certain salient aspects of Sanskritic culture are to be found all over the country. India is the sacred land not only of the Hindus but also of the Sikhs, Jains and Buddhists. The Muslims and Christians, too, have several sacred centres of pilgrimage in India. The institution of caste cuts across diverse religious groups and gives them all a common social idiom."

Srinivas further notes that India, as a secular state, tolerates diversity. The Five-Year Plans, the spread of egalitarian ideals, a single government and a common body of civil and criminal laws are enough evidence of India's plural character and oneness. However, one may not agree with Srinivas' observation regarding Hinduism in general and about the caste system, in particular. Orthodoxy of these two systems has, at times, endangered India's unity. The two have often been misused for suppression and exploitation of weaker sections of society, including women. Recently, the Noble laureate Amartya Sen, pleaded for a common civil code for all the communities, including Muslims.

The Constitution of independent India has established the 'rule of law' throughout the entire country. All citizens are equal and subject to the same authority. Birth-based privileges have been abolished. Religion, language, region, caste or community are no longer the basis of special powers and privileges. The weaker sections of society, the Scheduled Castes (SCs), the Scheduled Tribes (STs), and the Other Backward Classes (OBCs) have been given special concessions to bridge the gap between them and the upper castes and classes. Today, no caste or social group suffers from any kind of social disability. Women enjoy equal rights with men, in all respects. The policy of 'divide and rule', adopted by the British to rule this country, is no more in operation. Colonial exploitation has been replaced by processes of development and egalitarian ideology. However, despite constitutional and legal enactments, the weaker sections and women lag behind because of the deep-rooted entrenchment of the upper castes and patriarchy.

Factors of Disunity

Despite a rich cultural heritage, egalitarian policies and programmes, and the 'rule of law', narrow loyalties, parochial ties and primordial interests have also increased in the post-independence India. We find divisive forces in many parts of the country. India is a land of sharp contrasts having very rich, upper caste and class people on the one hand, and extremely poor, lower caste and class people on the other.

There are minority groups based on a variety of considerations such as religion, language, region, customs and traditions. Even, the so-called majority group, namely, the Hindus, are divided into several sects, castes, clans and linguistic groups. These groups have certain aspirations for their members in regard to better education, employment and a high standard of living. All members belonging to different castes and communities do not have equal chance or access, and hence they are denied 'distributive justice'. Such a situation of unequal opportunities in life, which itself is rooted into socially structured inequalities, aggravates tensions, mutual distrust and frustration.

The consciousness of unity and a feeling of Indianness are seriously hampered due to situations of hierarchy and inequality. Today, India is faced with this problem due to a lack of synchronisation between the form and contents of its social structure. There is an urgent need to reduce the hiatus between the ideal and the actual. National integration can be achieved by bridging up this gap, which is, in fact, between the strong and the weak, the rich and the poor, the educated and the uneducated, and between the upper caste and class and the lower caste and class people.

ETHNICITY

Defining Ethnicity

Literally speaking, the word 'ethnos' means nation, and the word 'ethnicity' is developed from it. However, ethnicity is not defined as nationhood. It is defined as a collectivity of people of a distinct nature in terms of race, descent and culture. Thus, an ethnic group is a social collectivity having certain shared historicity and common attributes, such as race, tribe, language, religion, dress, diet, etc. A combination of them in a group makes it an ethnic group, which is perceived as such by its members and by members of other groups. One may call this self-perception ethnic consciousness for status and for recognition as a distinct social entity. Ethnicity is not a static or pre-ordained category; it is a manifestation of the common economic, political, social and cultural interests and their protection by certain members in a plural society. Thus, ethnicity, at times, is used as an instrument of mobilisation for realising social, economic and political goals.

Ethnicity is a cultural phenomenon, and as such no culture is superior or inferior. Culture belongs to a people, and they endear it like any other people. E.B. Tylor defines culture as "that complex whole which includes knowledge, belief, art, morals, law, custom and any other capabilities and habits acquired by man as a member of society". Culture is the man-made part of the environment. Culture is social as it relates people in a variety of situations. Being a relational phenomenon, culture has instrumental significance. Therefore, all ethnic entities are cultural groupings, hence they enjoy the same position in terms of the normative orientations of different sets of people. The Constitution of India declares that India is a secular state in which distinctions and discriminations based on caste, creed, region, language, religion, etc., are not allowed. The people have been given 'fundamental rights', according to which, primordial or ascriptive considerations do not find any place in modern India.

Ethnicity and Culture

An ethnic group may think that it is a living being of a unique kind. Its members generally think in terms of a real or fictitious commonality based on common ancestory, cultural heritage, language, religion and even economic interests. Internally, all ethnic groups are stratified despite their claim of commonality in all respects. Ethnicity has also become a very sensitive aspect of India's social fabric because of ethnic cleavage, conflict, violence and hatred. Are ethnic groups classes? Are they the same groupings as of caste groups? A plural or multi-ethnic society like India would have an overlapping of ethnic, caste and class groupings. Contextuality of these groupings is important to distinguish among ethnicity, caste and class as three bases of social ranking and identification.

A given country consists of various communities; and facts about their origin and migration help understand the history of its civilization. The present population of India is over 1,000 million. More than 100 years ago, Sir Herbert Risley noted that there were 2,378 main castes among the Hindus in India. Certainly, this number must have reached over 3,000 by this time due to the processes of fission and social mobility. Marriage takes place in accordance with the rules of caste endogamy, clan exogamy and avoidance of relations on father's and mother's sides. Besides these caste groups, there are other communities, such as, Muslims, Christians, Sikhs, Parsis, Jains and many tribal groups, who limit marriage and social interaction to their own groups. However, inter-caste marriages are taking place, particularly among the educated urban middle and upper-middle class families. Resistance to such marriages is negligible due to weakening of the caste system.

Nature of Ethnic Conflict

At times, ethnic groups tend to operate as diametrically opposed groups due to clash of their real or supposed interests. Such a clash of interests may also take the form of communalism. Some groups may take undue advantage of their large numbers or of superior social origins to corner a major share of the national resources. The other communities with smaller populations may feel deprived of what they feel are their 'legitimate claims'. Situations of mutual distrust, disaffection and distance may arise between various ethnic groups. One perspective is that 'relative deprivation' is the root cause of all ethnic strife. The lack of distributive justice, differential accessibility to resources and cultural differences have been considered the main reasons of ethnic problems.

Sometimes ethnic conflict is due to the distinction made between 'outsiders' and 'insiders'. 'We' (insiders) against 'they' (outsiders) is an attitude found in all societies. Immigrants are treated as 'foreigners'. Such a problem arises when people speaking Assamese, Bengali, Gujarati, Oriya, Hindi, Kashmiri, Punjabi, Urdu, Marathi and Sindhi consider each other different in the national context. As such ethnic groups may be referred as 'primordial collectivities'. Members belonging to one state often consider members from other states as outsiders. They would not like them to seek employment in their state. Sub-regions, cities, towns and even villages are often used for drawing a line between the insiders and the outsiders. The question is: can we call it ethnicity? The answer is a clear no. India is a poly-ethnic society having distinctions based on race, caste, language, religion and territory.

RELIGION

Defining Religion

There are two types of values: (1) categorical or absolute values, and (2) instrumental values. The first refers to beliefs and practices relating to the supernatural powers. The second refers to norms and practices related to work, efficiency, productivity, etc. Religion falls in the first category of the value system. Religion may be defined as "beliefs and practices related to supernatural entities, spirits and powers, which are considered as ultimate in shaping human relations". Surjit Sinha refers to three components of the sociology of religion: (1) beliefs in supernatural entities, (2) specialists who create such beliefs, and (3) laity who receive these beliefs in various forms.

Religion has played an important part in Indian society from the earliest times. It has assumed numerous forms and nomenclatures in relation to different groups of people associated with it. India has been a poly-religious society. Transformations and changes in different religions have occurred from time to time vis-à-vis changes in intellectual climate and social structure. Religion in India has never been static. Today, it has made inroads into the arenas of politics and economic life. At times, affinity to religion is made an issue in elections; and in economic and business transactions.

Religious movements have been a perpetual feature of India's socio-cultural life. Pre-Vedic and Vedic religions, unorthodox religious currents led by Buddha and Mahavira, and theistic religions, including the element of Bhakti, characterize dynamics of religion in Indian society. Religious sects like Vaishnavism, Saivism and Saktism emerged as the components of orthodox Brahmanism. In addition to these ramifications of religion, several folk cults and religious practices were evolved by people in various parts of India.

Religious Communities and Diversity in India

According to the 1931 census, there were ten religious groups in India. These included: Hindus, Jains, Buddhists, Zoroastrians, Muslims, Sikhs, Christians, Jews, and other tribal and non-tribal religious groups. The census of 1961 listed only seven religious categories, namely, Hindus, Jains, Buddhists, Muslims, Christians, Sikhs and other religions and persuasions.

Religion is really a complex phenomenon in India. For example, elements of Sanskritic and tribal religion are found in a mixed form at various levels. So is the interaction between the 'great' and the 'little' traditions. Integration of Sanskritic Hindu religion and tribal religion is also found. The Santhals, for example, observe several high caste festivals. This is also the case with the lower and 'untouchable' castes. Some tribals worship Shiva. M.N. Srinivas (1952) writes: "Different tribes are Sanskritized in different degrees, and different sections of the same tribe may not be uniformly Sanskritized."

Conversion to Christianity and Islam has been a controversial issue over the past couple of decades. It is said that the members of the depressed classes and tribals have converted to Christianity, Islam and Sikhism in various parts of the country, particularly in the 1920s and also after independence. A good number of tribals have accepted Hindu rituals and religious practices in Bihar, Bengal, Assam and other areas. Thousands of Harijans have converted to Buddhism in Uttar Pradesh and Maharashtra. Induced or forced conversion is certainly against the spirit of the Constitution of India and the law of the land. There may be several factors responsible for change of religion. In recent years intense debate has occurred on religious conversions. One view is that the lower castes and communities are converting to Islam and Christianity because of the oppressive nature of Hinduism. Contrary to this is the view that conversions are being induced by the proponents of Islam and Christianity.

It has been reported that minority religions show a greater percentage of literacy than the majority religions. Parsis, Jains, Jews and Christians have shown this pattern. With the exception of Christians, these communities are also engaged in trade and business more than Hindus and Muslims. A study reveals that the Parsis, Jews and Jains are 'advanced' in business, though their activities are not diversified. Hindus and Muslims have a diversified occupational pattern because of their large numbers and spread all over the country. The minority groups are found in specific regions, sub-regions and cities, and therefore, they find themselves in an advantageous position. Syrian Christians, Moplas, Parsis and some other groups have been benefited because of their strategic locations in Kerala and Maharashtra.

Role of Religion in Social Integration

M.N. Srinivas (1952) examines the role of religion in social integration as a binding force amongst individuals and groups. However, it is more important to see how religion does this; how it functions. Karl Marx's dictum, "religion is the opiate of the masses", can be found true if religion becomes a tool of exploitation in the hands of a selected few who claim themselves its custodians and protectors. Srinivas, however, considers religious behaviour, as a part of social life. He refers to three points: (1) the relations between different castes and religious groups at the village and other local levels; (2) the role of religion in the economic development of the country; and (3) religion and socio-economic privileges. Religious ethic may be conducive to the development of capitalism as observed by Max Weber. Religion may be used as a solid so unifying force by white people in situations of crisis as explained by Emile Durkheim.

Multi-religious villages are not as conspicuous a phenomenon as multi-caste villages in India. However, in Uttar Pradesh, one can find Hindu tenants and Muslim landlords and vice versa. In a village in Karnataka, a few big Hindu landowners had Muslim tenants and servants, while Muslim landowners had Hindu servants. The Muslims were engaged in a variety of economic activities, as they did not own much land. The Hindus owned mango orchards, but the Muslims carried on the trade. Hindus and Muslims interacted on several occasions, including festivals and weddings. When a particular religious community has specialized in any economic field, its clientele belongs to various other religions.

In cities, Hindus and Muslims have been greeting each other on their festive occasions. In situations of riots and crises, they have come to each other's rescue. In the riots of November 1984 in Delhi and other places, a large number of Sikhs were given shelter and protection by Hindus. Similarly, in recent Gujarat riots, many Muslim families took refuge in houses owned by Hindus. Hindus and Muslims have lived in amity in the country for centuries. Inter-community marriages in Punjab are a well-established practice.

There is also association between religious communities and the specific economic functions they perform. For example, Parsis are in the liquor trade. Moplah traders are found in Kerala, Mysore, Chennai and Mumbai. Jain traders are found in Mumbai, Gujarat, Rajasthan, Karnataka and Bengal. Such an association is found even at the village level. From amongst the Hindus, Gujarati Banias, Telugu Komatis, Tamil Chettiars and Rajasthani Banias have played an important role in economic activities. However, from time to time, several new caste groups have entered into commerce and trade. Caste barriers have weakened, and spatial mobility is today far greater. The spread of various communities all over the country and diversification of their economic activities have strengthened the process of social integration.

The sociologist Max Weber was the first to mention a Hindu ethic consisting of the principles of *samsara* (belief in the transmigration of souls) and *karma* (doctrine of compensation). These two principles together formed the basis of the caste system. Consequent upon this, according to Weber, caste system did not have a this-worldly rational ethic. Weber based his analysis on extrapolation of textual notions of Hinduism. He perhaps looked at the traditionalism and irrationality of Hinduism from the point of view of the Protestant ethic and its relationship with the growth of capitalism in his own society. However, no necessary antithetical relationship has been seen by many scholars between religion and economic development.

Milton Singer (1972) has found religious/ideological bases of the *varna-jati* order, sects and tribalism and their relationship as functional with the processes of modernisation, nationalism, industrialisation and bureaucracy. However, it would be quite absurd to draw the conclusion that the Hindu ethic and caste system have essentially contributed to economic development in a positive way, and therefore, there is no need to change these systems. This view simply explains the resilient character of Hinduism and the caste system vis-à-vis changes in India's economy and polity.

Social Organisation of Hindu Religion

Hinduism is not a static religion. It has changed considerably due to the spread of scientific knowledge, technological advancement, improved means of communication and the process of secularism. Despite these changes, Hinduism remains a complex phenomenon. At the pan-Indian level, education, mass media, press and migration have promoted secular values. However, at the local level, religious practices remain unaffected to a large extent. We can see basic structural change in the countryside alongwith adherence to tradition and religious beliefs.

India has been characterised as a 'primary' or 'orthogenetic' civilisation, because it has its continuity; an uninterrupted history despite foreign invasions and wars between rulers within the country. The main source of strength of the Indian civilisation is the interaction between different parts of its traditions. The traditions, which are written, find a place in Hindu or Islamic literature, religious texts and scripts. These are called 'great traditions'. The traditions, which are unwritten and transmitted orally from one generation to another, are called 'little traditions'. These two are constantly interacting with each other. When the elements of a great tradition filter down to the people, the process of such a spread is known as *parochialisation*. When the elements of a little tradition become a part of a great (Sanskritic) tradition, the process is described as *universalisation*. To call a tradition great or little, in fact, amounts to designating people as great and little, because it is the people who are literate or unlettered. Traditions refer to norms of behaviour and interpersonal relations. They are symbiotic in nature, but their hierarchy refers to a hierarchy of human beings. To call illiterate folks little and the literate as great, even by implication, would involve a value judgement. Thus, religion is a very complex phenomenon. It is necessary to simplify it by clarifying those canons which put all the believers on the same wave-length without any discrimination whatsoever, based on caste, region, cultural heritage, economic position, educational status, etc.

Use of Religion in Fulfilling Narrow Ends

Though religion is an integrative mechanism, it has been used to fulfil narrow social and political ends. A number of associations and groups have been formed with religious names with a view to evoke religious consciousness for getting support or favour from members belonging to a particular religious group. The Hindu Mahasabha and Muslim League are glaring examples of this practice. Even educational institutions have Hindu, Jain, Muslim, Christian and Sikh names.

LANGUAGE

Defining Language

"A language is a system of arbitrary vocal symbols by which members of a social group cooperate and interact" (*Gazetteer of India*, Vol. I). Language as a system consists of a series of symbols, the meanings of which must be learned by all those who use that language. Language is an aspect of culture.... "by means of which the learning process is effectuated and a given way of life achieves both continuity and change" (ibid). The building-up of knowledge is not possible without language. As such language is not simply a construction comprising of words, phrases and sentences based on certain rules (grammar), it is a means of communication, and a mode of social relationship. Language is not monolithic, it is differentiated and hierarchical vis-à-vis ramifications of people in society.

Thus, language is also a social phenomenon in terms of its differential association with different social strata. Some people have command over both written and oral aspects of a given language; while others, being simple folks, have access only to the oral aspect. Sanskritic language or any other language may become a resource for some people, whereas a lack of knowledge of the same may prove an obstacle in social and cultural mobility. A linguistic group or collectivity becomes, at times, a strong primordial entity, and may turn into a sort of ethnic or communal group in opposition to some such other group.

Role of Language in Social Integration

Language is a living force; it is not a static phenomenon. It has changed with changes in social formations, ruling clans and with demands of specific historical situations. Pali and Prakrit languages were prominent in ancient India. Sanskrit enjoyed the status of carrying Hindu Sanskritic culture throughout the country. These were followed by modern Indo-Aryan languages like Assamese, Bengali, Gujarati, Hindi, Kashmiri, Marathi, Oriya, Punjabi, Sindhi and Urdu. The languages in peninsular India are of Dravidian stock (with the exception of Marathi). These include Tamil, Telugu, Malayalam and Kannada. Each of these languages, of both the stocks, have several dialects spoken by people living in different linguistic regions.

The rulers of medieval India brought new forms of religion, language, manners and customs compared to those of the orthogenetic culture and civilization. The institutional basis of social order and economic organisation remained unchanged to a large extent. The caste system and village economy continued to function considerably undisturbed during the medieval period. However, Indian culture and political power underwent transformation, influencing language, culture and religion. A 'Hindustani' way of life emerged in northern India. The writings and accounts of foreign travellers from Islamic countries promoted Arabic and Persian languages. Though the Hindu culture, caste system and village economy remained largely unaffected despite foreign rule, the Indo-Aryan languages rapidly developed into literary languages. With the emergence of these languages, cultural changes occurred, including diminishing upper caste domination, the decline of Sanskrit language, and waves of religious and social reforms, using popular idioms and the language of laity. The confrontation of Hindu and Muslim cultures led to interesting results and a mixed culture, particularly in North India.

Linguistic Structure of India

According to Grierson, India has 179 languages and 544 dialects. However, this estimate cannot be accepted as authentic since the dialects were counted under the head of 'languages'. The Constitution of India, in its Eighth Schedule, recognises two official and 22 national languages. The two official languages are English and Hindi (Devanagri script), whereas national languages include Assamese, Bengali, Gujarati, Hindi, Kannada, Kashmiri, Malayalam, Marathi, Oriya, Punjabi, Sanskrit, Sindhi, Tamil, Telugu, Urdu, Konkani, Manipuri, Nepali, Bodo, Maithali, Dogri and Santhali. In undivided India, over 73 per cent of the people spoke the Indo-Aryan languages, 20 per cent the Dravidian languages, 1.3 per cent the Austric languages and only 0.85 per cent spoke the Sino-Tibetan languages.

Language as the Basis of States Reorganisation

The present formation of India into states represents the language map of India. The States Reorganisation Commission (SRC) carved out states based on linguistic uniformity and continuity. There is an anomaly, however, in the ten Hindi-speaking states, namely, Bihar,

Jharkhand, Madhya Pradesh, Chhatisgarh, Uttar Pradesh, Uttranchal, Rajasthan, Himachal Pradesh, Haryana and Punjab. The spoken languages within these states have been clubbed under the broad head of Hindi. The rest of the states, namely, Assam, Bengal, Orissa, Andhra Pradesh, Gujarat, Maharashtra, Karnataka, Tamil Nadu and Kerala have a majority of people who speak Assamese, Bengali, Oriya, Telugu, Gujarati, Marathi, Kannada, Tamil and Malayalam, respectively.

Uttar Pradesh, Bihar, Madhya Pradesh and Rajasthan were large states. A demand for smaller states came up from time to time from the people of these states. The Adivasis of Chotanagpur, the Santhal Parganas of Bihar and the tribals of the adjoining areas of Bengal, Orissa and Madhya Pradesh demanded formation of a separate state of Jharkhand on the basis of not only their distinct language, culture, administrative viability and geographical contiguity but also their exploitation by the Dikkus (non-Adivasi zamindars, moneylenders and other exploiters). Consequently, three new states were carved out, namely, Jharkhand from Bihar, Uttranchal from Uttar Pradesh and Chhatisgarh from Madhya Pradesh.

The Language Problem

It seems that the root cause of the present language problem in India is the imposition of English by the British Raj in the country. Lord Macaulay said: "We must at present do our best to form a class who may be interpreters between us and the millions whom we govern; a class of persons, Indian in blood and colour, but English in taste, in opinions, in morals, and in intellect." He continued: "To that class we may leave it to refine the vernacular dialects of the country, to enrich those dialects with terms of science borrowed from western nomenclature, and to render them by degrees fit vehicles for conveying knowledge to the great mass of the population." This policy of imparting education in English proved fruitful for the Raj but not for the Indian masses. Universities and colleges were established for the express purpose of training individuals for subordinate ranks. Nationalist leaders viewed this policy as a device of the British to produce a 'baboo (clerks) class'. Jawaharlal Nehru (1956) writes: "The British had created a new caste or class in India; the English-educated class, which lived in a world of its own, cut off from the mass of the population, and looked always, even when protesting, towards its rulers." The indigenous elite were thus transformed into a class of clerks by Macaulay's policy of English education in India in the first half of the last century.

However, there is also a counter-view that India could join the world community only through its English education. The promotion of vernaculars would have been a threat to India's unity. The study of science and technology was made possible by the knowledge of English. We have already stated some limitations of the view which undermines the role of indigenous languages in 'emotional integration' and 'national consolidation'. Rabindranath Tagore writes: "A language is not like an umbrella or an overcoat, that can be borrowed by unconscious or deliberate mistake; it is like the living skin itself."

India has always been a multilingual civilisation with special elite languages and a constant interaction between local, regional and all-India languages. Unity and assimilation at various interactional levels have been specific features of the Indian sub-continent. Amidst vast diversities, the doctrine of a single language, essential for national identity, cohesiveness and unity, has been challenged from time to time. Since European countries are characterised by one dominant language, the problem of unity and cohesion is therefore different in Europe than in India. We have one nation-state, but many cultures, languages and religions. India's oneness lies in the community of the essence of all cultures and languages formed in different parts and regions.

About 90 per cent of the people claim national languages as their mother tongues. However, official (national) languages are Hindi and English according to the Eighth Schedule of India's Constitution. The fact is that even national languages are regional in scope. Even today, English is considered a necessary licence to get lucrative and prestigious jobs. English has thus created a hiatus between the elite and the masses. Regional and local leaders have, at times, demanded 'linguistic autonomy', with a view to replace English by Hindi or some other 'national' (regional) language. The carving out of states on the basis of language has certainly promoted regional linguistic autonomy. The 'three-language formula' was devised to counter the demand for 'Hindi only', and also to promote the use of a 'national' (regional) language in a given state in place of Hindi and English. These three languages were Hindi, English and the regional language, such as Telugu or Tamil.

Advocating Hindi as the official language for the entire country has evoked sharp protests in non-Hindi-speaking areas such as Andhra Pradesh, Tamil Nadu, Kerala, Karnataka, Bengal and Assam. On the other hand, the indigenous languages have received the attention required for their preservation and enrichment. One view is that the extended use of indigenous languages can bring about emotional integration and national consolidation, as this would be a direct attack on the small upper class, entrenched in administration, law-enforcement agencies, business and industry (as these use English as the basic instrument of communication). If English language is the medium of debate in Parliament or a State Assembly, the elected members cannot be considered true representatives of their people. Thus, it is argued that indigenous language should be used in administration and planning. Apparently, this seems to be a plausible way out, but it may block proper communication between the people speaking different national languages. Inter-language rivalries might also arise.

It is clear that the language situation in India is quite complicated and hazardous for national consolidation and development. The structure of linguistic states came into existence in India after a great deal of acrimony and bad feeling. Language riots in undivided Bombay state and anti-Hindi riots in Tamil Nadu are still fresh in our memory. The first Prime Minister of India, Jawaharlal Nehru, once suggested that the people in the north should learn one of the South Indian languages, and the people of the south should learn Hindi voluntarily. This has not happened. On the contrary, linguistic insulation is admired and used for political gains and cultural domination and identity.

Even in the heartland of Hindi (northern India), after six decades of India's independence, the English-knowing candidates are preferred for white-collar jobs. Demotion of English language logically amounts to the promotion of indigenous languages. However, the fact is that English continues to have its pride place, and at the same time, the regional languages are enjoying cultural and political significance.

In the absence of an all-India language as a unifying force, the formation of linguistic states has taken the country towards narrow sectionalism, provincialism and parochialism, endangering national integration. Caste, region and language tend to coincide in India to a great extent. Caste structure is broadly regional and goes along with the language boundaries. For example, a given number of sub-castes are found in Andhra Pradesh. They do not intermarry with the equivalent castes from outside Andhra Pradesh. The languages spoken by them are also different. Thus, caste, region and language coexist and have a certain degree of homogeneity. The absence of a single script for India has also accentuated the linguistic turmoil from time to time.

Language is a very sensitive aspect of people's lives. When, in accordance with the Official Languages Act of 1963, Hindi was declared the official language of India, serious riots broke out on 26 January 1965 in Tamil Nadu and spread to other non-Hindi-speaking states. Consequently, English was retained as an associate language for the non-Hindi speaking people as long as they wanted it. The three-language formula was introduced at this juncture.

We may sum up by stating that language, like ethnicity and region, is a primordial basis of collectivity, and therefore, it plays the same kind of role in various sectors of social life, including social ranking, economic development, education and politics. Language, being a cultural phenomenon, becomes a very sensitive issue on many occasions. Language disputes and riots have at times threatened national unity and solidarity. The three-language formula was introduced as a device to minimise such problems, and to strengthen the forces of national unity and integrity. Language, as a means of communication and accretion of knowledge, should not be allowed to become an instrument of power in a few hands. It should be accessible to all those who wish to learn as a skill and as a means for social development.

Conclusion

India can rightly be characterised as a society having unity in diversity and diversity in unity, as it is a plural society both in letter and spirit. Despite innumerable odds, India has maintained its unity. We find unity in India in all its historical and cultural facets. India is today a secular state. It has one Constitution and uniform rule of law for all its people living in different regions, speaking different languages, and believing in different religions and faiths. Today, Hindus, Jains, Muslims, Sikhs, Christians and people of other faiths participate together in administration, politics and public life. Ethnic, linguistic and religious diversities do not hinder the realisation of the common national goals. The cultural heritage of India has been a living example of the synthesis of different cultures.

Besides the Constitution of India, the Five-Year Plans, the spread of egalitarian values, a central government and a common body of civil and criminal laws strengthen India's unity and plural character. Distinctions based on caste, race and creed are no longer the basis of special powers and privileges. The weaker sections of society, including the SCs, the STs and the OBCs, have been granted special concessions and avenues for elevation of their depressed status and position. Women enjoy rights equal to men in all respects. Besides the legal provisions, various social movements and actions by the non-governmental organisations (NGOs) have created socio-political awakening among the deprived sections and victims of atrocities and exploitation.

We have discussed in this chapter the role and significance of ethnicity, religion and language. These are socio-cultural aspects of our society as well as its living forces. At times they are used to promote narrow parochial ends posing a threat to national integration. Ethnic conflict, communalism and language disputes have occurred from time to time. Educational institutions, elections and political parties have particularly been used for spreading communal feelings by the vested interests.

Exercises

1. Describe the physical and topographical features which have/had a direct or indirect bearing upon the history and civilisation of India.
2. Explain India's unity in diversity and diversity in unity. Give suitable examples from the socio-cultural life of the people of India.
3. What forces and factors threaten the unity of India today?
4. Define ethnicity. How is it different from caste? Give examples of ethnic conflict.
5. What role does religion play in Indian society?
6. Explain the following:
   (i) Religious movements
   (ii) Religious conversion
   (iii) Religion and national integration
   (iv) Religious harmony and tolerance
   (v) Main doctrines of Hinduism, Islam, Sikhism and Christianity
7. Discuss the following:
   (i) Great and little traditions
   (ii) Parochialisation and universalisation
8. Explain language as a socio-cultural force in national integration.
9. Discuss the linguistic basis for reorganisation of states in India.
10. What is the policy of government towards the promotion and use of Hindi, English and other national languages?
11. What are the main features of the present educational system in India? Explain the role of English language in contemporary India.

Select References

Bose, N.K., *Culture and Society in India*, Bombay: Asia Publishing House, 1967.

—, *Studies in Gandhism*, Ahmedabad: Navajivan Publishing House, 1972.

Harrison, Selig S., *India: The Most Dangerous Decades*, Madras: Oxford University Press, 1960.

Herskovits, Melville J., *Cultural Anthropology*, Calcutta: Oxford and IBH Publishing Co., 1955.

Kothari, Rajni, *Politics in India*, New Delhi: Orient Longman Ltd., 1970.

Myrdal, Gunnar, *Asian Drama: An Inquiry into the Poverty of Nations*, Vol. I, Penguin Books, 1968.

Nehru, Jawaharlal, *The Discovery of India*, 4th edn., London: Meridian Books Ltd., 1956.

Singer, Milton, *When a Great Tradition Modernises*, New York: Praeger Publishers, 1972.

Singh, Yogendra, *Modernization of Indian Tradition*, Jaipur: Rawat Publications, 1986.

Srinivas, M.N., *Religion and Society among the Coorgs of South India*, London: Oxford University Press, 1952.

—, "Social structure" in *The Gazetteer of India: Country and People*, Vol. I, The Government of India Publication, 1973, pp. 501-578.

The Gazetteer of India, Volume I and II.

2 Evolution of Indian Society: Socio-Cultural Dimensions

India is said to be a synthesis of diverse social and cultural elements. It is a synthesis of the Aryan and the Dravidian cultures. The unity between the village, the family, and the legal system was the outcome of this synthesis. The synthesis has created continuity from the ancient period till today – continuity from the time of Mohenjo-daro (2500 B.C.) through Jainism, Buddhism and Islam, and from the time of British rule to post-independence India. One finds the process of assimilation and synthesis in the fields of art, painting, music, religion, etc.

K.M. Panikkar (1967), a staunch nationalist, keeping in view the historicity of synthesis and assimilation writes: "I define culture as the complex of ideas, conceptions, developed qualities, and organised relationships and courtesies that exist generally in a society." He describes it as "a community of thought, a similarity of conduct and behaviour, a common general approach to fundamental problems, which arise from shared traditions and ideals". Indian culture has been modified continuously by outside contacts, but remains essentially Indian, based on doctrines and ideas developed indigenously. This form and substance of Indian culture are found in literature, art and architecture. India has had a tradition of religious and social tolerance. This tolerance has contributed to the richness and variety of social and cultural life in India.

SOCIETY IN ANCIENT INDIA

The main literary sources in the ancient period were written in Sanskrit and Sanskritic languages, and Dravidian languages. The Vedas, the Puranas and the Mahabharata, and the texts in Prakrit and Pali languages may be mentioned. The Ceylonese chronicles, the *Buddhacharita* and Jaina literature are the important historical works. In the medieval period, several historical works about the Chalukyas of Kalyana, Chatramanas, and the Palas of Bengal were written in the Sanskritic languages. The three well-known writings referring to these dynasties are the *Vikramankadevacharita*, the *Prathvirajavijaya*, and the *Ramacharita*, respectively. The Rajatarangini of Kashmir and the Gujarat chronicles are other important works. The Tamil, Kannada,, Telugu and Malayalam languages also produced important works in the period A.D. 1206-1761. The Persian and Arabic languages received a lot of encouragement.

Pre-historic and proto-historic periods are divided into the Stone Age, Copper Age and Iron Age. Such a classification refers to man's material and technological advancement. Knowledge of man's economic and social status and his environment needs greater attention. However, this periodisation does not provide adequate understanding. The following stages in man's progress are more indicative of the evolutionary process:

1. Primitive food collecting stage or early and middle stone ages.
2. Advanced food collecting stage or late stone age/mesolithic.
3. Transition to incipient food production or early neolithic.
4. Settled village communities or advanced neolithic/ chalcolithic.
5. Urbanisation or bronze age.

The Indus Valley Civilisation

We shall make a brief reference here to the Indus valley civilisation. The Indus valley civilisation was urban and it covered more area than the civilisations in the Nile, the Tigris-Euphrates valley or in the Yellow river valley. From west to east, the Indus valley civilisation covered a distance of over 1,550 km, and from north to south over 1,100 km. Systematic town planning is the most striking feature of this civilisation. Streets, lanes, bylanes and houses were in symmetry, and were built of kiln-burnt bricks. A house comprised a central courtyard, three to four living rooms, a bath and a kitchen; while the more elaborate ones contained even upto thirty rooms and were often two-storeyed. Many of the houses were provided with a well; and there was an excellent underground drainage system. The cities possibly had 'lower' and 'upper' parts. A 'college', a multi-pillared 'assembly hall', a public bath, a large granary and a citadel built with burnt-bricks with a wooden super-structure have been found.

There were bumper crops of wheat and barley, besides peas, melons and bananas. Cotton was also grown. Fish, fowl, mutton, beef and pork were also used. Cattle, cats, dogs and even elephants were commonly found. The *dhoti* and shawl were used as clothing. The womenfolk combed their hair with care and bedecked themselves with necklaces, bracelets, finger-rings, ear-rings, girdles and anklets. The Indus people lived in the full-fledged bronze age, as it is evident from the use of domestic objects like sows, sickles, chisels, fish-hooks, pins, mirrors and weapons made of bronze. Copper and gold were also used, but not produced locally. The objects of worship reveal that the Indus people comprised of Mediterraneans, Alpines, Proto-Australoids and Mongoloids. It was, in fact, a cosmopolitan civilisation.

The subsequent developments also testify to the existence of an 'organised civic life'. This included the planning of an entire township: a regular drainage system, standardisation of weights and measures and a system of writing. Arts and crafts began to develop. However, still people were in the 'primitive' era. By the time of the Atharva Veda, the Aryans were fully acquainted with metals and they drew distinctions between iron, bronze and copper.

The changes in Indian society have been slower than that in other civilisations. Each phase of cultural development tended to overlap the next, thus leading to a modicum of continuity and permanence. Despite regional differentiations and constant contact with outsiders, the Indus civilisation was essentially Indian in character. There are references to this effect in Vedic literature, Puranas and in the early Jaina and Buddhist texts.

A proper archaeological documentation is available about the Mauryan empire and various regional and local cultures. The use of iron is found all over India. The spread of Sanskrit also contributed to the fusion of cultures. Archaeological and linguistic materials testify to the evolution of pan-Indian culture. The sub-continent is Indian in essence because of its geographic isolation. The synthesis is the result of millennia of conflict and interaction of the various groups of people who migrated into this country. Linguistic integration was maximum as a result of contact with the foreigners. Racial and cultural synthesis is reflected in myths and legends narrated in the Puranas. 'Aryanisation' became widespread, covering Bihar and parts of West Bengal. Likewise, 'Indianisation' of foreign cultures also took place simultaneously. 'Aryanisation' refers to the impact of Aryans (foreigners) on the indigenous people; and 'Indianisation' refers to the process of adapting the styles of life of the native people by the Aryans. The two processes of change brought about accommodation and finally blending of the Aryan and the indigenous cultures.

The Vedic Civilisation

What is the relationship of the Indus valley civilisation with the Vedic civilisation of the Indo-Aryans? R.C. Majumdar, H.C. Raychaudhuri and Kalikinkar Datta write in *An Advanced History of India* (1970): "On the face of it there are striking differences between the two. The Vedic-Aryans were largely rural, while the characteristic features of the Indus valley civilisation are the amenities of a developed city life. The former probably knew of iron and defensive armour, which are totally absent in the latter. The horse played an eminent part in the Vedic civilisation but its early existence is doubted in the Indus valley. There were also important differences in respect of religious beliefs and practices."

The Vedas are the only literary source from where one learns about the Aryans in India. The *RgVeda Samhita* is the earliest book on the Aryans. Vedic society was rural and agricultural. Temples and schools emerged as the basic institutions of various socio-cultural and educational activities. The village was an autonomous unit. During the fourth century B.C., seven castes are reported by Megasthenes. However, intercaste marriages were quite common. The vices of drinking, gambling and prostitution were regulated by state licence.

Women had access to all branches of learning in Vedic times. They even composed Vedic hymns. Gargi and Maitreyi were eminent philosophers during the age of the Upanishads. The women of higher castes participated in *yajna* (sacrifice) with their husbands.. They had the right to own property and widows could remarry. A man could marry more than one woman, whereas a woman could marry only one man. However, in the Buddhist period, women lost their right to pursue Vedic studies. The situation changed considerably in the Gupta period. The *Svayamvara* (choice made by the bride for a groom after a test of valour) and *Gandharva* (free mutual choice) forms of marriage became unpopular, and *Arsa* and *Asura* marriages (with dowry) became popular. Woman had no right to own property and the widows were denied remarriage. The institutions of *purdah* and *sati* emerged.

The Post-Vedic Society and Culture

In the early centuries of the Christian era, foreign invaders mingled with Indian ruling families and came under their influence. The capitals of foreign dynasties became centres of a cultural synthesis which gave Indian civilisation a distinct cosmopolitan character. Puranic Hinduism rose during the Gupta Age. The Buddha was accepted as an incarnation of Lord Vishnu. Brahmanism and Buddhism were reconciled with each other. Hinduism, aboriginal beliefs and practices and foreign religious symbols came closer. Hindu society became a federation of cultural and social groups freely interchanging ideas and customs and living side by side in good neighbourly relations.

Fa-hien mentions that under the Gupta empire there was all round prosperity in northern India in the fifth century A.D. The merchant class amassed immense wealth. Trading and banking activities were at their peak. The wealthy people spent benevolently to build and run schools, monasteries, temples, hospitals and alms-houses. The Buddhist monastery at Pataliputra was a famous centre of learning. The people believed in omens and astrology. Music, dancing and feasting were common on social occasions and festivals. *Vasanta Utsava* (spring festival) was celebrated with enthusiasm and gaiety.

Dharma, and not law, was a real code of ethics for the harmonious functioning of the various divisions of society. "Dharma Sastra or Smritis laid down rules for every caste and vocation, for every relation in society – king and subjects, husband and wife, teacher and pupil. The rules were not rigid and were revised from time to time to meet new developments. Sometimes the law-givers and the priestly class introduced their own ideas and laid down strictures and taboos" (*The Gazetteer of India*, Vol. II). Hiuen Tsang, a Chinese traveller, who visited India in the seventh century A.D., wrote that the people were honest and were true to their word. They believed that a vice committed by a person could not go unpunished.

Social life was governed by the regulations of the Shastras. The Hindu society was divided into castes and sub-castes. Rules of social interaction and marriage (commensality and connubiality) were strictly followed. Sports and games, celebration of festivals and ceremonies, including *upanayana* (wearing of the sacred thread), were quite common. The atrocious caste rules resulted in the decadence of Indian society. The lower castes and the outcastes were humiliated. Women were suppressed. The corporate bodies, which were in existence, like *gana* (oligarchic states), *sreni* (craft guilds) and *sangha* (monastic orders), disintegrated. With the emergence of the caste system, social gradations became more significant than economic gradations. Al-Beruni reports that in the eleventh century A.D. foreigners were scorned by Indians.

Dignity of labour did not remain as a sign of self-respect. Society was highly differentiated. Enslavement, on account of non-payment of debt, became a common practice. The slaves were known as *Dasa*. The 'outcastes' were below the slaves. They were known as the *Chandalas*, *Pulkasas* and *Nisadas*. They were segregated from the higher castes. The caste system and slavery were found in the south almost in the same form as in the north. Village life and craft guilds were more autonomous in the south than in the north.

The *Varna* System

It seems to be a myth that pre-historic society was a casteless millennium of equality, plenty and piety. Division of society into Aryans and non-Aryans is the first indication of a stratified society as mentioned in the RgVeda. The Aryan 'Vis' or tribe was further divided into four groups based on the emergence of different pursuits such as agriculture, cattle-rearing and trade. Those who pursued activities related to trade and commerce were known as Vaisya. The surplus wealth was diverted towards the maintenance of the Brahmana and the Kshatriya. These three *varnas* (castes) were identified not by the colour of their skin but by their professions.

The Brahmana performed religious and ritual activities for the welfare of society. He studied the Vedas, and formulated norms (*dharma*) for all sections of society. The Kshatriya was assigned the task of defending the country and maintaining law and order. In course of time, these three *varnas* specialised in their functions, and formed a social hierarchy in which the Brahmanas were placed at the top, the Kshatriya ranked below and the Vaishya occupied the third rank. The fourth rank was of the Shudra or Dasa who served the three higher groups. The *Purusasukta* of the RgVeda gives a mythological story of the origin of the four *varnas* – from the mouth (Brahmanas), arms (Kshatriyas), thighs (Vaishyas) and feet (Shudras) of the Lord Brahma.

Varnas are different from caste groups. Varnas refer to broad divisions of Hindu society, whereas caste groups refer to specific endogamous groups, numbering more than three thousand. *Varnas* are an all-India general phenomenon, whereas castes are localised groups. The various caste groups which are found in Kerala or Tamil Nadu are not found in Gujarat and Rajasthan. Marriages took place among the members of a caste living in a given geographical area, as people did not know the antecedents of others living far away.

In the beginning, the vocations of the *varnas* were not hereditary. Not only was change of profession allowed, one could even improve one's status if one had the required talents and virtues. Demotion from higher to lower status could also occur. Later on, according to Smritis, *varna* and vocation became fixed and hereditary. The division of social and economic activities became a norm and a part of social device. The rise of individual enterprise resulted into private property. Thus, *varna* and property necessitated the coming of the state. State (country), patriarch and landlord became a sort of levels of identification for transacting economic and political activities. The king became the patriarch of the state and he appointed a battery of officers and councillors. The state started collecting land revenue and taxes. The *varna* system was projected as a functional way of fulfilling the needs of society.

Various *rishis* prescribed rigid norms for the four *varnas* including placing of restrictions on marriage and social relations between different groups. The Ramayana, the Mahabharata and the Jataka stories show that the Brahmana not only enjoyed the highest grade in the *varna* system, but also amassed wealth and power. They were assigned revenues of villages or tax-free lands, called *Brahnwdeva*, by royal charter. All Brahmana grantees were not engaged in study of the Vedas. Several of them followed Vaishya's activities. Brahmanas organised themselves into guilds like other professions. They used to quarrel among themselves for their respective shares. Brahmanas were not secularised, as they received a lot of charity from the kings and the laity. They became corrupt too as the Manu and Narad have reported.

The hereditary basis of *varna* did not apply strictly to the Kshatriyas and the Vaishyas. State-craft and military vocation were not confined to one group. There are numerous Brahmana, Vaishya and Shudra royal dynasties in the annals of India. The Satavahanas were Brahmanas, the Guptas were Vaishyas and the Nandas were Shudras. There were Yavana, Shaka and Kushana, who did not belong to any caste.

The Vaishyas were a highly differentiated group, as they consisted of a few wealthy families, small peasants, artisans, hawkers and petty officials. The Shudras had a perceptible class character. They served all the three *varnas*. Their economic standing was the lowest. They were practically 'servants' of the higher *varnas*. However, the 'exterior' groups were considered outside the *varna* system. As a result of this, differentiation, inter-mixing of groups through marriages, and formation of sub-castes emerged.

Did *varna* (caste) and class overlap in ancient India? Changes in a man's economic position did not affect his *varna* status. The two hierarchies, *varna* and class, did not coincide. The class hierarchy from top downwards consisted of (1) high officials, merchants, bankers and landlords, (2) small freeholders, artisans and ordinary officials, (3) labour without right and property, and (4) despised and segregated labour. The last two categories corresponded with the stated vocation of the Shudras and the Mlechha. However, the first two do not correspond with the stated vocations of the Brahmanas and the Kshatriyas. But there were also some who followed their stated vocations faithfully but could never become economically prosperous. Brahmanas and Kshatriyas enjoyed privileges, whereas the Vaishyas enjoyed wealth. The Brahmanas and the Kshatriyas commanded esteem and influence because of the high social and cultural value attached to their vocations. However, the *varna* system maintained its organic character and a balance of interests of the various sections of society.

The *Varnashrama* System

Hindu society's main stronghold was the system of *varnashrama dharma*. This refers to four different classes (*varnas*), which we have already discussed briefly, and four stages in man's life (*ashramas*). The four stages were: *Brahamacharya*, *Grahastha*, *Vanaprastha* and *Sanyas*. The Brahamacharya stage is one of learning and formation of good moral character and personality. The Grahastha specifies the obligations of a man to get married and look after his family as a religious duty. The Vanaprastha and Sanyas stages refer to the renunciation of the world for devoting oneself to the pursuit of spiritual knowledge and for attaining salvation. The *ashramas* were principles of equality and unity. They were devised to attain a full and complete life.

Along with these closely interlinked schemes was the scheme of the *purusharthas*, the basic principles of life, which defined the duties of a man towards himself, his family, and to the community. These are: *dharma*, *artha*, *kama* and *moksha*. These principles could rightly be called value-themes or goals of life arranged in a hierarchical order. Of these, *dharma* or moral duty is basic to all human activities.

Y. Singh (1973) has listed four hierarchies, namely, (1) role-institutionalisation (*varna*), (2) charismatic endowments (*guna*), (3) goal-orientations (*purushartha*), and (4) life-stages and its value-obligations (*ashrama*) as part of the Hindu concept of cultural order and its structure. Singh refers to both *order* and *change* as basic features of Indian tradition. Hierarchy, holism and continuity refer to 'order'. 'Change' is analysed in terms of transcendence or transformation. Everything is hierarchised in the Hindu tradition, including men and women, clothes, food, occupations, etc.

SOCIETY IN MEDIEVAL INDIA

Islamic Tradition and Culture

What is Islamic culture? Y. Singh (ibid) writes: "In contradistinction to the structure of the *Hindu great tradition*, the great tradition of Islam is founded on a world-view which is apparently non-hierarchical, is purely monotheistic and messianic-historical in ethos." The world-view of Islam proselytises in the sphere of religion. It also makes Islam holistic and socio-centric. In principle, there are no priests in Islam. Islam is an insular and exclusive religion. It is based on the unity of the Muslim Umma, "the collectivity of the faithful". The Quran (the holy book) and various Islamic traditions have contributed to this holism and collectivism. Thus, theoretically speaking, Islam has the elements of equality and egalitarianism. In the beginning, Islam spread among tribal people. However, subsequently, it became complex. From nomadism it turned to an agrarian and mercantile economy. Islam expanded its base in several countries. It acquired a feudal-authoritarian character.

Muslims are the second largest community in India. Historically too, they are the oldest group with the exception of Hindus. Hindus and Muslims have been living together for almost a millennium. The two represent two different cultures, world-views and ways of life. Islamic and Hindu traditions have interacted, synthesised and also remained insulated. Y. Singh (ibid.) mentions three major stages of Islamic traditions in India. These are: (1) the duration of Islamic rule in India, (2) during the British domination, and (3) during the Indian freedom movement and upto India's independence and the country's partition. The first stage is marked by conflict, tension, adaptation and cultural syncretism between the Hindu and the Islamic traditions. The Muslim rulers carried out religious warfare *(jihad)*, with the help of the Ulemas. Despite the conflict, the two traditions had changed their tribal egalitarian character due to their contact with Persian society. By this time, the social structure of Islam had distinctions based on status and honour.

The Islamic society was divided into priest, nobility, and all others. It also had hereditary succession in twelfth century A.D. The elite belonged to the upper-most segment of the indigenous people (non-convert foreigners). The Muslims (the *Ashrafs)* were of four grades: Sayyad, Sheikh, Mughal and Pathan. The Sayyads and Sheikhs belonged to the nobility of Muslims and occupied high religious offices. The Mughals and Pathans were warriors, feudal aristocrats and rulers. These groups later on evolved into a caste-like structure, and were guardians of the Islamic great tradition. The Sufi tradition had seventeen orders. Its emphasis on the ascetic ethic and on metaphysics impressed the Hindus.

Impact of Islam on Indian Society

Prior to the advent of Islam and after the reign of Harsha, India witnessed a spell of political disintegration and intellectual stagnation. The country was divided into several small states. People developed parochial outlooks and identities. Formalism and authoritarianism dominated religious and cultural life. Shaivism and Vaishnavism emerged as two distinct religious sects. No innovative religious writings, ideas or commentaries were contributed by the intellectual elite. The Shakas, Hunas and Gurjars put an end to the golden age of the Gupta dynasty. However, these foreigners gradually adopted Hindu religion and culture. These invaders called themselves descendants of the Kshatriyas. This was the beginning of Rajput culture, art, literature, poetry and drama. Malwa, Kanauj, Bengal, Kashmir, Ajmer, Gwalior, Chittor, Ranthambor and Mandu were the places not only of Rajput chivalry but also of new culture, architecture and literature. South India remained stable during this period and, therefore, did not experience political disintegration like the north. The Cholas ruled the whole of peninsular India.

The historian Tarachand, in his book, *The Influence of Islam on Indian Culture,* observes that social and cultural revivalism in the south was due to the impact of Islamic culture. Muslim Arabs had trade relations with south India for many centuries before the emergence of Islam in India. Indo-Iranian maritime trade had reached its peak. Some of these foreign traders had even settled in Sri Lanka and on the coast of Malabar. Some Arab Muslims also came to Sind and Gujarat, but their impact was limited. However, from the twelfth century A.D., a definite impact of Islamic culture on Indian society is evident.

H.V. Sreenivasa Murthy and S.U. Kamath (1976) have highlighted both negative and positive aspects of the impact of Islam on Indian society. They write: "Islam was indirectly responsible for making Hindu society caste ridden and exclusive. The

Hindu woman was veiled and sati was made more strict. Child marriage became more popular."

Synthesis of Hindu and Muslim Cultures

With the Sufis started writing in Hindi, Hindi literature thus developed. Urdu also grew as a hybrid of Hindi and Persian. Arabic words crept into this new language. Indian music was also much influenced by Islam. New schools, like *Khayal*, developed in Hindustani music due to the influence of Persian music. New instruments like the *tabla* and *sitar* evolved. In architecture, the Indo-Saracenic style appeared, with spacious interiors, massive domes, arches and minars. Sufism was highly influenced by the mysticism of the Hindus. The monotheistic ideas of Islam influenced Hindu society, some of the leaders of the Bhakti movement like Kabir were influenced by the ideology of monotheism. The rise of the Bhakti cult was unique development of the Mughal period. Leaders of the movement were mystic saints. They emphasised on oneness of God. Universality, love and equality were publicised as attributes of God. The Vaishnavites were the main followers of this cult. South India was the main seat of the Bhakti movement. The Nayanars (Saivas) and Alwars (Vaishnavas) of Tamil Nadu popularised the movement by singing devotional songs. The saints like Ramanuja and Madhwa were its main architects. Ramanuja propagated *Visishtadvaita* (qualified monism), and Madhwa taught *Dwaita* (dualism). *Veerasaivism*, a zealous *Saiva* cult, was propagated by Basava in the twelfth century A.D. Ramananda (a propagator of Rama Bhakti), Kabir, Gyanadeva and Raidas were other Bhakti saints who propagated oneness of God in north India. Meera, Vishnu and Rama Bhakti were their main concerns. Bhakti was no religion. Kabir Panth advocated universal brotherhood and love, amity between Hindus and Muslims. Chaitanya Prabhu, Tulsidas, Surdas and Meera enriched the Bhakti movement and Hindi literature.

It has been mentioned earlier that Akbar strived at a synthesis of Hinduism, Jainism, Islam and Zorastrianism by introducing *Din-e-Illahi*, a new faith. Amir Khusro, a literary figure, tried to incorporate Hinduism in the Muslim culture. Several poets wrote in Hindi. Many of them made appeals for cultural integration of the two religions. Along with such cultural synthesis, Islam continued on orthodox lines with the support of the administration and the Muslim clergy. Muslim *qazis* (judges), *muftis* (preachers), *faujdars* (district administrators) and *durbaris* (courtiers) held positions with economic advantages and power, and contributed to the emulation of the Islamic culture.

Changes in the Islamic Tradition

The Muslims lost their prestige and power during the British period. Loss of political power and legitimacy was a severe jolt to the Muslim elite and the Islamic tradition. Poverty descended upon them and their educational pattern underwent a considerable change. The syncretic and liberal tendencies of Islam were undermined and were being replaced by the orthodoxy and revivalism of the eighth century A.D. Y. Singh (1973) observes that the reform movement in the nineteenth century A.D. had two polar views: (1) for liberalism and peaceful reform, and (2) for more orthodoxy and militancy. Perhaps, the latter was responsible for the creation of Pakistan. Singh mentions two levels of relationships regarding struggle for independence: (1) the relationship between the secular-minded and the orthodox Muslim elite, and (2) the relationship between the Hindu and the Muslim elite. The Muslims aspired for equal power and political parity in free India. Fearing that they would not get this, they agitated for the creation of a Muslim state—Pakistan. Besides gaining the lost power and prestige by having a Muslim state, they also thought of revivalism of the Islamic tradition, culture and nationalism.

Y. Singh (ibid.) distinguishes between the little and great traditions in the context of the Islamic tradition as follows: "the former is rural, mass-based, consisting of the unlettered and less formalised; whereas the latter is elite-based, urban, reflective and formalized." The little tradition of Islam consists mainly of the converts from Hinduism. It also includes descendants of those

Muslims who slided down to lower status. Islamisation has been a fact in at least three ways: (1) as an upward cultural and social mobility in the status of groups through conversion to Islam, (2) as a movement for restoring orthodoxy among the converts, and (3) in terms of adoption of some Islamic cultural values by non-Muslims.

Islamisation was a sort of sanskritisation until the coming of the British. In both the British period and in the post-independence India it is more of a revivalistic movement. However, conversion to a religion generally results in change in socio-cultural status, and sometimes in economic advantage and psychic gratification. Generally, the lower Hindu castes with their degraded status converted to Islam, and in the recent decades to Christianity to achieve equality of status and economic gain. However, the converts have rarely been accepted either as equal to those whom they have theoretically joined or to those whose ranks they have left. In regard to endogamy and hypergamy, they are still guided by rules of their original castes/communities.

Even today, Muslims in India are a conservative lot. Economic inequalities are more pronounced among the Muslims. They are very sensitive about personal laws, the system of *purdah*, and family planning. Muslims are generally more 'backward' than the Hindus in cultural matters as the latter have shown more adaptive capacities. Muslims also suffer from fear and suspicion of the Hindu majority. With the formation of Pakistan some sections of Hindus feel that the Muslims of India should blend into India's mainstream of national life. The Hindu community can certainly play a constructive role in generating confidence among the Muslims.

SOCIETY IN BRITISH INDIA

It is generally accepted that society in India was nearly stagnant at the time of the British intrusion. The British were advised not to interfere with the social customs and religious beliefs of the Hindus. L'Abbe Dubois observed that "the day the British interfered will be the last of its existence as a political power". The Mughal rulers were also not generally interested in conversion as a means of social change. However, some sort of a synthesis emerged during the medieval period (we have discussed it in the last section of this chapter). Caste and class structures in rural India were rigid and stagnant at the beginning of the British rule. The individual was considered subordinate to the caste, the family and the village panchayat. Economy was archaic. People lacked national consciousness. At such a time, the advent of the British created a new situation.

British Impact on Indian Society

The British government, Christian missions and English education were three main sources of British impact on Indian society. The British government replaced the indigenous systems of administration and governance. The missions made efforts to convert Indians to Christianity. British educationists tried to spread education to bring about a change in the outlook of the indigenous population. The British community in India also had an influence on the people in different parts of the country. The port towns and coastal areas were more affected, at least in the beginning of the British Raj. The emergence of a national consciousness, the realisation of the value of organisation and of the importance of agitation led to the formation of the Indian National Congress in 1885. K.M. Panikkar notes that "the most notable achievement of British rule was the unification of India". This was done unconsciously by the British in the interest of the Indian people. They were interested in spreading and consolidating their rule throughout the country. The same argument can be made about the introduction of western education, means of transport, communication, technology and judiciary.

Y. Singh (1973) observes that "the contact of the Indian (Hindu) tradition with the West was of a different and radical sociological significance ... Historically, it was a contact between a pre-modern and a modernizing cultural system". The western tradition had "the scientific and technological world-view based on rationalism, equality and freedom". Consequently, the Indian tradition, which already had a sort of 'breakdown', became further open, liberal, equalitarian and humanistic. The western (British) tradition posed a serious challenge to the Indian tradition. Hierarchy, the principle of social ranking based on birth in a particular caste group, and holism, the 'organic' interdependence between different caste groups, based on norms relating to performances of the assigned functions and duties by various groups, were considerably affected by the western tradition.

Westernisation

M.N Srinivas (1966) defines 'westernisation' in terms of the change in Indian society due to the impact of British rule in India. The areas of change include technology, dress, food, and changes in the habits and lifestyles of people. Westernisation takes place at three levels: (1) primary, (2) secondary, and (3) tertiary. At the primary level were a minority of people who first came into contact with western culture, and were its first beneficiaries. The secondary level of westernisation refers to those sections of Indian society who came into direct contact with the primary beneficiaries. At the tertiary level are those who came to know indirectly about the devices introduced by the British. However, the spread of westernisation has been uneven and unequal among different sections of Indian society. Though Srinivas has mentioned humanitarianism and egalitarianism as its positive features, there are others who consider westernisation as a process of cultural and cognitive colonialism and as a model of an "impersonal, non-cultural and non-sovereign state".

Westernisation has contributed to the re-emergence of a pan-Indian culture on new grounds. Some areas of western impact include education, law, science, technology, new forms of politicisation, urbanisation, industrialisation, the press, means of transport and communication. Y. Singh calls the re-emergence of these institutional foci as the process of 'cultural modernisation'. The western impact has brought about "a new great tradition of modernisation". Certainly, this poses the problem of conflict between the indigenous tradition and the western tradition on

Indian soil. A synthesis between the two has occurred, particularly in regard to the elite sections of Indian society. Today, 'globalisation' has far more impact on Indian society. In fact, India is in the process of becoming a global market/centre of economic and professional activities.

At the initial stage, the western impact was peripheral and localised, as it remained confined to middle class people in the cities of Calcutta, Bombay and Madras. Today, these cities are named as Kolkata, Mumbai and Chennai, respectively. Educational institutions were also centred around these three cities. English education had two-fold impact: (i) inculcation of the western values and ideologies among the educated people, and (ii) the rise of social and cultural reformation movements. We shall discuss the latter in the next chapter. Education was confined to the upper and middle class urban people. The British rule created a new consciousness and structure of values. Westernisation has created the following as observed by Y. Singh (1973): (1) the growth of a universalistic legal superstructure, (2) expansion of education, (3) urbanisation and industrialisation, (4) increased network of communication, and (5) growth of nationalism and politicisation of the society. These elements contributed to modernisation throughout the country.

The judiciary, law courts, legislations (for prohibiting child marriage, infanticide and *sati*, etc.), law commissions and several other legal innovations relating to rules of marriage, family, divorce, adoption, inheritance, minorities, land rights, trade, commerce, industries, labour, etc., were enacted.

Impact on Education

Macaulay's policy of 1835 to promote English education and language, the emergence of missions to spread education and the first Indian Education Commission of 1882 are the highlights of the British period. The British policy put more emphasis on higher education. Education at the primary and secondary levels was considerably neglected. Even today, in terms of course contents and management of educational institutions, India continues to follow the British model. The Education Commissions, set up in 1948 and 1964, under the chairmanship of Dr. S. Radhakrishnan and Dr. D.S. Kothari, respectively, have not produced the desired results. However, courses in some universities in social sciences and humanities have been indigenised in recent years.

Urbanisation and Industrialisation

Urbanisation and industrialisation in India are generally concomitant. Several studies have shown that both the processes reinforce tradition. Urbanisation is a slow process in India compared to the developed countries. However, urban population has increased over the years. Cities or urban centres have a concentration of all the major infrastructural facilities and highly skilled professionals. Urbanisation has been uneven for different cities and regions, and so is in the case of industrialisation. A number of institutional factors have hindered the rapid growth of industrialisation in the past. However, studies by Richard Lambert, Milton Singer, N.R. Seth, etc., have shown that caste, joint family and other traditional values have not obstructed a healthy pattern of social relations in factories and industrial organisations.

Impact of the Means of Transport and Communication

Means of transport and communication have really ushered in an era of new social and cultural contacts. Newspapers, periodicals and magazines, particularly in the regional languages, postal services, movies and radio were all introduced by the British. The same is true of the railways, roadways and airways. These new devices weakened the institution of caste, notions of pollution-purity and hinderances in migration. Spatial mobility was undoubtedly a concrete gain of these means, but 'psychic mobility' also became a fact of life.

Impact of National and Social Awakening

Finally, national and social awakening was created by the British. Raja Ram Mohan Roy and Mahatma Gandhi borrowed several humanistic elements from the British tradition and used them for creating national feelings and political consciousness. The ideas of communalism, secularism and nationalism borrowed from the western philosophers proved very useful.

INDIA SINCE INDEPENDENCE

India won freedom mainly through a sustained, non-violent struggle involving the sacrifice of thousands of people, mainly under the leadership of Tilak, Gandhi, Nehru and Bose.

India became a free country on 15 August 1947. India was partitioned, and a new nation – Pakistan – was created. India has adopted a democratic-socialist path for its development and progress. It adopted a new Constitution which was implemented on 26 January 1950. The Constitution guarantees fundamental rights to the citizens of India, ensuring equality, freedom and justice. Besides the fundamental rights, the Constitution also outlines directives for state policy with a view to give a desired direction to social and economic change in India.

Equality before Law

Today, there is 'rule of law' in India. All citizens are equal and subject to the jurisdiction of the same authority. Even, the privy purses, granted to the princes and feudal lords, were abolished in the late sixties. Birth is no more the basis of recognising status and power. Religion, language, caste or ethnicity are no longer considerations for providing social honour and privileges. However, the weaker sections of Indian society, particularly the Scheduled Castes (SCs), the Scheduled Tribes (STs), and Other Backward Classes (OBCs), have been provided special facilities and provisions for their upliftment. They are protected against discrimination and exploitation by the dominant sections of Indian society. Women have equality with men. All the citizens of India have the right to vote at all the levels of our political system.

Progress in Education

There has been tremendous progress in the field of education. More than 100 million children receive education at the primary level.

The increase in numbers at the secondary stage is also impressive. Education at college and university levels has also increased enormously. Today, there are about 300 universities in India. Diversification of education at senior school, college and university levels has also been taken up by the Government of India. Basic education is being provided at the elementary level. Today, at senior school and university levels, emphasis is being put on vocationalisation, computer studies, applied sciences, management and on some other relevant and gainful fields of knowledge to tackle the problem of unemployment among the educated young men and women.

In 1986, a new Education Policy was implemented by the Government of India placing greater emphasis on the quality of education particularly at the school level. Special attention has been given to the education of the SCs and STs, women and backward sections. Education has promoted migration of people from villages to towns and cities. There is an increased emphasis on Hindi and other national languages. The policy of learning three languages at the school level has been implemented in all the states of the Union of India.

National Consolidation

States of India were reorganised in 1955 on the basis of the recommendations made by the States Reorganisation Commission. Since this was done on the basis of the language spoken by the people, each state has some cultural cohesiveness. India was characterised by the unique type of feudalism under which the *rajas*, *thikanedars*, *jagirdars* and *zamindars* were treated as *Mai-Bap* (parents). To begin with, the government abolished such patrimonial feudalism, and subsequently also abolished the privy purses and compensations granted to the *rajas*. This was really a 'revolutionary' step as the tenants were granted ownership rights. The institution of *zamindars* as intermediaries was removed with the stroke of a pen. Later on, the consolidation of small landholdings and ceilings on maximum landholdings were taken up as measures of land reforms. The Green Revolution has been made possible because of these reforms, and also because of adoption of new technology, fertilisers and seeds in the field of agriculture. India is today self-sufficient in foodgrains, whereas in the fifties and early sixties it depended upon the United States of America and some other countries for its requirement of foodgrains.

Five-Year Plans and Socio-Economic Changes

In the field of industry as well, India has made a lot of progress since independence. Heavy industries at Hatia, Rourkela, Bokaro, Sindri, Bangalore and other places were established in the fifties and sixties. Small-scale and cottage industries have also received the attention of the government. Industrialisation has been possible because India adopted the path of planned economic development and social change. The Planning Commission of India was assigned the task of planning. The government has adopted the policy of 'mixed economy', a policy of balanced growth of the private, the public, and the joint sectors.

The Community Development Programmes (CDPs) were started on 2 October 1952 for the uplift of the rural people. To overcome some of the impediments in the implementation of these schemes, the Panchayati Raj scheme was introduced on 2 October 1959, initially in the states of Rajasthan and Andhra Pradesh. The elected leaders of the rural people at three levels, viz., the village, the block and the district, were given the responsibility of implementing the developmental schemes in view of the 'felt needs' of the rural classes. Several schemes were executed for the welfare of the urban people and of those working in industries. Today, the Panchayati Raj Institutions (PRIs) enjoy statutory status like the legislatures and Lok Sabha based on the provisions of the Constitutional Amendment of 1993.

Social Legislations and Progress

The British enacted social legislations, particularly for preventing child marriages, *sati*, infanticide, and for encouraging widow remarriages, etc. The Government of India passed the Hindu Marriage Act in 1955 and the Hindu Succession Act in 1956. Legislation also was enacted to discourage child labour. There is now stringent legislation against the institution of dowry. According to the Constitution of India, untouchability is a criminal offence. The legislation for giving fair wages to wage-earners and to eliminate the intermediaries and the institution of *zamindari* have helped poor workers in towns and villages to get minimum wages.

Despite these healthy developments in the post-independence period, the concentration of economic power in the hands of a few families and individuals has increased. The poor are not yet getting their due share. Their living conditions are quite appalling. The poor are, even today, victims of the dictates of the rich upper caste and class landlords. Dowry is still a serious evil, particularly in towns. Social consciousness about these problems is still lacking.

Religion, ethnicity and caste are considered important factors in elections. Much reliance is placed upon one's caste members to win an election. Factional disputes originate from alliances based on caste, religion and community-based affiliations. Even urban and educated people are not free from these problems.

Conclusion

We have analysed socio-cultural dynamics in Indian society from ancient to modern times. Our effort in this exercise was to understand the patterns of continuity and change. Traditional society in India was characterised by division of labour, virtues in social life, and recognition of man's virtues and objectives of life. Life was not static; it had both order and change as its essential features. Cultural synthesis and transmission of cultural traits from one period to another have been possible because of the co-existence of stability and change in Indian society and culture. The synthesis of Hindu and Muslim cultures in the fields of music, language, architecture and Bhakti movements which started a couple of centuries ago, is evident even today. We have discussed the interaction between Islamic and Hindu cultures, and the interaction of the two with other cultures in India. Impact of Islamisation as a process of change in other communities was also discussed.

British rule in India, Christian missions and English education have brought about noticeable changes in Indian society. In a way the British tradition posed a serious challenge to the Indian (Hindu) tradition. The ethos of Indian culture and society underwent drastic change due to the impact of British rule. Land tenure systems, the new educational system, systems of judiciary and administration have all altered the structure of Indian society. Many scholars attribute some positive results to this impact, but others think otherwise. We have discussed the process of 'westernisation' in the context of education, judiciary, urbanisation, industrialisation, means of transport and communication and national and social awakening.

Today, India is a free country. It has its Constitution which guarantees rule of law to its citizens. Five-Year Plans and other developmental schemes are implemented for making progress in the fields of education, industry, upliftment of weaker sections and women. However, it has not been possible, so far, to provide 'distributive justice' to all citizens of India. Casteism, factionalism, communalism and regionalism at times hamper the progress of the country. In some cases, the benefits have not reached the needy and the downtrodden. Social legislations have also remained somewhat ineffective.

Exercises

1. Explain the following:
   - (i) The concept of culture
   - (ii) The literary sources in the ancient period
   - (iii) Stages of man's progress
2. Write a note on the quality of life in the Indus valley civilisation.
3. Bring out the main points of distinction between the Vedic civilisation and the post-Vedic civilisation.

4. Write notes on the following:
    (i) The Vedas
    (ii) Status of women in the Vedic period
    (iii) Dharma
    (iv) Cultural synthesis
5. Define *varna*. Distinguish it from caste.
6. Explain the *varnashrama* system in terms of division of society into varnas and four stages in man's life (*ashramas*).
7. What is Islamic culture and tradition?
8. Critically discuss the impact of Islam on Indian society.
9. What major challenges were faced by Indian society in face of the British rule in India?
10. Explain the process of westernisation in the context of the imbalances it created in Indian society.
11. What are the main social and cultural changes noticed in India since independence?
12. Discuss the main reasons which obstructed implementation of policies and programmes for the upliftment of the weaker sections of Indian society.

Select References

Bettelheim, Charles, *India Independent*, London: MacGibbon and Kee Ltd., 1968.

Desai, A.R., *Social Background of Indian Nationalism*, Bombay: Popular Prakashan, 1976.

Hussain, S. Abid, *The National Culture of India*, New Delhi: National Book Trust, India, 1956.

Majumdar, R.C., Roychaudhuri, H.C. and Datta, Kalikinkar, *An Advanced History of India*, London: Macmillan and Co. Ltd., 1970.

Panikkar, K.M., *Essential Features of Indian Culture*, Bombay: Bharatiya Vidya Bhavan, 1967.

Prabhu, P.N., *Hindu Social Organisation*, Bombay: Popular Book Depot, 1954.

Singh, Y., *Modernization of Indian Tradition*, Jaipur: Rawat Publications, 1986.

Smith, Vincent, A., *The Oxford History of India*, London: Oxford University Press, 1970.

Sreenivasa Murthy, H.V. and Kammath, S.V., *Studies in Indian Culture*, Bombay: Asia Publishing House, 1976.

Srinivas, M.N., *Social Change in Modern India*, Berkeley: University of California Press, 1966.

Tarachand, 1967, *History of Freedom Movement in India*, Volume II, New Delhi, Govt. of India Publication.

—, 1963, *Influence of Islam on Indian Culture*, Allahabad: Indian Press Publication.

The Gazetteer of India, Vol. II, New Delhi: The Government of India Publication, 1973.

3 Socio-Religious Reform Movements

Socio-religious reforms in British India were felt necessary due to three reasons: (1) the selection of texts from various commentaries on the code of Manu had not always been enlightened; (2) the reliance on law courts for interpretation had resulted in greater conservatism; and (3) the law, as applied by the law courts and British judges, was a combination of ancient Hindu and Victorian English conservatism, particularly in regard to women, inheritance, marriage and the rights of married women. The right to property of individual members in a joint family or the granting of property right to women took many years from their acceptance in letter to their actual acceptance. The joint family, caste and Hinduism have always been the pivotal institutions and have discouraged any legislations which would weaken them manifestly or even latently.

Besides these reasons, there were several socio-cultural and economic problems which demanded mass mobilisation, awakening and action against the British Raj, feudals and upper sections of society. There was a need to attack the institutional mechanisms, which had made society rigid and exploitative.

A.R. Desai considers religious reform movements as an expression of national awakening due to contradictions between the old value system and new socio-economic realities. The aim of these movements was to revive the old religion in the context of nationalism and democracy as the cardinal principles for the emergence of modern India. Desai (1976) writes: "Modern society established liberty, freedom of competition, contact and freedom of the individual to own and manipulate property at will. Individualism was its keynote in contrast to the pre-capitalist society which was authoritarian in character, maintained social distinctions based on birth and sex, and subordinated the individual to caste and the joint family system. The new society demanded, as the very condition of its development, the abolition of privileges based on birth or sex." The reform movements were against medievalism in socio-cultural realms. They attacked the caste system and its allied institutions, polytheism, superfluous religious rites and dogmas. These religio-reform movements were national in content but religious in form. Here, in this chapter, besides the Brahmo Samaj, the Prarthana Samaj, the Arya Samaj, the Ramakrishna Mission, the Servants of India Society, we will also briefly discuss several other movements, including the Theosophical Society, reform movements among Muslims and Sikhs, the Swadeshi movement, the Satyashodhak Samaj movement, Sri Narayana Dharma Paripalana (SNDP) movement and tribal movements.

The Brahmo Samaj

Raja Ram Mohan Roy is considered to be the father of modern Indian renaissance. He was born in an orthodox and well-to-do Brahmana family in a village in the Burdwan district of West Bengal in 1772, and died in 1833. Besides English and Bengali, Ram Mohan Roy acquired knowledge of Sanskrit, Persian and Arabic. He also knew Hebrew, Latin and Greek. He made a deep study of Hindu and Muslim laws, literature and philosophy. He believed in the progressive reform of religion and a society with a liberal outlook. Ram Mohan Roy did not believe in worshipping the images of God. Monotheism was his main slogan.

On 20 August 1828, he founded the Brahmo Samaj, the literal meaning of which is "One God Society". The orthodox Hindus did not cherish the ideals of this institution, but generally people welcomed this new organisation. Ram Mohan Roy was a secularist as he was inspired by Christianity, Islam and the Upanishads. He had great faith in the uncompromising monotheism of Islam. He learnt about the concept of the unity of God as an essence of Hinduism from the study of the Upanishads, Brahma Sutras and Gita.

Ram Mohan Roy thought that without sacrificing or discarding the genuine spiritual and cultural heritage, India could not have a new philosophy, absorbing and assimilating the modernism imported from the west. He strongly advocated use of modern science and technology in education and also use of the English language. Ram Mohan Roy was, in fact, a rationalist and a pioneer of English education and enlightened journalism. He championed the cause of the exploited peasantry. His main aim was to relate religion to all aspects of life – individual, social and national. Universal theism was his message. He, however, used the Vedas and the Upanishads, in worship, sermons and devotional music, with emphasis on the universality of their contents.

Ram Mohan Roy worked against irrational institutions like *sati* and child marriage. He was champion of the cause of women. Through the Brahmo Samaj, he advocated widow remarriage, divorce, civil marriage, and education for women. Inheritance of property for women, and inter-caste marriages were special programmes undertaken by the Brahmo Samaj. He was against the caste system, as it put barriers in the ways of growth of Indian society. Ram Mohan Roy was essentially a democrat and humanist.

He did not hesitate in borrowing good from the British Raj and western culture. The Brahmo Samaj was an institution for all sorts of people, without distinction, for the worship of the one Supreme God, without idolatory. However, the historians – R.C. Majumdar, H.C. Roychaudhuri and Kalikinker Datta are of the view that Ram Mohan Roy never regarded himself as anything but a Hindu. He stoutly denied that he had founded a different sect. He always entertained the recital of the Vedas even by orthodox Brahmanas. No non-Brahmana was allowed in the Brahmo Sabha room.

Ram Mohan Roy himself wore the sacred thread of the Brahmanas upto his death.

Debendranath Tagore (1817-1905) provided a solid organisational set-up to the Brahmo Samaj after the death of Ram Mohan Roy in England. He decided to make the propagation of 'Brahmo Dharma' the main programme of the Brahmo Samaj. His *Tattvabodhini Sabha*, or Truth Teaching Society, preached the Vedas and Vedantism as the basis of the Samaj. The system of initiation and form of divine service were introduced by the new leader. He maintained and carried the best traditions of the days of Ram Mohan Roy. Upto 1866, Debendranath remained the leader of the movement at Calcutta (now Kolkata). He gave a new direction to Brahmanism by abandoning belief in the infallibility of scriptures. The Samaj continued to work for ameliorating the condition of women and children and for modernisation of education.

A new phase began with the emergence of the dynamic personality of Keshub Chandra Sen (1838-84). He joined the Brahmo Samaj in 1857. Sen advocated radical reforms with the zeal of a missionary. His mission was to broaden the activities of the Brahmo movement and to extend it to other parts of the country. In 1867, the Brahmo Samaj started functioning at Bombay under the leadership of Ranade and Bhandarkar. It organised several programmes in Madras (now Chennai). In 1866 alone, 54 activities of the Samaj were organised in different parts of the country. Keshub's fervent devotion, passionate enthusiasm and powerful eloquence gave a new life to the Samaj. His rationalistic principles reached new heights. The true spirit of repentance and devotional fervour increased the strength of the movement. He toured Madras and Bombay and other places to propagate the ideals of the Samaj.

Debendranath and Keshub soon fell out, as the two cherished different ways of functioning within the Samaj. Debendranath was for a slow and cautious move, while Keshub advocated a radical approach. In 1866, Keshub established the Brahmo Samaj of India. The parent body was known as the Adi Brahmo Samaj. The new organisation tried to foster the sense of spiritual and national unity in India. Keshub's visit to England in 1869 spread the message of the Samaj in the West.

The splinter Samaj advocated radical changes, including complete abolition of the caste system. Female emancipation and female education received top priority. Due to Christian influence, greater emphasis was put on the sense of sin, the spirit of repentance, and the efficacy of prayer. Religion was treated as a practical recourse to solve human problems rather than a dogmatic doctrine. His thesis of 'New Dispensation' (*Nava Vidhan*) declared on 25 January 1880 promoted a new synthesis of different religions.

The fourth phase in the Brahmo Samaj emerged when some followers of Keshub Chandra Sen left him and founded the Sadharan Brahmo Samaj on 15 May 1878. The new organisation was formed for the following reasons: (1) the demand for the introduction of a new constitution was not accepted, (2) there was disagreement on the question of *adesha* or Divine Command; and (3) Keshub Chandra Sen's daughter was married to the prince of Cooch Bihar, in violation of the Native Marriage Act of 1872.

The founders adopted a new constitution based on universal adult franchise. The old organisation went into oblivion. The new Samaj is active even today, with its branches all over the country. It has followed the path of constitutionalism and radical reformism. Its programmes include the removal of the *purdah* system, introduction of widow remarriage, abolition of polygamy and early marriage and provision of higher education for women. It has attacked rigidities based on the caste system. Inter-caste commensal relations, such as eating and drinking water, have been encouraged by the Samaj. Emphasis on monotheism continues to be its primary ideal.

The Prarthana Samaj

The Prarthana Samaj, an offshoot of the Brahmo Samaj, came into existence in 1867 under the leadership of Justice Mahadev Govinda Ranade. Keshub was a source of inspiration for this organisation. The followers of the Prarthana Samaj never looked upon themselves as adherents of a new religion or of a new sect, outside and alongside the general Hindu body, but saw it simply as a movement within it. They were staunch theists in the Vaishnavite tradition of Maharashtra. The saints, like Namdeo, Tukaram and Ramdas influenced them to a large extent. They devoted themselves to social reforms such as inter-caste dining and marriages, remarriage of widows, and improvement of the lot of women and depressed classes. The Samaj founded the following organisations and institutions: (1) an asylum and orphanage at Pandharpur; (2) night schools; (3) a widows home; and (4) a depressed classes mission.

Justice Ranade devoted his life to the Prarthana Samaj. He contributed to the formation of the Widow Marriage Association in 1861, and the Deccan Education Society in 1884-85. Ranade conveyed two things: (1) the whole man was his concern; and (2) there was continuity even in face of radical transformation. He advocated that these two should become a part of the reformist philosophy.

The Arya Samaj

The Arya Samaj was founded in 1875 by Swami Dayananda Saraswati (1824-83). He was a Sanskrit scholar with no English education. He gave the call "Go back to the Vedas". He had no regard for the Puranas. Swami received education on Vedanta from a blind teacher named Swami Virajananda at Mathura. His views were similar to that of Ram Mohan Roy. Disbelief in polytheism and image worship, opposition to caste-based restrictions, child marriage, opposition to the prohibition of sea voyages, and advocating female education and widow remarriage were important programmes common to the followers of Brahmo Samaj and Arya Samaj. Like other reformers of his times, Swami Dayananda Saraswati regarded the Vedas as eternal and infallible. His monumental work – *Satyartha Prakash* is an interpretation of the Vedas. Swami considered the epics – the *Ramayana* and the *Mahabharata* – as literary treasures.

Swami launched the *Shuddhi* (purification) movement, conversion of non-Hindus to Hinduism. This was begun to realise the ideal of unifying India notionally, socially, and religiously. Direct contact with the masses swelled the number of his followers in a short time. His teachings had immense impact in the Punjab and the United Provinces. The Vedas had all the truth. Every modern thing could be found in them. Swami strongly attacked the hereditary basis of the caste system, idolatry and the belief in the superiority of Brahmanas over other caste groups. He rejected untouchability and pleaded that the study of the Vedas be made open to all. The work of the Swami after his death was carried forward by Lala Hansraj, Pandit Guru Dutt, Lala Lajpat Rai and Swami Sraddhananda.

The Samaj, to prevent child marriage, fixed the minimum marriageable age at 25 years for boys and 16 for girls. Inter-caste marriage and widow remarriage were encouraged. Even today, Arya Samaj Mandirs (temples) perform such acts with sincerity and promptness. Equal status for women was their demand, both in letter and spirit. The Samaj also helped the people in crises like floods, famines and earthquakes. The Samaj opened orphanages and widow homes at various religious places. The Samaj has also attempted to give a new direction to education. The revival of the 'Gurukula' pattern, an ancient system of Hindu education, has been its goal. However, at the higher level, the value of English education was recognised. Today, the Arya Samaj has a widespread network of Dayanand Anglo-Vedic (DAV) schools and colleges throughout India.

The Ramakrishna Mission

The Ramakrishna Mission is an embodiment of the synthesis of ancient Indian and modern western cultures. Ramakrishna Paramahamsa (1836-86) was the founder of this socio-religious movement. He was a poor priest in a temple at Dakshineshwar near Calcutta. He had no formal education. He had faith in all religions and performed religious exercises in accordance with Hinduism,

Islam and Christianity. All the different religious views are different ways leading to the same goal — was the message of Ramakrishna. He (God) is both one and many. He has form and is also without it. This message is a great universal spirit as well as a constellation of symbols. Thus, catholicity was the essence of the Mission's founder. He led a life of a secluded saint with broad catholicity, mysticism and spirituality.

Formally, the Mission was founded in May 1897 by Paramahamsa's disciple, Narendranath Dutta, who was later on known as Swami Vivekananda (1863-1902). Vivekananda was a graduate of Calcutta University. Two objectives of the Mission are: (1) to bring into existence a band of monks dedicated to a life of renunciation and practical spirituality, from among whom teachers and workers would be sent out to spread the universal message of Vedanta as illustrated in the life of Ramakrishna; and (2) in conjunction with lay disciples, to carry on preaching, philanthropic and charitable works, looking upon all men, women and children, irrespective of caste, creed or colour, as veritable manifestations of the Divine.

Paramahamsa himself founded the Ramakrishna Math with his young monastic disciples as a nucleus to fulfil the first objective. The second objective was taken up by Swami Vivekananda after Ramakrishna's death. Vivekananda carried the message of Ramakrishna all over India. He was an eloquent speaker with a charming personality. Vivekananda's followers included people of all strata including princes and priests. In 1893, he attended the famous "Parliament of Religions" at Chicago. He delivered lectures on Hindu philosophy as enunciated by Ramakrishna Paramahamsa at various places in the UK and the USA.

The headquarters of the Ramakrishna Math and Mission are at Belur, near Kolkata. This centre was established in 1898 by Swami Vivekananda. The Math is a religious trust dedicated to the nursing of the inner spiritual life of the members of the monastery. The Mission is a charitable society dedicated to the expression of inner spiritual life in outward collective action in the service of men. The

Belur Math is the headquarters of both the Math and the Mission. Both the organisations have close links, and are almost inseparable from each other. The Mission stands for religious and social reforms. The Vedantic doctrine is its ideal. Its emphasis is on the development of the highest spirituality inherent in man. Certain spiritual experiences of Ramakrishna, the teachings of the Upanishads and the Gita, and the examples of the Buddha and Jesus are the basis of Vivekananda's message to the world about human values. He wanted to make the Vedanta practical. His mission was to bridge the gulf between *paramartha* (service) and *vyavahara* (behaviour), and between spirituality and day-to-day life. He advocated the doctrine of service – the service of all beings. The service of *jiva* (living objects) is the worship of Siva. Life itself is religion. By service, the Divine exists within man. Vivekananda was for using technology and modern sciences in the service of mankind.

The Mission has been in existence for more than a century. It has now developed into a worldwide organisation. The Mission is a deeply religious body; but it is not a proselytising body. It is not a sect of Hinduism. In fact, this is one of the strong reasons for the success of the Mission. The Mission has given top priority to the idea of social service, both in terms of philanthropic work and upliftment of religious and spiritual life. It has been successful in propagating the universal principle of Vedanta and giving a true picture of India to the western world. It believes that the philosophy of Vedanta will make a Christian a better Christian and a Hindu a better Hindu.

The Mission has opened many schools and dispensaries, and helped the victims of natural calamities. Millions of men and women suffering from dumbness have been helped by the Mission. There were over 138 branches of the Mission in 1961. Of these 102 were in India and the rest of them were in other countries, including the US, England, France, Sri Lanka, Pakistan, Burma and Singapore. In 1961, there were 12 indoor hospitals and 68 outdoor dispensaries run by the Mission. About 65,000 boys and girls studied in the Mission's schools and colleges in 1961. The Mission has published books on the Vedanta, and it also publishes about ten journals and magazines in English and other Indian languages.

The Servants of India Society

Like other nineteenth century organisations for socio-religious reforms, the Servants of India Society undertook various welfare programmes in the early twentieth century. Gopal Krishna Gokhale, a liberal leader of the Indian National Congress, founded the Society in 1905 with the aim to train "national missionaries for the service of India, and to promote, by all constitutional means, the true interests of the Indian people". Its members were called upon "to devote their lives to the cause of the country in a religious spirit". It was a society dedicated to the service of the country. Its aim was to prepare a cadre of selfless workers.

Srinivasa Shastri succeeded Gokhale as its president, after Gokhale's death in 1915. Some of the members devoted themselves to selfless politics, others took up welfare activities. In 1911, Narayan Malhar Joshi, a follower of Gokhale, founded the Social Service League in Bombay. Its aim was "to secure for the masses of the people better and reasonable conditions of life and work". In 1926, they ran 17 night schools, 3 free day schools, 11 libraries and reading rooms and 2 day nurseries. They organised over a hundred cooperative societies. Other activities included Police Court Agent's work, legal advice and aid to the poor and illiterate, excursions for slum-dwellers, facilities for gymnasia and theatrical performances, sanitary work, medical relief and Boys' Clubs and Scout Corps. Joshi also founded the All-India Trade Union Congress in 1920.

The Theosophical Society

The Theosophical Society was founded in 1886 by Madam H.P. Blavatsky and Colonel H.S. Olcott. Later on, Mrs Annie Besant took up the leadership of this organisation to revive and strengthen Hinduism, Zorastrianism and Buddhism.

Bipin Chandra Pal, Aurobindo Ghose, Bal Gangadhar Tilak and Mahatma Gandhi also made use of the Upanishads and the epics for making India a secular state, and for effecting social reforms. Gandhi did tremendous work for the removal of untouchability.

Reform Movements among Muslims, Sikhs and Parsis

The Muslims had four revivalistic movements: (1) the Ahmedia movement; (2) the Aligarh movement; (3) Sir Mohammad Iqbal's movement; and (4) Shaikh Abdul Halim Sharar's movement. These movements stressed upon universal brotherhood, liberal education and liberal interpretation of the Quran. The Aligarh Muslim University came into being in 1920. An All-India Muslim Educational Conference was also organised. Sayed Ahmad Khan was the leader of the Aligarh-based movement.

Parsis and Sikhs also launched several socio-religious reforms in their respective communities. Parsis vowed to discard orthodoxy, particularly in regard to education of women, marriage and social position of women. The Sikhs did a lot of work to reform the management of the Gurudwaras. There was practically a revolt against the Mahants of these shrines. The Khalsa College at Amritsar was established by the end of the nineteenth century.

The Swadeshi Movement

The Swadeshi movement aimed at the indigenisation by discarding use of foreign goods and inculcation of nationalist spirit among the people of India. 'Lokahitawadi', a reformer in Maharashtra, an ardent advocate of the Swadeshi movement, listed the following points for reforming society:

1. all should devoutly worship God;
2. all ceremonies, except those connected with initiation, marriage and death should be abolished. Ceremonials and prayers should be performed in one's own language;
3. every person should have liberty to act, speak and write according to what he thinks;

4. men and women should have equal rights in social and religious functions;
5. morality is higher than performance of ritual;
6. no person is to be treated with contempt. Pride of caste is unbecoming. All men are to be treated with charity. Do good to all;
7. love of the motherland and good of the country should always be borne in mind;
8. the rights of the people are higher than those of the government,
9. the rules laid down by the government and rules suggested by reason should be observed;
10. everybody should strive for the growth of learning; and
11. truth should be the abiding principle of conduct.

These canons of conduct show that India was trying to rejuvenate its socio-cultural fabric and make a dignified place for itself in the changed circumstances. It had become necessary to change, to discard and to adopt some elements simultaneously. Striving for synthesis had become a necessity. Condemnation of ritual paraphernalia, caste system, rules of marriage, and of differences between the sexes had become absolutely necessary.

The Satyashodhak Samaj Movement

Jotiba Phule organised a powerful movement against the Brahmanas in Maharashtra. He started a school for girls, and one for the 'untouchables', and also a home for widows. He challenged the supremacy of the Brahmanas. His two writings – *Sarvajanik Satyadharma Pustak* and *Gulamgiri* became sources of inspiration for the common masses. He founded the Satyashodhak Samaj (Truth Seekers' Society) to carry out his crusade against the Brahmana hegemony. The Satyashodhak Samaj, besides being anti-Brahmanic, had a programme of positive action for women's liberation, propagating education, and for economic betterment. Mahatma Phule used the symbol of Rajah Bali as opposed to the Brahamana's symbol of Rama. The middle castes, the Kunbis, Malis and Dhangars, developed a sense of identity as a class against Brahmanas, who were thought of as exploiters. In the 1900s, the Maharaja of Kolhapur encouraged the non-Brahmana movement. The movement spread to the southern states in the first decade of twentieth century. Kammas, Reddis and Vellalas, the powerful intermediate castes, joined hands against the Brahmanas. Muslims also joined them.

The SNDP Movement

A number of backward class movements were launched in the pre-independence period. The backward classes organised themselves against the Brahmanas in particular as they thought that most of the socio-economic advantages were cornered by them depriving the agricultural intermediate castes and communities. We have discussed these movements in detail in Chapter 11. These were similar to Jotiba Phule's Satyashodhak Samaj movement, with the similar aim of ending oppression by the Brahmanas. The Brahmanas were the first to exploit modern educational and employment opportunities. The upper non-Brahmana castes failed to get access to these opportunities. The Sri Narayana Dharma Paripalana (SNDP) movement, among the Ezhavas of Kerala, is an example of conflict between the depressed classes and the upper non-Brahmana castes. The Ezhavas were a caste of toddy-tappers in Kerala. They were like the Nadars of Tamil Nadu and the Idigas of Karnataka. The Ezhavas were the largest single caste group constituting 26 per cent of the total population of Kerala. In a developing country like India, movements led by the backward classes speak of their low status, disadvantages, discriminations and deprivations which they suffered for a long time at the hands of the ruling classes and communities.

The SNDP movement is an example of a 'regional' movement. It pertains to the Ezhavas of Kerala who were untouchables. The ideology of the movement was formulated by Sri Narayana Guru Swamy. He formed a programme of action known as the 'SNDP Yogam'. The Yogam took up several issues, including the right of admission to public schools, recruitment to government employment, entry into temples, on roads and political representation. Most of these objectives were realised. The movement, as a whole, brought about transformative structural changes which included upward social mobility, a shift in the traditional distribution of power, and a federation of 'backward castes' into a large conglomeration.

Caste reforms and mobility movements were launched in almost all parts of India during the British period. These movements had two objectives: (1) to protest against the hegemony of Brahmanas in particular and of other upper castes in general; and (2) to elevate the position of the backward castes in the caste hierarchy by imitating lifestyles of the upper castes, including having higher education and prestigious jobs. These movements invariably created 'ethnic' awareness and politicisation among various caste groups.

Tribal Movements

Several tribal movements began, making demands for formation of a separate state, greater autonomy, development of a script and for independent identity. Such movements were related to cultural and political revivalism. For example, the Khasi, Garo, Bodo-Kachari and Ahom tribes of the North-East made such demands from time to time. Tribal movements in the states of Bihar, Bengal, Madhya Pradesh and Orissa were regarding political autonomy, the right to agrarian and forest-based produce and socio-religious, cultural and linguistic problems. Sub-regional identity was the main focus of these movements. Some of these movements started and died out in the pre-independence era. But some movements in the North-East are still alive. The movements such as Jharkhand, Chhatisgarh, and Uttrakhand are no more because demand for formation of separate states has already been meted out

A number of organisations and associations have been formed such as the Mizo Union, the Garo National Council, the East-India Tribal Union and the All-Party Hill Leaders Conference. Restoration of autonomy has been the hallmark of a large number of tribal movements. The tribals had full control over the forests before the advent of the British. These organisations have mobilised the tribals to demand their right to manage forests and forest produces.

Though initially, a number of movements started with some cultural goals in view, but subsequently they expressed political goals, like statehood and autonomy. The states of Nagaland, Manipur, Mizoram and Arunachal Pradesh are the concrete results of these tribal movements. However, some movements are certainly cultural, as they are confined to ethnic identity, revival of culture, script and language. The Bhagat movement in Bihar, Rajasthan, Gujarat and Madhya Pradesh by the tribal people involves the imitation of the socio-cultural practices of upper caste Hindus. The imitation implies adoption of vegetarianism, teetotalism and worship of Hindu gods. Gonds, Kharwas, Oraons, Gahiras, Bhils, Meenas and some other tribes have become Bhagats (saints) in large numbers.

Impact on Social Structure

The greatest impact of the nineteenth century socio-religious reform movements was: (1) the creation of national awakening among the masses; (2) the revival of Hinduism as a tolerant, rational religion to restore its lost prestige in the wake of Islam in the past and Christianity in the nineteenth century; (3) an onslaught on the indignities committed on women, untouchables and other oppressed and depressed sections of Indian society; (4) the creation of the feelings of sacrifice, service and rationalism; (5) an attack on the hereditary character and rigidities of the caste system; and finally (6) a sense of equality, indigenisation and co-existence of cultures and religions.

It has been noted earlier that atrocities on women through *purdah*, child marriage, hypergamy, dowry and sex-based inequality in regard to division of work, education, occupation, freedom, etc., moved all the reformists. Not only were legislations against these ills passed, but concrete social actions were also taken to ameliorate the plight of women. It was an era of new enlightenment, of indigenisation with an open mind, welfarism, liberalism and equalitarianism. This sort of awakening contributed a lot to India's freedom struggle.

These socio-religious movements were for introducing humanistic social reforms by stopping the moral and material decadence of India. Even radical westernisation was pleaded for by Ram Mohan Roy as a means to rejuvenate the decaying Indian culture and society. These movements did not have an all-India character. They were localised in Bengal, Maharashtra, Punjab, etc. Their impact was generally limited to the educated, upper middle and middle classes. Assimilation of the values of rationalism, universal brotherhood, freedom of man and equality of sexes was not so easy with the Indian tradition and culture. These movements have been called "denationalised and hyper-westernised" by some critics. It is certainly undeniable that these movements made tremendous and everlasting impact in terms of socio-cultural awakening against social evils.

Conclusion

We have discussed in detail some selected socio-religious reform movements, namely, the Brahmo Samaj, the Prarthana Samaj, the Arya Samaj, the Ramakrishna Mission, the Servants of India Society, the Theosophical Society, movements among Muslims, Sikhs and Parsis, Swadeshi movement, Satyashodhak Samaj movement, the SNDP movement and tribal movements in the pre-independence period. These movements strived at a synthesis of traditional and modern values. All of them discarded dogmatism, ritualism and orthodoxy, and worked for the welfare of women and deprived sections of society. They were all against British colonialism and its negative effects on Indian society. Social evils, like *sati*, child marriage, *purdah*, etc., were condemned. Widow remarriage, women's education, inheritance of property for women and inter-caste marriages were encouraged. Education, social awakening, national pride and egalitarianism were promoted by various organisations by introduction of several welfare projects.

Exercises

1. Bring out the salient features of the Brahmo Samaj.
2. Was Ram Mohan Roy truly the Father of modern Indian renaissance?
3. One common goal of all the socio-religious reform movements was the achievement of synthesis of traditional and modern values. Comment.
4. In what way did various movements advocate the upliftment of women and backward classes?
5. Explain the following:
   (i) Cultural movement
   (ii) Political movement
   (iii) Reform movement
6. Discuss similarities and differences between the Brahmo Samaj and the Arya Samaj.
7. In what way was the Ramakrishna Mission a mix of Hinduism, Islam and Christianity?
8. Prepare notes on the following:
   (i) The philosophy of Vedanta
   (ii) Sati
   (iii) Child marriage
   (iv) The SNDP movement
   (v) Mahatma Jotiba Phule
   (vi) Hinduism

Select References

Chandra, Bipan, *Modern India*, New Delhi: NCERT, 1976.

Chand, Tara, *History of the Freedom Movement in India*, Volume II, New Delhi: Government of India Publication, 1967.

Desai, A.R., *Social Background of Indian Nationalism*, Bombay: Popular Prakashan, 1976.

Majumdar, R.C., Roychaudhuri, H.C. and Datta, Kalikinker, *An Advanced History of India*, London: Macmillan Co., 1970.

Murthy, H.V.S. and Kamath, S.U., *Studies in Indian Culture*, Bombay: Asia Publishing House, 1976.

Singh, Yogendra, *Modernization of Indian Tradition*, Jaipur: Rawat Publications, 1986.

The Gazetteer of India, Volume II, New Delhi: Government of India Publication, 1973.

4 National Movement: Its Sociological Implications

Indian society had divisions based on religion, region, tribe, caste and language; and the British not only perpetuated these divisions but accentuated them further so that the Indian people could not unite against the British rule. Various castes and communities were allowed to retain their names and titles. Associations, institutions and regiments were named after particular castes and communities. Muslims were encouraged initially to make demand for separate electorates, and later on a demand for the formation of Pakistan. Muslim communalism was mainly a product of the British policy of "divide and rule". In this chapter we will discuss the early phase of national awakening, the emergence of the Indian National Congress, the role of the 'moderates' and the 'extremists' in the Congress, the emergence of Mahatma Gandhi, and above all the communalistic and divisive policy of the British.

In this context, political awakening, education, communalism and caste have been identified as major sociological facts of India's struggle against the British for achieving freedom. In fact, these are not independent phenomena. At times they cut across each other and find themselves in contradistinction, but they have also been found co-existent during the national movement for India's freedom.

Socio-Economic Conditions at the Advent of the British

The British Raj had to overcome several administrative difficulties arising from the divisions in Indian society based on religion, region, tribe, language and caste. At the same time, the British did not want India to modernise, fearing revolts against themselves. In many ways, they, in fact, encouraged the divisive tendencies to prevent unity among various sections of Indian society. The British did their best to keep the people divided on the basis of caste, community, religion and region.

The caste system was the essence of the social life of the Hindus. Caste panchayats regulated its members in regard to choice of occupations, selection of mates, inter-caste relations and channels for social mobility. Caste prejudices were very strong. Even in the army, Brahmanas and Rajputs were allowed to observe their caste rules and regulations. They had their own separate cooking pots and *lotas* (jugs). Sea voyage was regarded as defilement. The British gave army regiments names such as Rajput Rifles and Jat Regiment. Some communities, such as the Yadavas, have for a long time been demanding a regiment named after their caste.

The native princely states and their feudatories supported these reactionary policies of the British Raj. The trading communities and the service classes were also not averse to the retrograde steps taken by the government. The government did it with its notorious policy of "divide and rule". Whatever the reformers were doing was being undone by the British. After the revolt of 1857, the British government made a show of adopting a policy of greater respect for Indian usages and customs and of non-interference with religious beliefs and worship. The princes were assured of the continuity of all the treaties and agreements made with them by the East India Company. Hence, they did not bother about the social and cultural conditions and the policy of the Raj towards these conditions.

The Muslims were also divided on the basis of caste, sect, tribe and economic status. The Shias and the Sunnis used to quarrel with each other. Both the communities (Hindus and Muslims) observed *purdah*, and practised early marriage. The Hindus continued to practise sati, and imposed restrictions upon widow remarriage (among the upper caste Hindus in particular).

The British Raj also changed the judicial system. A highly bureaucratised imperial administrative system was affected. Economic development and modernised communications unified the country and brought it closer to the British empire. The railways and telegraph system also contributed to the spread and consolidation of the Raj in India. It seems that national awakening was generated more by the British educational policy than any other single factor.

Macaulay's policy (1835) necessitated opening of universities and colleges in the country. In 1857, the universities of Calcutta, Madras and Bombay were founded. In 1882, the Hunter Commission recommended the reorganisation of the educational services. English education was intended to provide English knowing people to staff law courts and various departments of the government. However, it unwittingly brought to India political ideas of the West along with the knowledge of western science. The British educational system created a sizeable educated middle class who shared English language and the liberal ideas of the West. This class, with the help of the railways, the telegraph and the press, acted on an all-India basis to stir up national feelings and ideas.

Early Phase of Nationalism

The following developments may be noted as a result of the early phase of nationalism in India:

1. In 1876, Surendranath Banerjea founded the Indian Association in Calcutta (now Kolkata) with a mission for the admission of Indians to the civil service. This association also protested against several reactionary measures taken by the British government in India.
2. In 1883, the Indian National Conference was founded in Calcutta with members from all over the country.

3. In 1885, the Indian National Congress was founded at Bombay (now Mumbai), and the Indian National Conference merged into this new organisation. The Muslims, however, kept themselves aloof from the Congress under the leadership of Sir Syed Ahmed Khan.
4. Under Lord Curzon, administrative and economic reforms were initiated to strengthen the Raj. The Indian Police was reorganised. He reduced the burden of taxes on the peasants and protected them against eviction by the moneylenders. He also encouraged cooperative credit societies and agricultural banks. The Department of Agriculture and the Agricultural Research Institute were started by him. Irrigation was promoted. A Department of Commerce and Industry was also created. More railway lines were constructed. Efforts were made to preserve the monuments of India. The Archaeology Department and the Imperial Library at Calcutta were significant developments. All this was done to instil a feeling of goodwill for the British rulers in India.
5. In 1902, an Education Commission was formed to reform university education. The control of the government was increased by appointing Vice-Chancellors selected by the government. The Universities Act of 1904 was opposed by the educated middle class as it interfered with the autonomy of the universities and higher institutions of learning.
6. The Swadeshi movement and the boycott of foreign goods also started in the first decade of the twentieth century.

The year 1905 is important at least for two reasons. Firstly, Bengal was partitioned, and secondly, open conflicts and tensions began within the Indian National Congress in 1905. The second was directly related to the national movement.

The Partition of Bengal

Lord Curzon came to India (1899-1905) with a strong determination to stem the rising tide of nationalism. The Calcutta Cooperation Act, the Indian Universities Act (1904), and the

Official Secrets Act (1904) were some of the measures through which Curzon sought to curb the growing nationalistic and patriotic spirit. The partition of Bengal was Curzon's most unpopular measure. On 20 July 1905, Lord Curzon announced the partition of Bengal into two parts: Eastern Bengal and Assam (one part) and the rest of Bengal (the other part). Curzon announced the partition on the pretext of administrative convenience as he considered the existing province of Bengal too big and unwieldy to be effectively administered. However, the Indian National Congress and nationalists saw that it was a part of the policy of "divide and rule".

This measure provoked violent opposition from the people of Bengal as they felt humiliated and insulted. The anti-partition movement was started on 7 August 1905 at Calcutta to boycott English goods, and adopt 'swadeshi' (indigenous) goods.

The response of the people was speedy and spontaneous. A day of national mourning was observed throughout Bengal as the partition took effect on 16 October 1905. Rabindranath Tagore composed a national song for the occasion. The streets of Calcutta rang with the cries of *Bande Mataram*. It was followed by hundreds of public meetings, demonstrations, picketing of shops, bonfires of foreign goods, clashes with the police, imprisonment of volunteers, and expulsion of students from colleges and universities.

A remarkable aspect of the Swadeshi movement was the active participation of women, prominent Muslims like Abdul Rasul, Liaquat Husain Guznavi, and particularly of students. It was the students who showed the greatest enthusiasm and created 'swadeshi' spirit in Bengal during the agitation. However, the movement did not really involve or affect the masses of Bengal.

The Swadeshi movement spread to other parts of India towards the end of 1905. Tilak played a leading role in giving the movement an all-India character. Bal Gangadhar Tilak, Bipin Chandra Pal and Aurobindo Ghose were dissatisfied with the old leadership (moderates) of the Congress party and its policy of constitutional protest. They wanted to force the government to extort concessions not by prayer but by action. The leadership of the Anti-Partition Movement soon passed to militant nationalists.

The differences between the extremists and the moderates came to a head at the Surat session of Congress in 1907.

Congress was ideologically divided into 'moderates' and 'extremists'. The leaders of the moderate group (*naram dal*) were Pherozeshah Mehta, Surendranath Banerjea and Gopal Krishna Gokhale. They admired British political institutions and trusted British rulers. Constitutionalism was their approach for enacting reforms. The extremists (*garam dal*) did not approve of the policy of the lawyer-dominated politics of petition and prayer. Pressure and active resistance were adopted as their main tactics. Bal Gangadhar Tilak, Lala Lajpat Rai and Bipin Chandra Pal were the leaders of the extremists, and they believed in militant means for achieving wider national goals. They boycotted British goods. However, upto 1916, the moderates remained in a commanding position in the Indian National Congress.

Discontentment emerged in western India, Bengal and Punjab due to popular sentiments against the British. This heightened national consciousness. It resulted into quick action by the Raj to enact reforms and political change. Every British thing (not only goods) was boycotted – the boycott being extended to government and government-aided educational institutions, courts and executive bodies. Such aversion to British things led to constructive and nation-building efforts on the one hand and glorification of the Indian (specially Hindu) heritage on the other.

Muslim separatism crystallised with the formation of the Muslim League in 1906. Since the League was opposed to Hindu domination, it supported the partition of Bengal and opposed the anti-British boycott. A demand was made for separate electorates for Muslims. Finally, the Indian National Congress was also influenced by developments in the international arena.

Constitutional and Other Reforms

In 1909, the Morley-Minto Reforms were initiated under which (1) the principle of election to the central legislature, provincial legislatures, municipalities, district boards, chambers of commerce and universities was recognised, and the landholders and others were granted the right to vote; and (2) a communal electorate by creating a number of Muslim constituencies for the Centre as well as provinces was introduced.

In 1919, the Montague-Chelmsford Reforms were approved, under which the bicameral system was introduced at the Centre: (1) the Council of States, and (2) the Legislative Assembly. About 70 per cent of the members were elected to these councils. The principle of direct election was recognised. Separate electorates were maintained for Muslims, Anglo-Indians, Europeans, Sikhs and Christians, and for non-Brahmanas in Madras (now Chennai). Tilak and Mahatma Gandhi were of the view that the reforms should be implemented on a trial basis.

In 1920, Gandhi launched a non-violent and Non-Cooperation Movement, and at the same time rejected the reforms. The Ali brothers (Shaukat Ali and Muhammad Ali), the pioneers of the Khilafat movement, joined hands with the Mahatma in the national struggle against the British. The peasants and workers were also drawn into the struggle against the British. The Non-Cooperation Movement, a revised form of the Swadeshi movement, urged people to resign from government offices, shun the law courts, withdraw from English schools and colleges, and boycott elections. The use of indigenous goods, khadi and home-spun cloth was strongly advocated. Gandhi was arrested in 1924, for steering the Non-Cooperation Movement.

By this time, the Congress party was a divided house consisting of (1) the Swaraj Party led by Motilal Nehru and C.R. Das; (2) the followers of Tilak; (3) the Justice Party of Madras; and (4) the independents led by Jinnah. Consequently, there was no cohesion in the Indian National Congress. Communal riots broke out in 1924. However, the Mahatma dedicated himself for restoration of communal harmony and for the upliftment of Harijans. The Hindu Mahasabha, which was formed in 1915, also became active as a result of communal disturbances.

The government, without bothering about the popular sentiments against its policies, implemented the reforms of 1919.

Elections were held. The central and the provincial governments were reconstituted. The Moplah rising (August 1921) worsened communal relations. The Non-Cooperation Movement was reactivated. A violent incident occurred at Chauri Chaura in Uttar Pradesh. The Khilafat movement weakened. Gandhi was arrested in 1922, and with his arrest the Non-Cooperation Movement came to a standstill. The Indian National Congress became weaker. Communalism raised its ugly head. Elections were fought on communal lines. Nationalist forces lost their vigour.

Jallianwala Bagh Massacre

In 1919, the British government passed the Rowlatt Act, which was an extremely repressive measure. This Act authorised the government to imprison any person without trial and conviction in a court of law. Gandhi started 'satyagraha' and called for a countrywide passive resistance movement in protest against the Act. To put down this movement, the government decided to meet the protest with repression, particularly in Punjab, under its Lieutenant-Governor, Sir Michael O'Dyer. At the same time, two prominent leaders, Dr. Saifuddin Kitchlu and Dr. Satyapal, were arrested in Punjab. In protest against these arrests, an unarmed and defenceless crowd gathered on 13 April 1919 in Jallianwala Bagh at Amritsar. Under the orders of General R.E.H. Dyer, British troops surrounded the Bagh, closed the only exit and mercilessly fired on the peaceful gathering. Thousands were killed and wounded. The Jallianwala Bagh massacre was indeed a dark tragedy. After this massacre, martial law was proclaimed in Punjab and people were submitted to the most inhuman atrocities and humiliating punishments. There were indiscriminate arrests, confiscation of property, floggings and whippings and cutting off of water and electric supplies.

All these outrages shocked the people of India and raised a strong wave of discontent throughout the country. Rabindranath Tagore renounced his knighthood in protest against the Punjab tragedy. Congress boycotted the special committee headed by Lord Hunter to enquire into the killings. When Gandhi came to know about the atrocities in Punjab, he decided to break off his relations with the British, and started a non-violent campaign of non-cooperation against the British government.

Reactions to the Reforms

The visit of the Simon Commission to India to review the reforms of 1919 sparked off a new phase of nationalist agitation. A nationwide agitation to boycott the Commission was launched. All the groups and factions, ignoring their differences, joined this protest. Since the Commission did not include a single Indian, it was greeted with black flags, strikes and mass demonstrations. Motilal Nehru emerged as a national leader. He prepared a report which opposed separate electorates. Jinnah decided to dissociate himself from this and joined hands with the Muslim separatists. A dominion status was demanded for India by an All Parties Conference. The British government rejected the demand. Congress observed 'Independence Day' on January 26, 1930, and Mahatma Gandhi started his Dandi Satyagraha (civil disobedience) on 12 March 1930. This aimed at making salt in defiance of the salt law. The Civil Disobedience Movement spread all over the country. Gandhi was arrested. Over 60,000 people were arrested and several killed.

The princes and the non-Congress political parties and groups collaborated with the British Raj. In the first Round Table Conference in 1930-31, Congress was not represented, but the princes and other political parties and groups participated. Congress was represented in the second Round Table Conference, but to counter its weight, the Raj involved the non-Congress parties in a big way. The Simon Commission had proposed self-government in the provinces and a federation of British India and the princes at the Centre, but the proposal could not materalise due to lack of support from the Congress. Under the Gandhi-Irwin Pact, Gandhi and all the detainees were released, and the Civil Disobedience Movement was called off. But no solution could be found for electoral representation. Consequently, the Civil Disobedience Movement started again, and Gandhi was arrested shortly after his return from England. Lord Irwin's successor, Lord Wellington, was hostile to the Congress. It was banned and over 1,20,000 persons were arrested. Gandhi also opposed to the formation of a separate electorate for 'backward classes' as decided by the British Prime Minister, Ramsay Macdonald in August 1932.

Formation of Congress Ministries in Provinces

After the end of the Civil Disobedience Movement in May 1934, Congress decided to launch a programme to bring about constitutional changes. In the meanwhile the Parliament passed the Government of India Act, 1935, making a provision for an all-India federation and provincial autonomy. The federal part of the Act was never introduced but provincial autonomy came into operation from 1937. Though new constitutional reforms fell far short of India's national aspirations, Congress decided to contest the elections to the assemblies in the provinces under the new Act of 1935. In the elections, Congress obtained an overwhelming majority in most of the provinces. The Muslim League fared badly even in provinces predominantly inhabited by Muslims. After a deadlock over the question of the exercise of the special powers of interference by the Governor of a province and clarification of the position by the Viceroy, Congress decided to work in the provinces. Congress ministries were formed in July 1937 in several provinces, including the United Provinces, Madras, the Central Provinces, Bombay, Bihar, Orissa, and after sometime in the North-West Frontier Provinces (NWFP). It also formed coalition ministries in Sind and Assam. Only Bengal and Punjab had non-Congress ministries.

The result of the elections widened the rift between the Congress and the Muslim League. The phenomenal success of the Congress alarmed M.A. Jinnah and consequently he started to denounce the policies and activities of Congress ministries and openly declared that "the Muslims can expect neither justice nor fair play under Congress government". The majority of Muslims accepted this view and Jinnah became the undisputed leader of the League.

When the Second World War broke out in 1939, and England declared war against Nazi Germany without consulting either the Central Legislature or the provincial governments, the Viceroy declared India to be a belligerent country on the side of the British. The Congress Working Committee called upon all the ministers to resign from their posts. The Muslim League observed a 'Day of Deliverance', as a mark of relief after the resignation of the Congress ministries in the provinces.

The Act of 1935 was a culmination of the developments listed above. Under this Act, provinces were granted autonomy. The Governor was assisted by a legislature. As stated earlier, the provinces had a bicameral system. However, the communal basis of voting was retained. The Governor still enjoyed the power to control key sectors of administration.

The nationalist fervour hardened in the thirties. Leftism grew both within the Congress and outside it. The leftist forces within the Congress pleaded for a radical policy and militant action. They supported a strong Civil Disobedience Movement. Jawaharlal Nehru and Subhash Chandra Bose were eminent leftist leaders within the Congress. Nehru accepted Mahatma Gandhi's leadership, but Bose believed in an armed struggle against the British. A socialist group emerged in the Congress under the leadership of Nehru, Jai Prakash Narain and Acharya Narendra Deva. The All-India Trade Union Congress was founded in 1920. The All-India Kisan Sabha was founded in 1936. The terrorism of the 1920s was transformed by revolutionary leftism in the 1930s.

Thus, Congress simultaneously faced ultra-leftism and communalism. Communalism was, in fact, a more serious problem. The 'nationalist' Muslims supported Congress, but they were too few to become an effective voice. The Muslims resigned from the Congress ministries in the provinces. In 1940, the Muslim League declared formation of Pakistan as its ultimate goal. The League also demanded equal share with the Hindus in the proposed national government.

On 9 August 1942, Congress called upon the British to relinquish power and to quit India. Congress leaders were arrested and the party was banned. Violent clashes took place between the people and the police. The Communist Party of India kept itself out of the Quit India Movement. Subhash Chandra Bose escaped from India in 1941, and formed the Azad Hind Fauz (Indian National Army) in 1943. He also established the Azad Hind Government with its headquarters at Rangoon.

Indian National Army

The major inspiration for carrying on a relentless struggle against Britain came from Subhash Chandra Bose's adventures abroad. During World War II Bose escaped from India and went to Italy, Germany and Japan. With the help of Japanese, he formed the Azad Hind Fauz (the Indian National Army, INA) in Singapore on 21 October 1943. Its purpose was to conduct a military campaign for the liberation of India. He gave his famous call of "Delhi Chalo". He was assisted by Rash Behari Bose, an old revolutionary. A large number of Indian prisoners of war in Japanese camps and Indians of trading communities settled in South-East Asia joined the INA. The INA fought on the side of the Japanese to defeat the British and to liberate the country. Bose invaded the British on Indian territory and had some initial success. Later on, his army had to surrender. Bose is reported to have died in an air crash in 1945. He was undoubtedly an ardent patriot, and by organising the Azad Hind Fauz he set an inspiring example of patriotism before the Indian people and the Indian Army.

The RIN Mutiny

On 18 February 1946, the ratings of the Royal Indian Navy (RIN) in the signals training establishment *Talwar* went on a hunger-strike in protest against bad food, weakening of the old military tradition of recruitment and racist insults. It was a heroic rising against a long series of unsettled grievances. The rising was mainly centred in Bombay. By 19 February, it had spread to all the 20,000 ratings in the twelve shore establishments in Bombay and its suburbs as well as to the twenty ships in the harbour. The ratings elected a Naval Central Strike Committee and formulated a charter of demands which included the national political slogans for the release of INA and other political prisoners. The ratings fought a seven-hour battle with the army and navy on 21 February. Finally, on 23 February, Vallabhabhai Patel managed to persuade the ratings to surrender by giving an assurance that "the Congress will do its level best to see that there is no victimisation". This was followed by a similar assurance from the Muslim League.

Political Awakening

The real beginning of the nationalist fervour dates back to the second half of the nineteenth century. Earlier, in the pre-1857 period, two contradictory ideas were expressed: (1) anti-British, and (2) pro-British. The pro-British ideas led to the emergence of nationalism and patriotism as a reaction to the devotion of the people to the principles of British administration and English education. The anti-British ideas resulted in several political and civil movements and uprisings. Both the stances were, in effect, against the British Raj and for freedom of India. The atrocities perpetrated by the Raj generated the ideas of political awakening. The demand for political rights and social justice became a valued idea. The leaders of the freedom movement became eager for emancipation from the British yoke.

The revolt of 1857, also known as the first war of India's independence, was the first signal expression of people's opposition to British rule in India. It is said: "What began as a fight for religion ended as a war of independence, for there is not the slightest doubt that the rebels wanted to get rid of the alien government and restore the old order in which the emperor of Delhi was the 'rightful representative'. 'March to Delhi' was the call given by the leaders of the Mutiny".

The revolt of 1857 succeeded in winning over the zamindars, merchants, public servants, pundits and fakirs as they thought that their interests could be protected by restoration of the pre-British rule. The sepoys were fighting for their castes, the chiefs for their kingdoms, the landed classes for their estates, the masses for fear of conversion to Christianity and the Muslims in particular for the restoration of their old sway. Yet, all in their own way were fighting against the English. Thus, the revolt of 1857 involved all sections of Indian society under the leadership of the military. The revolt was followed by rebellions in several parts of Bengal, Bihar and Punjab in particular. Organisations such as the Arya Samaj, the Theosophical Society and the Ramakrishna Mission also fostered political awakening through their religious and cultural preachings.

The intelligentsia were dead set against the British Raj. The economic ruin of the country, the chronic poverty of the people and the recurrence of famines were some of the factors responsible for political awakening among the people. Insults to their pride also angered the intelligentsia against the British. Rude behaviour towards Indians, brutal assaults, maltreatment of servants and men in the street were common occurrences. Englishmen were not punished for such violations and offences. This discriminatory policy encouraged educated Indians to fight against the British rule. Such a policy of discrimination against Indians was effectively implemented in recruitment of services including the Indian Civil Service. Indians were humiliated and dehumanised by the British to an unlimited extent. The British Indian Association was formed by educated Indians to fight these evils.

Prominent leaders of the early phase of political and national awakening were W.C. Banerjee, Dadabhai Naoroji, Surendranath Banerjea, Pherozeshah Mehta and Rajnarain Basu. In 1874, Kristodas Pal demanded Home Rule for India. In Maharashtra, M.G. Ranade gave the lead to the process of political awakening. In the north, the Arya Samaj leader Swami Dayananda Saraswati created anti-British feelings by giving a call "go back to the Vedas".

The Indian National Congress was founded by A.O. Hume in 1885 for the mental, moral, social and political regeneration of the people of India. Hume, in consultation with leaders like Dadabhai Naoroji, Badruddin Tyabji, Pherozeshah Mehta and others, organised a conference at Bombay in 1885. The Congress developed into a powerful political organisation. It focussed on the political ideas of English-educated Indians and gave them definite shape and form. Liberalism and a sense of justice were accepted as the cherished ideals of the Congress leaders. The Congress helped the political advancement of the country, gave reality to the ideals of Indian unity, developed patriotic feelings and awakened political consciousness. However, several people made bitter and unfriendly criticism of the policies and actions of the Congress. The Muslims and Englishmen both considered it a threat to their existence. The Congress, despite the criticism, continued to work for the liberation and upliftment of the country.

Bankim Chandra Chatterji (1838-94), the author of *Anandamath*, ridiculed Congress policies. So did Aurobindo Ghose (1872-1950). Bal Gangadhar Tilak (1856-1920), however, upheld the mission of the Congress. A great scholar, politician and a man of action, Tilak devoted himself to liberating his countrymen from foreign rule. Tilak is known as the "Father of Indian Unrest". He spread the spirit of patriotism and nationalism among the masses. He made Shivaji a symbol of these virtues. Tilak, through his newspapers, *Kesari* (in Marathi) and *Mahratta* (in English), advocated nationalist fervour through strong constitutional means. He decried the policy of mendicancy followed by the Congress. In Bengal, Bipin Chandra Pal (1858-32), and in Punjab, Lajpat Rai (1865-1928), followed Tilak's policy, and criticised Congress policy as that of one confined to a few English-educated persons. They also worked against the use of the English language and against support to the ruling authorities. Tilak demanded 'swaraj' (self-government) rather than reforms in administration. He also gave a call for self-help and political agitation by the masses.

Thus, Tilak gave a new direction to politics. He disliked the attitude of prayerfulness and importunity and the method of political mendicancy of the Congress. He always thought of involving the mass of people in the nationalist movement. It has been said that "Tilak brought political philosophy in India from heaven to earth, from the Council Hall or the Congress Mandap to the street and the market". Force and vitality in politics were Tilak's sanguine contribution to Indian nationalism. Tilak said: "Swaraj is my birth-right and I will have it." While drawing a line between the moderates and Tilak's policy, it is stated: "Formerly it was a Congress of petitioners, now it is a Congress of men and women determined to win their freedom." Ganapati and Shivaji festivals in modern Maharashtra are symbolic of Tilak's philosophy and practice.

The British government made all-round efforts to repress the revolutionaries, particularly in Maharashtra and West Bengal. Several legislations were passed to curb their activities. The newspapers and magazines managed by the revolutionaries were censored. Several people were hanged and killed on charge of sedition. The British adopted the policy of "divide and rule" to put the extremists against the moderates and the Hindus against the Muslims. This policy also meant passing of the Acts of 1909 and 1919 which appeased the moderates in the Congress. The revolutionary group in the Congress generated intense feelings of patriotism and nationalism, but did not produce any tangible results.

Mohandas Karamchand Gandhi (1869-1948) then emerged on the Congress scene as leader of the moderates. He launched 'satyagraha' in South Africa against the humiliation of Indians. He also gave top priority to the cause of Hindu-Muslim unity which was endangered by the British rulers. The Lucknow session of the Congress in 1916 commented on the impaired relations between the two communities. Separate electorates for Muslims and Hindus were accepted at this session. Mahatma Gandhi's leadership of Congress was, in fact, the beginning of the constitutional reforms. However, Gandhi started 'satyagraha' and Non-Cooperation Movements (alongwith acceptance of legislative reforms) whenever he thought injustices were committed by the British Raj.

Gandhi transformed the Indian national movement into a people's movement for liberty. He supported the Khilafat cause, and hence strived for Hindu-Muslim unity. Non-Cooperation Movement was launched by Gandhi in 1920. Under his leadership, the people surrendered titles and honorary offices and resigned their posts as nominated members in local bodies, law courts and legislatures. Innumerable people boycotted foreign goods, adopted 'swadeshi' cloth and refused to pay taxes.

It was decided to attain 'swaraj' by all legitimate and peaceful means. Students left colleges and schools in large numbers. Lawyers gave up practice and people boycotted the elections held in 1920. The Indian National Congress also started constructive work to create feelings of self-help and discipline. The message of passive resistance and civil disobedience reached every part of the country. Gandhi toured various parts of the country to spread his philosophy among the masses.

In 1927, S. Srinivas Iyengar, Jawaharlal Nehru and Subhas Chandra Bose advocated 'complete independence' instead of 'dominion status' for India (as was demanded in 1917). This demand was reinforced in 1929 at the Lahore session of the Congress. Industrial workers, women and other sections of Indian society also started participating in India's struggle for independence. Civil disobedience and non-payment of unjust taxes had been adopted as an instrument to fight against the British Raj. The British rulers, fearing a serious threat from the Congress, engineered a split between the Muslims and the Hindus by giving a communal award in 1932. Gandhi worked towards unity between the two communities. However, the British were successful in propounding the 'two-nation theory'. The communal situation deteriorated further due to the British policy of "divide and rule". The last phase of political awakening is reflected in the Quit India Movement launched on 9 August 1942. British rulers were called upon to leave India. The movement was a mass upheaval in which youth and students played a major role in threatening the Raj.

Education

A.R. Desai (1976) refers to three main agencies of modern education: (1) the foreign Christian missionaries, (2) the British government, and (3) the progressive Indians. The missionaries attacked polytheism and the caste-based inequalities and lured people towards Christianity. They imparted education through mission schools, but only a few people converted to Christianity. The British government opened a large number of universities, colleges and schools which imparted modern knowledge. Liberal and technical ideas were spread by education despite hostility of the British government to the rising wave of Indian nationalism. The British government spread modern education to produce clerks, managers and agents who would carry out the British Raj's work in India, but the same educated Indians turned against the Raj at the opportune time. They boycotted schools and colleges, resigned jobs, and joined the national movement. The call for 'swadeshi' was welcomed by these young educated men and women.

The British believed that an English medium education for these young men and women was a political and economic necessity. However, Raja Ram Mohan Roy and several other reformers who were English-educated emerged as saviours of India's cultural heritage and fighters against the social evils of Indian society. Deshmukh, Karve, Tilak, Gokhale, Malaviya and Gandhi were all educated in the English medium, but they were staunch nationalists. The national movement made them strong in their nationalist conviction. They not only emphasised on the study of the Vedas, but they also studied the Quran and the Bible to have a more complete view of religion.

The Arya Samaj, which emphasised rejuvenation of Vedic culture, opened a chain of colleges and schools throughout the country. The Deccan Education Society, opened by Tilak and Agarkar, was another example of the nationalist ethos. It aim was to prepare a band of people who could undertake educational reforms and national work for the upliftment of the country. Nationalist leaders opened *vidyapiths* in various states, such as Gujarat and Uttar Pradesh. Vishwa Bharati at Shantiniketan, the S.N.D.T. Women's University and the Jamia Millia are also examples of such an effort by some dedicated Indians.

The British educational system was divorced from the realities of Indian society. It was made an instrument for training people who could serve the Raj. There was no emphasis on Indian culture, art, painting, people, economy, polity and religion. Educated Indian people did not know about their own society and culture. Nationalist leaders very well realised this lacuna. There was nothing 'national' in the education imparted by British colleges and schools. Nor could English education become mass education. Thus, widespread mass education, with a nationalist ethos, became the central concern of Indian nationalist forces.

Communalism

Communalism was mainly the result of the peculiar development of the Indian social economy under British rule, of the uneven economic and cultural development of different communities, and of the action of the strategy both of the British government and the vested interests within those communities. The British thrived on communal divisions in India. They introduced the institutions of 'communal award', 'communal electorate', 'communal representation' and also engineered 'communal troubles' and ensured that such troubles escalated. These are the observations made by A.R. Desai (1976) and some other scholars. The national movement leaders had to fight the British on the one hand, and the forces which divided the country, on the other. The British rulers themselves were a big force that sponsored communal troubles in India, in accordance with their policy of "divide and rule".

The leaders of the Indian National Congress, under its programme of the Non-Cooperation Movement, strived for a united action of the Hindu and Muslim communities. However, some among the Hindus and some among the Muslims (who adhered to the ideology of the Hindu Mahasabha and the Muslim League, respectively) indulged in spreading communal hatred in their respective communities against each other. Communal clashes occurred at various places in 1924-25. Since communalism proved to be a cancer to India's struggle for independence, the national leaders decided to curb it effectively. The Indian national leaders realised that religious feelings and sentiments were being exploited not only by the British rulers but also by the reactionary elements within these two communities. They, therefore, assured the people that religion and particular beliefs and practices of the two communities would be respected, and religion would not be allowed to become an instrument of expression of political and economic expectations and aspirations.

The Muslims in India have been (the major minority group) at loggerheads with Hindus. At times they have feared repression, and at times the Hindus have been uneasy with the Muslims. This situation of mutual distrust was created by the British rulers through their policy of "divide and rule". The Muslims were not a monolithic community in India. They were divided into landlords and princes, professional groups, shopkeepers, moneylenders, peasants and workers. These classes, like those among the Hindus, had divergent and even conflicting interests. Muslims did not share a common territory, language and standard of living. There was rivalry between the upper sections among the Muslims and their counterparts among the Hindus.

In general, the Muslims had lagged behind the Hindus. Jawaharlal Nehru has rightly observed in his book *The Discovery of India* (1956) that because the Muslims remained behind the Hindus by a generation or two, they have developed a psychology of fear. Nehru also observed in some other context that communal leaders inevitably tended to become reactionaries in political and economic matters. They used communal or religious demands as a cover for their own class interests. Their demands had nothing to do with the masses. This is how communalism was fostered by vested interests from amongst Hindus and Muslims in India.

The Wahabi Movement was the first organised effort by the Muslims for religious reforms. Subsequently, this movement turned into a political, anti-British movement. However, it could not survive after the revolt of 1857. Sir Syed Ahmed Khan (1817-98) organised the Muslims and urged them to adopt western education and culture. He was loyal to the British Raj. Khan founded the Mohammedan Anglo-Oriental College at Aligarh, which later was transformed into the Aligarh Muslim University. He opposed the Indian National Congress and dissuaded Muslims from joining it.

Khan became the advocate of the Muslim middle classes and professional groups. He also supported communal electorates. A social and political awakening among the Muslim middle classes and their affiliation with the Raj were some of the concrete results of Sir Syed's movement.

The Muslim League was founded in 1906. It was 'communal', and its leadership belonged to the upper classes of the Muslims. The League demanded separate representation for Muslims. It expressed feelings of loyalty of the Muslims to the British government. It aimed at protecting the political and economic rights, and also at having friendly ties with other communities. At its Amritsar session in 1908, the League demanded representation for Muslims on the local boards and on the privy council and a percentage of the available government jobs.

The Morley-Minto Reforms of 1909 introduced a system of separate electorates and representation for the Muslims. Later on, this was extended to the Sikhs, the depressed classes, and other minority groups. The Act of 1935 provided separate electorates for several communities. The British Raj also provided separate electorates for landholders, Europeans, merchants and industrialists. Thus, the Raj created political and economic divisions in terms of communities, classes, and interests. In this way, the Raj was successful in putting one group against the other and in perpetuating its interests in India. The Muslims of India contributed a lot to the maintenance of British paramountcy by asking for separate representation and electorates.

A number of associations, interests and classes emerged demanding their shares in services and other arenas. Communal, caste, class and religious divisions were thus superimposed by the British rulers. Militancy among the Indian Muslims was an offshoot of this development. The Indian National Congress, though realising its dangers, accepted the principle of separate electorates in 1916 at its Lucknow session. The nationalist Muslims became weak in the face of the rising wave of militancy among the hardcore of communalist Muslims. However, the League was also affected by socialist and nationalist thinking. In 1918, at its Delhi session, the League demanded self-determination for India.

The Khilafat Movement was a struggle for the boycott of British goods and non-cooperation with the government. Gandhi and Congress supported this movement. Support was also extended to the League in their demand for the restoration of the Holy Lands, and for certain other demands. The Ali brothers were staunch advocates of the nationalist forces among the Indian Muslims. However, the Hindu-Muslim unity was short-lived and dwindled after the Non-Cooperation Movement of 1920. The 'backward' Muslims were not instilled with a deep national consciousness, and the nationalist Muslim leaders were not able to give them a suitable programme of action. Gandhi's constructive programme could cover only the lower sections of Hindu society. A.R. Desai (1976) observes: "Communalism was only the disguised expression of the struggle between the vested interests belonging to different faiths who gave a communal form to that struggle. It also was the form within which the struggle of the professional classes of different communities over posts and seats was carried on. One of the most effective methods to combat communalism was to unite the lower strata of different communities in a movement for securing their common economic and other interests."

The proletariat from amongst the Muslims and the Hindus and other communities have never united in India. Groups with unequal statuses within the Muslims and the Hindus have, however, separately united at times to press for their demands against each other. Even economic demands have been presented through communal idiom. It is true that upper sections of both the communities have raised the bogey of communalism in the British period. Some of them do it even today after nearly six decades of India's independence.

The Simon Commission was welcomed by one section of the Muslim leadership, whereas it was boycotted by all other political parties and groups. Jinnah decided to boycott the Simon Commission, but prepared a charter of fourteen points to present to the Commission on behalf of the League. He demanded the establishment of a federal state, one-third representation of Muslims in the Central Legislature, separate electorates, and the inclusion of one-third Muslim ministers in Central and Provincial Councils of Ministers. On this basis, Ramsay Macdonald, the British Prime Minister, granted the communal award in 1932, and Jinnah emerged as the spokesman of the Muslims. Jinnah expressed his dissatisfaction with the results of the 1937 elections. The Muslim League, at its Lahore session in 1940, demanded the formation of Pakistan as the only way of meeting the aspirations of Indian Muslims. Gandhi was always unhappy with such a complex communal situation and had always fought against communalism. Besides economic and political factors, there were some other structural factors which created communal disharmony. These factors included uneven demographic structure, composition of Hindus and Muslims, disparity in their economic positions and social and cultural heritage.

Gandhi tried to restore communal harmony, but Jinnah did not agree to abandon elections based on communal basis. The ultimate result was India's partition in 1947. India and Pakistan were formed as two nations on 15 August 1947.

Caste

Caste was an obstacle to the national movement, as it divided people into high and low positions, and prohibited commensal and connubial relations between members of different caste groups. The caste system was thus based upon deep-seated inequalities – social, cultural, political and economic. Change in the system was not permitted as caste ranks were based on birth. The national movement could become effective if it involved people from all sections of Indian society, particularly the Hindus. So long as the caste system continued, it was not possible to make the movement widespread, egalitarian and democratic.

The English educational system no doubt spread ideas of rationalism, individualism, liberty and equality among people, but modern education did not reach the lower strata of Indian society. On the other hand, British rulers encouraged the caste-based distinctions with a view to keep the people divided and disunited. They adopted discriminatory policies towards various castes, communities, classes and associations. Some castes were granted decrees for higher status to create cleavages among them and those whose claims were not accepted.

The British declared that the caste system was a very positive and useful arrangement for the Hindus. The Census of 1901, under the supervision of Sir Herbert H. Risley, placed all castes in a rank-order based on commensal ties. J.J. Hutton, the Commissioner for the 1931 Census, pronounced the caste system as positive as it performed functions for good of the people and Indian society as a whole. They maintained details of each caste group in the census records. Their sole purpose was not to allow the emergence of a national consciousness against the British. However, the national movement was able to weaken the parochial, caste, religious and regional considerations. The leaders of the national movement and other organisations decried caste and communal considerations by projecting secular values.

Social reform movements like the Arya Samaj, the Brahmo Samaj and the Prarthana Samaj attacked caste-based inequality and segregation. They attacked the theory of karma, pollution-purity, untouchability, hereditary division of labour and birth as the basis of status determination. In an earlier chapter, we have discussed the anti-caste stance of these reform organisations. However, there were certain organisations which advocated perpetuation of the caste system. The communal award of 1932, separate electorates for Muslims, Sikhs and other groups and classes were the main obstacles in the freedom struggle.

The policy and attitude of the British Raj towards the caste system encouraged mobility movements within the caste hierarchy. These movements strengthened the caste system rather than weakening it. Apparently, the process of 'sanskritisation', under which lower caste people imitate the lifestyles of upper caste people, attacks the dominant position of the latter, but in reality such a process of change causes even more dissensions and divisions in the existing caste system. In this process, the lower caste people discard their traditional occupations and lifestyles to copy the occupations and lifestyles of the upper castes. They are generally not successful in getting better alternative sources of livelihood. What they achieve is an imitation of some cultural traits of the upper castes, but the upper castes immediately stop emphasising these traits. Thus, the net result of such a process of caste mobility is horizontal change, that is, change within the system, and not of the system.

Mahatma Gandhi fought against the caste system as it degraded and dehumanised the lower and the 'untouchable' castes. He gave the name 'Harijan', i.e., children of God, to the 'untouchable' caste groups. Gandhi founded the All-India Harijan Sangh for this purpose in 1932. Gandhi's greatest mission was his crusade against untouchability. He did his best to upgrade the Harijans by keeping them in the forefront of the national movement.

B.R. Ambedkar, a Harijan himself, joined Gandhi in this endeavour of Harijan upliftment. Ambedkar fought against caste tyranny and the disabilities imposed upon the Harijans. He demanded entry of Harijans into temples and other religious and public places. The Constitution of India has also a provision for the abolition of untouchability. The practice of untouchability today is a cognizable criminal offence under the law of the country.

Conclusion

In this chapter we have discussed major sociological trends during the freedom struggle. The main point is that the British tried to block the emergence of egalitarian values, national consciousness and a united front against their rule in India. They promoted communal, caste, regional and religious forces to keep the people fighting among themselves and to remain divided against the British Raj. The nationalist forces fought against the British despite these heavy odds. They also fought against the social evils of Indian society which obstructed the freedom struggle. In fact, the freedom struggle proved to be a struggle not only against British rule, but also against the caste system, untouchability, oppression of women and

Harijans, communalism and regionalism. It was, in fact, a movement towards regeneration of the people and their nationalist sentiments to fight against the British Raj.

Exercises

1. Describe the socio-economic and political conditions at the beginning of the British rule in India.
2. Bring out the main features of the early phase of nationalism.
3. Discuss the following:
   (i) Partition of Bengal
   (ii) Factionalism in the Congress in the early period
   (iii) Constitutional reforms of 1909 and 1919
   (iv) Jallianwala Bagh massacre
   (v) Formation of Congress ministries in provinces in 1937
   (vi) Indian National Army (INA)
   (vii) Communal Award by the British
4. Write an essay on the role of Gandhiji in India's struggle for freedom.
5. Discuss the main points of political awakening in India.
6. Highlight the main features of the educational system in the British period and its impact on Indian society.
7. Explain the historical and social factors of communalism in India.
8. In what way was the caste system not conducive to the cause of India's freedom struggle?

Select References

Chandra, Bipin, *Modern India*, New Delhi: NCERT, 1976.

Chand, Tara, *History of the Freedom Movement in India*, Volume 2, New Delhi: Government of India Publication, 1967.

Desai, A.R., *Social Background of Indian Nationalism*, Bombay: Popular Prakashan, 1976.

Nehru, Jawaharlal, *The Discovery of India* (4th edition), London: Meridian Books Ltd., 1956.

The Gazetteer of India, Volume II, New Delhi: Government of India Publication, 1973.

5 Tribal Life in India

Tribal settlements, villages and towns are the three main components of India's social formation. A sharp distinction between tribal settlement and village and between village and town cannot, however, be easily drawn due to some common characteristics shared by them. There are big tribal villages in some parts of the country and they are not significantly different from non-tribal, multi-caste villages. Distinctions based on kinship, wealth and power among some tribal villages are as sharp as we find among the non-tribal villages. Tribals are not, theoretically, a part of Hindu social organisation, but they have always been in touch with wider society in India. They have been exploited economically and socially by the non-tribals living in tribal areas. A number of tribes have revolted against their exploitation.

Tribal Identity in India

Article 46 of India's Constitution states: "The State shall promote with special care the educational and economic interests of the weaker sections of the people, and, in particular, of the Scheduled Castes and the Scheduled Tribes and shall protect them from social injustice and all forms of exploitation." There are, however, tribes which are not Scheduled Tribes (STs) and are generally weaker sections of India's population, like the Scheduled Castes (SCs). The tribes are backward, particularly in regard to education and economic standing. They were exploited in the past (and even today they are exploited), by the dominant sections of Indian society, namely, Hindu landlords, moneylenders and industrialists who purchased their lands to establish industries in tribal areas. Forest produces, which tribals bring to the markets for sale, are bought at throwaway prices.

A number of tribes have 'Hinduised' or converted to Christianity or Islam to break away from their tribal identity, to get redemption from exploitation and to elevate their status and honour. Sometimes it becomes difficult to draw a clear line between a tribal and a caste group. There are hunters and food gatherers among the tribals on the one end, and there are tribals settled in villages, practically functioning as 'caste groups' on the other.

Tribals have a strong sense of their distinctiveness and separate themselves from non-tribals, *jatis*, Christians and Muslims. Language is one of the strong traits by which they identify themselves. Mundas, Santhals and Hos are identified as distinct tribes on the basis of their spoken languages (besides other attributes). A large number of tribals in India live in hilly and forested areas where population is sparse and communication is difficult. They are spread over the entire sub-continent, but are found mainly in the states of West Bengal, Jharkhand, Orissa, Chhatisgarh, Rajasthan, Gujarat and Maharashtra.

Defining Tribal Society

D.G. Mandelbaum (1972) writes: "In tribal life the principal links for the whole society are based on kinship." Kinship is not simply a principle of social organisation, it is also a principle of inheritance, division of labour and distribution of power and privileges. Tribal societies are small in size. They possess a morality, religion and worldview of their own, corresponding to their social relations. However, some tribes such as Santhals, Gonds and Bhils are quite large.

Theodore Sahlins writes that the term 'tribal society' should be restricted to 'segmentary systems'. The segmentary systems have relations on a small scale. They enjoy autonomy, and are independent of each other in a given region. We may observe this about the Santhals, Oraons and Mundas of Jharkhand or about the Bhils, Bhil Meenas and Garasias of Rajasthan. Contrary to tribes, castes are 'organic' in nature, as each caste is part of an organic whole in terms of the 'jajmani' system, commensality and connubiality. The principle of organic relationship explains interdependence of various caste groups upon each other in social life. Caste groups are hierarchically arranged on the basis of certain ascriptive criteria. These criteria do not apply to tribes in India.

Distinctions between 'folk', 'peasant' and 'urban', or between 'tribal', 'folk' and 'elite', are not very useful for the understanding of tribes in India. For example, the tribes of Jharkhand have been interacting and cooperating with each other, despite geographical barriers, problems of communication, relative cultural autonomy and economic self-reliance because they faced a common external threat to their traditional system of land relations, economy and cultural autonomy. The Hindu zamindars, Bengali moneylenders and the British administration exploited them, pushing them to the point of extinction and utter dehumanisation. There was never inter-tribal isolation and cultural exclusiveness. The tribals of Jharkhand mobilised their members against their exploiters. They interacted with the administration, town elite and outsiders. The Jharkhand (earlier part of Bihar state), which contains numerous tribes, is a tribal cultural zone comprising several tribal sub-cultures. The Mundas, Oraons, Hos and Santhals – the major tribes of this region – depend upon forest produce, settled agriculture, employment in industries, coal mines and government jobs. Some have settled in towns, others are in villages, and some of the latter are economically very well off. Thus, tribal culture is in part a peasant culture and in part an urban culture.

Tribal exclusiveness, intact tribal solidarity and tribal consciousness on the one hand, and dependence upon towns and cities, administration and mobilisation against their exploiters on the other, have existed simultaneously among the tribal people. Even the revival of tribal aboriginality has been expressed in the form of an instrument of protest against the external intrusions and impositions of rules and regulations. The tribals of Jharkhand are peasants to a large extent, and therefore, their 'peasant qualities' should become the basis to understand their economic problems. The characteristics of peasant societies, outlined by Theodore Sahlins, aptly apply to the tribals of Jharkhand. These are: (1) the peasant family farm is the basic unit of a multi-dimensional social organisation; (2) land husbandry is the main means of livelihood, directly providing the major part of the consumption needs; (3) specific traditional culture is related to the way of life of small communities; and (4) the peasants have the underdog position, domination of peasants by others. The tribes of Jharkhand have been called peasants by S.C. Roy (1970). They have fought against feudalism for 300 years. Today, they are facing problems emerging out of industrial urbanisation in the Jharkhand region.

Tribal Social Structure

D.G. Mandelbaum (1972) mentions the following characteristics of Indian tribes: (1) kinship as an instrument of social bonds; (2) lack of hierarchy (rigid status distinctions) among men and groups (clans and lineages); (3) absence of strong, complex, formal organisations; (4) communitarian basis of landholding; (5) segmentary character; (6) little value on surplus accumulation, on the use of capital, and on market-trading; (7) lack of distinction between form and substance of religion; and (8) a distinct psychological make-up for enjoying life.

Tribes have been separated from other social categories on the basis of these features. In India, the British conducted a detailed enumeration of the tribals in the 1930s. Tribes were distinguished from castes on the basis of their religious and ecological conditions.

However, tribals are also peasants, as a good number of them today live in villages and have been engaged in agriculture and allied occupations, just like peasants belonging to various castes and communities. According to the 1991 census there are more than 67 million tribals divided into 427 tribes. They form about 8 per cent of the total population. There is vast diversity among the tribes in terms of habitation, ecology, economic pursuits, language, religion and contacts with the outside world. Each tribe is internally stratified. It may be that members of a given tribe do not have a clear perception about their existential conditions or that they have a distorted or false consciousness.

The large tribes of India are the Gonds of Chhatisgarh (formerly part of Madhya Pradesh), Maharashtra and Andhra Pradesh; the Bhils of Rajasthan, Gujarat, Maharashtra and Madhya Pradesh; and the Santhals of Jharkhand (formerly part of Bihar), Orissa and West Bengal. The Gonds and the Bhils are more than four million each. The Santhals are more than three million.

B.K. Roy Burman (1972) divides tribal communities into five territorial groupings, taking into account their historical, ethnic and socio-cultural relations. These are as follows: (1) north-east India, comprising Assam, Arunachal Pradesh, Nagaland, Manipur and Tripura; (2) the sub-Himalayan region of north and north-west India, comprising hill districts of Uttar Pradesh and Himachal Pradesh; (3) Central and East India, comprising West Bengal, Bihar (now Jharkhand), Orissa, Madhya Pradesh (now Chhatisgarh) and Andhra Pradesh; (4) south India comprising Tamil Nadu, Kerala and Karnataka; and (5) western India, comprising Rajasthan, Gujarat and Maharashtra.

Tribes in India differ from one another in racial traits, language, social organisation, cultural patterns, etc. The dominant racial type among tribes is the proto-Australoid. In the sub-Himalayan belt, the Mongoloid type is preponderant. The Mediterranean and the Negrito are found in other regions. Tribal languages belong to all the types: the Austric, the Dravidian, and the Tibeto-Chinese. Tribal people are generally bilingual. Some tribes have been assimilated into the Hindu-fold, like the Bhumij and the Bhils. Some have been attracted by Christianity. The main occupations of the tribes are: (1) forestry and food gathering; (2) shifting cultivation; (3) settled agriculture; (4) agricultural labour; (5) animal husbandry; and (6) household industry.

Social Stratification among Tribes of India

Andre Beteille (1974), following N.K. Bose's classification, mentions language, religion and the degree of isolation as the main bases of classification of tribes. Beteille, however, considers the manner in which they make their living as the plainest way to arrange them into categories. Bose (1972) classifies the tribal people into three main categories: (1) hunters, fishers and gatherers; (2) shifting cultivators; and (3) settled agriculturists, using the plough and plough-cattle. Santhals, Gonds, Bhils, Oraons and Mundas fall into the last category. Their peasantry is not substantially different from the non-tribal peasants. These tribals are also categorised as cultivators, agricultural labourers and workers. They are working in factories in Jharkhand, Bengal, Orissa and Chhatisgarh, and in plantations in Assam, Bengal and some southern states. S.C. Roy (1970) describes the Oraon and Munda villagers as peasants. Furer-Haimendorf (1982) describes the Raj Gonds of Adilabad as peasants. F.G. Bailey (1957) refers to the Konds of Orissa as peasants.

Several anthropologists have observed social stratification among the members of a specific tribe. S.C. Roy (1970) has listed a number of groups in an Oraon village in terms of their different occupations. The Oraons have also been classified on the basis of their tenurial status. Roy mentions the presence of 'peasant proprietors' or various categories of *raiyats*. There are various endogamous groups such as Mahalis, Ghasis and Lohars. The Mundas too have settled agriculture and division of labour within the family. The Mundas had the 'Khuntkatti' system of land tenure. Under this system, there were: (1) the Khuntkattidars, (2) the *parjas* or *raiyats*, and (3) the subsidiary castes (service groups). The Khuntkatti system lost its significance due to the introduction of individual ownership of land and the intervention by moneylenders and zamindars into tribal life (during British Raj). G.S. Ghurye (1969) calls tribal people as 'backward Hindus'.

Tribe and Caste

Mandelbaum (1972) observes a slow shift from tribe to caste. He writes: "There is no absolute cultural or social distinction between all tribal and all caste peoples, but rather a range of variation between tribal and caste traits." Tribes and castes have certain cultural traits in common, in regard to the nature of ritual, purity and pollution, the worship of local spirits, and in kinship practices. The broad aspects of distinction between the two are: (1) social; (2) political; (3) economic; (4) religious; and (5) psychological. Despite distinction in these aspects, there is a shift toward *jati* values. The shift is in the areas of styles of life, customs, dietary patterns, rituals, hierarchy, factions and feuds, sanskritic religion and worldview. Tribal groups have imitated caste groups in these spheres.

Historian D.D. Kosambi reports that the tribes of the Gangetic plain were conquered by and assimilated into the kingdoms of Kosala and Magadha in the sixth century B.C. From ancient times until the British Raj, tribals were frequently raided by non-tribals. The British deplored the assimilation of tribal groups into the caste system. They might have thought of this combination of tribe and caste as a serious threat. It was their political move to stop the integration of tribes and castes. Sir Herbert H. Risley observed that the tribes were transforming into castes since 1873. This process of transformation might be termed as 'sanskritisation'.

Tribal Problems

K.S. Singh's edited volume *Tribal Situation in India* (1972) gives a detailed account of various tribes in different regions regarding social and cultural communications, policy, politics, administration, agrarian issues, economic development, movements, leadership, and problems of integration. The survey by B.K. Roy Burman also shows that the tribals are the most backward. The rate of literacy is low, and their economy is primitive. In as many as 285 taluqas (sub-divisions), they constitute 50 per cent or more of the total population. The tribal situation is not uniform in all the parts of

India. In the north-east, the situation has been disturbed for several years, whereas in the mainland (central India) problems related to poverty, unemployment, indebtedness, backwardness and ignorance are acute. The tribals of the north-east have a high level of politicisation, literacy and a high standard of living compared to their counterparts in other parts.

Process of Change among Tribes of India

Tribes are becoming conscious, both socially and politically, of maintaining and preserving their ethnic and cultural identity and also of protecting themselves against exploitation by *dikkus* (outsiders). They have stressed their political solidarity. This may, however, result in a new form of ecological-cultural isolation. Tribes have generally taken such steps due to their economic backwardness and a feeling of frustration.

To integrate the tribes with the mainstream, special economic opportunities are offered to them. The 'assimilationist' model of the tribes' integration with non-tribal India demands structural linkages of the tribes with the non-tribes. The 'isolationist' model would not be much relevant today in the face of rapid changes in Indian society. Despite vast changes taking place in India, tribal consciousness has been strengthened mainly to project tribes as distinct components of Indian society. Industrialisation in Jharkhand, for example, has promoted both tribal consciousness and integration with the non-tribal sections in the region. The demand for autonomy by tribals has originated from their fear of loss of cultural autonomy and of exploitation

To Niharanjan Ray (1972), the very expressions – 'tribes', 'criminal tribes', 'scheduled tribes' and 'scheduled castes' are misleading. He believes that these expressions are unfortunate and unwise. "It has conditioned our attitude towards these communities of peoples and our approach towards the solution of their problems which are theirs as much as of the rest of the Indian population." From the point of view of Indian nationalism Ray makes the following observations:

1. Tribes are *janas* or peoples, just like the peoples of other territorial and cultural regions of India. Tribes or *janas* differ from other communities in terms of the socio-economic system of *jati* to which non-tribal Hindu communities belong. Ray writes: "*Jati* is not caste nor is it just a socio-religious system; it is also an economic system, hereditarily and hierarchically organised according to groups recruited by birth".
2. There is a sharp distinction between 'incorporation' and 'integration'. The tribes have been incorporated rather than integrated into the *jati*-fold by placing them at different hierarchical levels of the system, generally at the lower levels. Even this process has been slow, and it has also become redundant because of considerable fluidity in the caste system. There is a need, therefore, to draw them into the new techno-economy, a new production system.
3. There is a need to understand the stresses and strains being suffered by the tribals due to the quicker tempo of modern life, new legal, administrative and economic systems.
4. The tribal people have migrated to other places from their birth places due to economic and other hardships. They have also joined the army.
5. The nomenclatures such as 'scheduled tribes', 'denotified tribes' and 'scheduled castes' have inherent seeds of division.
6. Tribes today are in search of a sense of identity, of a sense of belonging and for self-determination in a new social order. Several new states have been formed in the north-eastern region. The demand for the formation of a separate state of Jharkhand for tribals of Bihar and adjoining districts of other states was indicative of this new identity.

Ray (1972) writes: "Any consideration in the contemporary context, of the traditional Hindu method of tribal absorption is therefore sheer madness to my mind. In the present context this is simply anachronistic." But, the fact of the matter is that a large number of major tribes have either Hinduised or converted to Christianity and Islam. These processes of change and mobility have no doubt reduced the gap between tribals and non-tribals, but have also created factions and feuds between the non-converts and the converts. A sharp line is drawn in Jharkhand between the tribals converted to Christianity and those who continue to adhere to their traditional way of life.

Conclusion

Tribes are generally backward, economically as well as educationally. To protect against injustices done to them and to bring them up with other sections of society, the Constitution of India has granted them special concessions for their upliftment. However, there are some tribes who have not been 'scheduled' as such sections by the Constitution. Generally, tribes are distinct from non-tribes, particularly from caste groups and other non-caste communities like Muslims, Christians, Sikhs, etc. Tribal people have been victims of exploitation by non-tribals for centuries.

A strong sense of identity is prevalent among the tribes of India. Language, religious and magical beliefs and practices, food habits, styles of dress, patterns of habitation and dependence upon forest produce are important features of their life which make them distinct from non-tribal groups. Kinship is the key principle of social organisation, as it governs major social, juridical, economic and political activities of their life.

Tribal societies are generally of a small size. There is not much social interaction between people of different tribes. However, intra-tribal solidarity has been strong. Tribal culture is in part peasant culture, in part it has its exclusiveness, and in part it has taken elements from urban culture. Tribal people are differentiated like non-tribal people in terms of wealth, power and accessibility to resources and opportunities. We have mentioned broad distinctions between tribe and caste, and also the direction of change from tribe to caste. Today, the main problem of tribals is not of integration or assimilation with castes and communities in India. Their main problems are of poverty, unemployment, indebtedness, backwardness and ignorance. There are indications of inter-tribal solidarity, movements, and concerted action against their exploitation and suppression.

Exercises

1. List the main socio-cultural characteristics of tribes in India.
2. Explain the following:
   (i) Kinship
   (ii) Segmentary and organic systems
   (iii) Inter-tribal and intra-tribal solidarity
3. In what ways are tribes different from caste groups?
4. Bring out distinctions between tribal, peasant and urban cultures.
5. What are the main bases of social stratification among the tribes of India?
6. Discuss processes of change among the tribes, with particular reference to isolationist and assimilationist perspectives.
7. Write an essay on the major economic problems of the tribal people in India.

Select References

Bailey, F.G., *Caste and the Economic Frontier*, Manchester: Manchester University Press, 1957.

Beteille, Andre, *Six Essays in Comparative Sociology*, New Delhi: Oxford University Press, 1974.

Bose, N.K., *Tribal Life in India*, New Delhi: National Book Trust, India, 1971.

—, *Some Indian Tribes*, New Delhi: National Book Trust, India, 1972.

Furer-Haimendorf, C. Von, *Tribes of India: The Struggle for Survival*, Delhi: Oxford University Press, 1982.

Ghurye, G.S., *Caste and Race in India*, Bombay: Popular Prakashan, 1969.

—, *The Scheduled Tribes*, Bombay: Popular Book Depot, 1969.

Mandelbaum, D.G., *Society in India*, Bombay: Popular Prakashan, 1972.

Ray, Niharanjan, "Introductory Address", in K.S. Singh (ed.), *Tribal Situation in India*, Simla, 1972.

Roy Burman, B.K., "Tribal Demography: A Preliminary Survey", in K.S. Singh (ed.), *Tribal Situation in India*, Indian Institute of Advanced Study, Simla, 1972.

Roy, S.C., *The Mundas and their Country* (reprint), Bombay: Asia Publishing House, 1970.

Sahlins, M., *Tribesmen*, Prentice Hall, Englewood Clife, 1966.

Singh, K.S. (ed.), *Tribal Situation in India*, Indian Institute of Advanced Study, Simla, 1972.

6 Village and Urban Communities in India

There are some common characteristics of village and town. The two are dependent upon each other, particularly in the field of economy. People from villages migrate to towns and townsmen depend upon them for manual labour and produces like foodgrains, milk and raw materials. Despite this dependence between these two components, there are some distinctive features which separate them from each other in terms of their cultural ethos, styles of life, economy, employment and social relations. In this chapter we will discuss village and urban social structure, their interrelations, changes in the village community and urbanisation.

THE VILLAGE COMMUNITY

It is rightly said that India is a country of villages. There are more than six lakh villages. Village, caste and joint family are three crucial institutions of India's social life. They have survived not only the onslaught of foreign invasion and internal contradictions, but have also absorbed new forces of social and cultural change and adapted themselves to the demands and challenges posed to them. We will discuss the caste system and joint family later on. Here, we provide a bird's eye-view of the salient features of the Indian village community and its nexus with urban India.

Village Community in Ancient India

According to *Apastamba Dharma Sutra*, state officials *(Adhyaksas* or *Adhipals)* were to be appointed by the kings for towns and villages with well-defined jurisdictions. In *Visnu Smrti*, it is written that a chain of officials is to be placed by the king in charge of 1, 10, and 100 villages as well as of the whole rural area. According to Kautilya, three tiers of officials were to be in charge of the rural as well as the urban areas. The *Samaharta* or the *Pradesta* was in charge of the *janpada* or the rural area. Each of its four divisions was entrusted to a *Sthanika*, and units of five or ten villages were in charge of *Gopas*. The officers were primarily concerned with the protection of the lives and property of the subjects. The officer of lower rank was required to report to his superior officer if he failed in the tasks assigned to him. Kautilya reports that the officers were individually responsible for protecting people's lives, maintaining records of revenues, dues and remissions, and deciding civil and criminal suits at the headquarters of ten, four hundred, and eight hundred villages.

According to the *Dharma Sutras*, the headman is appointed by the king. According to Kautilya's *Arthasastra*, the office of headman was hereditary, subject to confirmation by the king. *Jatak* story mentions village assemblies for managing village affairs. Under the rule of the Pandyas and the Cholas, well-organised assemblies, with wide powers of self-government, functioned with an executive body or various executive committees. Executive committees were elected by the members according to rules framed by themselves. The assemblies enjoyed a high reputation for integrity and honesty. They enjoyed the king's patronage and managed temple funds. The assemblies decided disputes, granted lands, founded and maintained hospitals, took charge of charitable endowments and controlled taxes.

At the time of the Buddha (in the sixth century B.C.), the village was an autonomous unit of corporate life ministering to its own needs of taxation, education, settlement of disputes and public works. One finds a lot of change in village life during this period. In

Pali texts the *Gamabhojaka* (person who received village revenues by royal charter) appears as a tyrant who fleeced people with arbitrary exactions and sometimes interfered with the autonomous and associate life of the village. People during this period amused themselves at fairs and carnivals where animal fights, acrobatic and magical feats, dances and dramatic performances were held for entertainment. Prostitution, drinking and gambling were common vices.

The accounts given by Megasthenes report the existence of seven castes, namely, Brahmanas or philosophers, cultivators of land, herdsmen and hunters, artisans and traders, soldiers, spies and councillors (officers of the king). These were in fact vocational groups rather than castes based on heredity. Inter-caste marriages were quite common. It seems that this was the period when socio-cultural distinctions arose. However, distinctions in terms of the ruler and the ruled existed earlier in the Indian village. Inter-village ties always existed. The villages had connections with the king and townsmen. Both were governed by the king and the officers appointed by him.

Village Community in Medieval India

The village scene underwent a sea-change in the medieval period. The temple and the village council (panchayat) emerged as the most effective institutions. Medieval Hindu rulers neglected their obligations to their subjects. The people were left with no choice except to search for their own means of improving their lot. The temple and the panchayat emerged as the means to a happy, healthy and productive life. The panchayat protected people from exploitation by the government. The temples maintained a good number of employees, patronised scholars, and served as seminaries of higher knowledge and the fine arts. They also served as bankers and farmers, daily feeding thousands of people, besides carrying on a variety of religious, educational and cultural activities. Many mosques also served as seminaries and they had government patronage. Temples and panchayats no doubt filled up the socio-cultural vacuum created by the rulers, but they also created a static culture in India. The economy became stagnant. No new changes, innovations and devices for advancement of society were introduced.

In the early medieval period, the majority of people lived in villages with agriculture as their principal occupation. The agriculturists were required to pay land revenue to the state through different types of intermediaries. The land-man ratio was low, food was plentiful and cheap. Life in the villages was isolated and unprogressive, and extremely simple and unchanging. The village economy was largely self-sufficient. The village artisans and servants, the priest and the moneylender satisfied all his (the villager's) requirements. The joint family system afforded him protection; the village panchayat gave his minor grievances a just redress. The village with its caste panchayats and headman was an autonomous unit of the state which carried out its activities unmindful of what happened to the central government. Thus, medieval India had a different village scene from that of ancient India. The stagnant village economy during the medieval period created several misconceptions about Indian village among the British administrators and ethnographers. In the following paragraphs we will give a brief account of some of these distorted views.

Village Community in Modern India

The study of the Indian village began in the eighteenth century, with intensive survey work regarding landholdings. Intensive empirical studies of village social life became popular in the twentieth century. The studies by Munro, Metcalfe, Maine, Marx and Baden-Powell considered the Indian village as a 'closed' and 'isolated' system, Sir Charles Metcalfe considered the Indian village a monolithic, atomistic and unchanging entity. Metcalfe writes: "The village communities are little republics, having nearly everything that they want within themselves and almost independent of any foreign relations." Further, Metcalfe states that wars pass over it, regimes come and go, but the village as a society always emerges "unchanged, unshaken and self-sufficient".

The question is: Is this characterisation of a typical Indian village appropriate and true? Several anthropologists and sociologists have vehemently refuted this view. A large number of studies had been carried out in the fifties with the assumption that the Indian village was not 'static', 'isolated' and 'homogeneous', but it was changing, had connections with wider society, and had social differentiation. Migration, village exogamy, inter-village economic ties (through the *jajmani* system), dependence upon towns for markets, division of labour and visits to religious places have also been basic features of the Indian village, breaking its isolation and separation from its vicinity and the wider world.

The *jajmani* system refers to a system of social, cultural and economic ties between different caste groups. Under this system, some castes are patrons and others are service castes. The service castes offer their services to the landowning upper castes and in turn are paid both in cash and kind. These castes are generally under obligation to serve the patron castes and their families. Sometimes, particularly on festivals and auspicious occasions, they also get 'gifts' from their *jajmans* (patrons). The *jajmani* system has been weakening due to market forces, contacts with towns, migration, education, and social and cultural awareness on the part of the functionary (service) castes. Today, village people are dependent upon towns and cities for the services which they used to get earlier from the functionary castes.

Thus, the village is linked by many ties to other villages, towns and cities, Mandelbaum (1972) writes: "A village is not a neatly separable social and conceptual package but it is nonetheless a fundamental social unit." It is increasingly becoming the part of the wider society.

Village as a Social Unit

The famous French sociologist Louis Dumont (1972) refers to three meanings of the term 'village community': (1) as a political society, (2) as a body of co-owners of the soil, and (3) as the emblem of traditional economy and polity, "a watchword of Indian patriotism". Thus, according to this view, the village community in India has been a part of India's polity and economy. "A village is far more than a locale, more than just a collection of houses, lanes and fields." These reactions have come up because of an exaggerated notion of the independence of Indian villages. The village exists even today as a cohesive territorial unit. However, village identity, solidarity and loyalty cut across caste and community. There are factions and feuding groups within villages and between villages. Land reforms, Panchayati Raj, sanskritisation and other structural and cultural changes have brought about significant changes within its social structure and in its relations with the wider world. Mandelbaum further observes: "A village is clearly an important and viable social entity to its people, who also take part in the larger society and share in the pattern of the civilisation." In some cases, the village may be isolated for the purpose of studies, in others it is not. Therefore, the village needs to be studied in its local milieu as well as in a wider perspective.

The British themselves created a new pattern of social differentiation by introducing *zamindari* and *raiyatwari* systems of land-tenure. The zamindars were generally upper caste men who were assigned the task of collecting revenue from village people on behalf of the British government. They received commission for this assignment. Their status was not the same as they were assigned this task on different scales. The *raiyats* were peasant-proprietors who were granted 'occupancy' rights by the government after they had paid a certain amount of money for getting this right. They were not subjected to the control of zamindars because they dealt with the government directly under the rules of occupancy right. With the abolition of these systems of land tenure, the traditional pattern of inequalities came under severe strain in the 1950s and 1960s. The village had a new pattern of administration and relations with the revenue officials.

Changes in Village Communities

In the 1950s, a large number of studies were undertaken on the Indian village community. In the year 1955 alone, S.C. Dube's

Indian Village, M.N. Srinivas' (ed.) *India's Villages*, D.N. Majumdar's (ed.) *Rural Profiles* and McKim Marriott's (ed.) *Village India* were published. All these studies have analysed structure and process of change in village India. The main aspects covered are caste system, family, *jajmani* system, religious practices and rituals, health conditions, village and caste panchayats, social mobility among different caste groups, and the impact of adult franchise, education, development programmes and Panchayati Raj on the rural people. The impact is uneven on different villages and on different castes, communities and families within the villages. B.R. Chauhan (1974) refers to four different situations: (1) one village and one caste, (2) one village and many castes, (3) one caste and many villages, and (4) many castes and many villages. Thus, there is a bewildering variety and complexity in village life. A typology of India's villages cannot easily be made out due to its historical and cultural ramifications.

The Indian village has undergone significant changes, particularly since independence. Caste system is not confined simply to *jajmani*-based social and economic relations. The fact is that the *jajmani* system itself has declined to a large extent due to increased contact with towns and the introduction of technological devices in agriculture. Market economy has shattered the traditional arrangement. Caste is still a noticeable source of socio-cultural groupings at the time of birth, marriage, death, and on other social occasions. Caste endogamy, clan exogamy and other allied rules are still adhered to in deciding marriages. While caste endogamy refers to marrying within one's own caste, clan exogamy refers to marrying within one's own caste but outside one's own clan. A given caste or sub-caste has a number of clans *(gotras)*. Those who belong to one's own *gotra* and also those on the maternal side are generally avoided as marriage partners.

Despite these patterns of caste continuities, inter-caste relations have become segmentary, that is, inter-caste interdependence has lessened, tensions have increased, and competition between different castes for a major share of the village's resources has heightened. Castes, and even different clans and lineages within specific castes, sometimes function as factions and warring groups. At times votes are cast in panchayat elections on caste lines. Castes have in a way become interest groups.

Caste panchayats have become almost ineffective in day-to-day affairs of members of a caste. However, on certain occasions, particularly in matters of grave consequence for the entire caste, a caste council (an informal group of dominant members from the caste) comes up to decide upon conflicting or controversial issues. Normally, such occasions are very rare. Matters of daily routine are taken up informally by the village elders. If a particular problem is to be referred to the statutory village panchayat, it is screened by the informal group, consisting of members of a given caste as well as some others from other caste groups. The power dynamics in a village could be seen in terms of such conflicts, decision-making and voting patterns.

The economic scene today is different in villages due to education, migration, change in the cropping pattern, electrification, irrigation and contact with towns and cities. The traditional pattern of lending has also changed to a large extent due to alternate channels of borrowing money. The wages of agricultural workers have gone up. They have acquired some bargaining power too. Economic dominance of the intermediate castes and classes such as Jats, Ahirs, Kurmis, Reddis, Patels, etc., has increased due to land reforms and green revolution. Green revolution is defined in terms of tangible changes in the agricultural sector, brought about through the adoption of new technology, seeds, fertilisers, etc. They have also become politically stronger due to their larger numbers. The lower castes have also come closer to other sections of people in the village community. Untouchability is not a rigid institution as it used to be before independence. They have become conscious of their position in independent India. A large number of people from these groups have migrated to towns and cities for better employment. Despite these changes in the village's social structure and economy, the village remains somewhat different from towns and cities in its ethos, way of life and interpersonal relations. In fact, the village represents a structural pattern different to that of the town.

URBAN LIFE IN INDIA

At least two trends are clear regarding urban life: (1) dependence upon agriculture for livelihood has steadily decreased; and (2) population of towns and cities has increased over the years. Both the trends indicate an increase in the processes of industrialisation and urbanisation. Towns and cities offer jobs and better amenities, whereas people in villages live a hard life. Due to urbanisation, traditional bonds based on religion, caste and family have weakened in the village. Anonymity, as found in towns, is absent in rural areas. City life creates a personality of its own, different from the one which is the product of rural life.

Structure or Towns and Cities

A city is defined as a place having a population of 1,00,000 or more. Places with a population of 5,000 and more are classified as towns. Three conditions for a place being classified as a town are: (1) the population is more than 5,000; (2) the density is not less than 400 per sq. km., and (3) not less than 75 per cent of the adult male population is engaged in non-agricultural activities.

The ratio of rural population to the urban population has not changed drastically since 1901, but there is a trend towards its perceptible decline. Today, cities are overcrowded. They contain many more people than the number for whom they can comfortably provide civic amenities. Cities which are state's capitals have become overburdened. The cities of Delhi, Bangalore and Jaipur, for example, have shown rapid increase in their populations over the past three decades. All towns and cities do not have a uniform pattern of population growth and development.

In 1981, there were 216 cities of one lakh population or more (Class I), containing 94 million people. Of these, 27 per cent lived in 12 big cities (with one million or more people). Of these, 12 cities even grew by less than 48 per cent in the decade up to 1981.

Of the other five, two had just 48 per cent growth, two were between 55 and 65 per cent, and only one, namely, Bangalore, grew very fast. The unevenness in the growth can be seen in terms of some more data. Eight cities grew more slowly than the urban population as a whole, and nine at less than the rate of increase for all Class I cities. Delhi and Bangalore exhibited rapid growth. Of the three cities which crossed the one million mark, Jaipur grew slightly faster than Class I cities, Nagpur slightly slower, and Lucknow at below the rate of natural increase for India.

There were 50 cities (Class I) that grew very rapidly in the decade 1971 to 1981. Only 12 were big cities, and 38 had under half a million population each. One view is that rural exodus has not contributed to population growth in cities as much as it has often stated. Cities in India have grown much less fast than cities in America. America has one-third of India's population, and of this, 166 million live in 290 Class I cities, and 55 per cent of them live in 38 big cities. Thus, India's urbanisation is actually taking place at a very slow rate. Urban growth is mainly due to natural growth of cities, and there we find real cause of unevenness.

Table 1

Some Majorly Populated Indian Cities

Name	*Population*	
	1991 Census	*2001 Censuss*
Greater Mumbai (Bombay)	9,925,891	11,914,398
Delhi	7,206,704	9,817,439
Kolkata (Calcutta)	4,399,819	4,580,544
Bangalore	2,660,088	4,292,223
Chennai (Madras)	3,841,396	4,216,268
Ahmedabad	2,876,710	3,515,361
Hyderabad	2,964,638	3,449,878
Pune	1,566,651	2,540,069
Kanpur	1,874,409	2,532,138

Source: Census of India 2001

The number of largest cities in 1991 and 2001 went up from 9 to 35. Because of the numerical increase of cities, the percentage share of these individual cities declined whereas overall urban population increased as it was 25.72 per cent in 1991 and 27.78 per cent in 2001. The increase in urban population is shared by medium and small towns.

Urban centres are divided into six categories on the basis of size. These are: (1) 1,00,000 and above, (2) 50,000-1,00,000, (3) 20,000-50,000, (4) 10,000-20,000, (5) 5,000-10,000, and (6) less than 5,000. Besides these, there are metropolitan cities like Delhi, Kolkata, Mumbai, Chennai, Ahmedabad, Hyderabad, Bangalore and Kanpur. The number of Class V and VI towns has shown a marked decline after independence. Industrial towns have come up in all the states, particularly in the states of West Bengal, Jharkhand and Orissa.

Table 2

Percentage of Population in the Metropolitan Cities to the Total Urban Population (India), 1991, 2001

Name of City	*Urban Population*		*% Share of Urban Population*	
	1991	*2001*	*1991*	*2001*
1. Greater Mumbai	12596000	16368084	7.90	5.74
2. Kolkata	11021198	13216546	6.91	4.63
3. Delhi	8419084	12791458	5.28	4.48
4. Chennai	5421985	6424624	3.40	2.25
5. Bangalore	4130288	5686844	2.59	1.99
6. Hyderabad	4344432	5533640	2.72	1.94
7. Ahmedabad	3586685	4519278	2.25	1.58
8. Pune	2493987	3755525	1.56	1.32
9. Surat	1518950	2811466	0.95	0.99
10. Kanpur	2029889	2590485	1.27	0.91
11. Jaipur	1518235	2324319	0.95	0.81

Contd...

Contd...

12. Lucknow	1669204	2256933	1.05	0.79
13. Nagpur	1669204	2122965	1.05	0.74
14. Patna	1099647	1707429	0.69	0.60
15. Indore	1109056	1639044	0.70	0.57
16. Bhopal	1062771	1454830	0.67	0.51
17. Coimbatore	816321	1446034	0.51	0.51
18. Ludhiana	1042740	1395053	0.65	0.49
19. Cochin	1140505	1255406	0.72	0.44
20. Vishakapatnam	1057118	1329472	0.66	0.47
21. Agra	948063	1321410	0.59	0.46
22. Vadodara	1125824	NA	0.71	0.00
23. Varanasi	1030863	1211749	0.65	0.42
24. Madurai	1085914	1194665	0.68	0.42
25. Meerut	849799	1167399	0.53	0.41
26. Nasik	725341	1152048	0.45	0.40
27. Jabalpur	888916	1117200	0.56	0.39
28. Jamshedpur	829171	1101804	0.52	0.39
29. Asansol	763939	1090171	0.48	0.38
30. Dhanbad	815005	1064357	0.51	0.37
31. Faridabad	617717	1054981	0.39	0.37
32. Allahabad	844546	1049579	0.53	0.37
33. Amritsar	708835	1011327	0.44	0.35
34. Vijayavada	845758	1011152	0.53	0.35
35. Rajkot	654490	1002160	0.41	0.35
Total	80481480	106179437	50.47	37.21
Total Urban Population, India	159462547	285354954		

Source: Calculated from Census of India, 1991, 2001.

Towns and cities are not an offshoot of industrialisation in India. The Indus Valley civilisation was basically a civilisation of towns. In pre-industrial India, there were pilgrim centres, capital towns, centres of trade and commerce and towns having universities and facilities for academic activities. Varanasi, Allahabad,

Table 3

Metropolitan Cities of India, 2001

City	Locational Extent		Total Population		Decadal Growth Rate (%) 1991-2001
	Latitude (N)	Longitude (E)	1991	2001	
1. Greater Mumbai	18.55	72.54	12596000	16368084	33.69
2. Kolkata	22.34	88.24	11021198	13216546	19.88
3. Delhi	28.38	77.12	8419084	12791458	46.95
4. Chennai	13.04	80.17	5421985	6424624	26.41
5. Bangalore	12.58	77.38	4130288	5686844	41.36
6. Hyderabad	17.20	78.30	4344432	5533640	66.60
7. Ahmedabad	23.03	72.40	3586685	4519278	29.51
8. Pune	18.31	73.55	2493987	3755525	44.82
9. Surat	21.12	72.52	1518950	2811466	64.41
10. Kanpur	26.28	80.24	2029889	2690486	23.84
11. Jaipur	26.55	75.52	1518235	2324319	49.56
12. Lucknow	26.55	80.59	1669204	2266933	65.66
13. Nagpur	21.09	79.09	1669204	2122965	36.45
14. Patna	25.37	85.13	1099647	1707429	19.67
15. Indore	19.03	81.00	1109056	1639044	33.73
16. Bhopal	23.16	77.36	1062771	1454830	58.38
17. Coimbatore	11.00	77.00	816321	1446034	15.87
18. Ludhiana	30.55	75.54	1042740	1395053	71.77
19. Cochin	9.58	76.17	1140605	1255406	38.27
20. Vishakapatnam	17.42	83.20	1057118	1329472	75.13
21. Agra	27.10	78.05	948063	1321410	26.86
22. Vadodara	22.00	73.16	1126824	NA	44.02
23. Varanasi	25.20	83.00	1030863	1211749	29.32
24. Madurai	9.58	78.10	1085914	1194665	19.73
25. Meerut	29.01	77.45	849799	1167399	56.50

Contd...

Contd...

26. Nasik	20.02	73.50	725341	1152048	63.43
27. Jabalpur	23.10	79.59	888916	1117200	17.38
28. Jamshedpur	22.50	86.10	829171	1101804	21.93
29. Asansol	23.42	87.01	763939	1090171	52.01
30. Dhanbad	23.47	86.30	815005	1064357	18.94
31. Faridabad	28.25	77.22	617717	1054981	86.70
32. Allahabad	25.28	81.54	844546	1049579	29.92
33. Amritsar	31.37	74.55	708835	1011327	19.16
34. Vijayavada	16.31	80.39	845756	1011152	37.81
35. Rajkot	22.18	70.56	654490	1002160	47.05
Total Urban Population of India			159462547 (25.72%)	285354954 (27.78%)	

Tirupati, Amritsar, Ajmer, Haridwar, Delhi, Agra, Hyderabad, Poona, Dacca, Nalanda and Taxila were well-known towns before the dawn of industrialisation. Today, the pilgrim towns also tend to have become centres of trade and commerce. The capital towns housed army, police, bureaucracy and intelligentsia. They also attracted artists, singers, musicians and scholars. With the coming of the British, port towns became important centres of trade and commerce, but later on the same towns, namely, Kolkata, Mumbai, and Chennai also became places of higher education and centres of legal profession.

URBANISATION

Urbanisation is a universal process implying economic development and social change. Urbanisation also means, according to one view, "a breakdown of traditional social institutions and values". However, in India, one cannot say that urbanisation has resulted in the caste system being transformed into the class system, the joint family transforming into the nuclear family, and religion becoming secularised. M.S.A. Rao (1974) observes that the 'breakdown' hypothesis originated from the western experience, and it ignores the fact of 'traditional urbanisation' in India. 'Modern urbanisation' is different from the traditional urbanisation.

Urban centres in traditional India were important places of worship, annual congregations, trade and navigation. They had a stable population. Today, cities have come up as places of industry, headquarters of districts and states or as centres of higher education. A city has a highly diversified population. Chandigarh, Gandhinagar, Bokaro, Bhilai and Sindri are examples of new towns and cities. Some towns have lost their traditional significance, whereas some have acquired added importance because of economic and political factors.

Rao classifies urban studies into three categories: (1) those concerned with the institutional approaches, (2) those treating cities and their growth in the general context of history of civilisations, and (3) those which formulate the cultural role of cities in the context of social organisation of the great tradition. The first category of studies highlights on economic institutions (such as the emergence of a middle class and a commercial organisation) and religion. For Pirenne, the city consisted of middle classes and groups engaged in trade and commerce. For Coulanges, an ancient city was a religious community. Max Weber's emphasis was on social action and autonomous city government. The institutionalists, thus, look for specific causes and conditions for the growth of cities in different contexts. Secondly, Spengler, Toynbee, Geddes, Ghurye, Mumford and Wirth look for an explanation for the growth of civilization in general. They consider world history in terms of city history. The city is a mirror of civilisation. Thirdly, Robert Redfield (1956) has provided a typology of the city in terms of orthogenetic and heterogenetic processes of change in the organisation of tradition and culture. Milton Singer (1972) observes that the great tradition is basically an urban phenomenon, and transformation of the little tradition into the great tradition refers to the process of urbanisation. However, the great tradition has also been undergoing significant change, hence individualism, freedom and fluidity in traditional norms and values.

Gideon Sjoberg (1960) distinguishes cities into: (1) pre-industrial, and (2) industrial. The pre-industrial city was a feudal one. There are two limitations to this approach: (1) feudalism was not the only basis of city formation, and (2) today, the modern city is found in existence due to other factors too, in addition to industrialisation. Even some very important towns and cities are devoid of the industrialisation which one finds in Bokaro, Bhilai, Jamshedpur, Ranchi, Faridabad, Ahmedabad, Mumbai and Pune.

Urbanisation in India

The following points have been made about the nature of urbanisation in India: (1) whether the nature of urbanisation is coterminus with westernisation; (2) can a valid distinction be made between villages and cities; (3) urbanisation is seen in relation to social change, hence urbanisation is not an independent variable of social change; and (4) urbanisation has brought new forms of social organisation and association.

Since caste, joint family and folk-culture continue to exist in India's towns and cities, urbanisation is not coterminus with westernisation. In the pre-westernisation period, there were urban centres in India, and people flocked to them from different parts of the country. There is a valid distinction between village and city in terms of two different ethos of life, cultural patterns, socio-cultural groupings and modes of earning. However, there are also structural similarities between the two in regard to patterns of caste, kinship, rules of marriage and observance of religious practices. Migration, educational institutions, employment opportunities and administration are other institutional sources of linkages between villages and cities.

Thus, villages and towns cannot be seen as dichotomous entities. They are interlinked and yet distinct from each other. It is a fact that urbanisation itself is a result of advancement in science and technology and some other factors. But, once urbanisation becomes a fact in itself, it brings about formal associations and institutions, organised means of transport and communication, and creates problems of slums, overcrowding and crime. In fact, urbanisation is a dependent variable initially, but it tends to become a causative factor subsequently. There is a sort of 'circular causation' in the process of urbanisation.

An operational definition of urbanisation is given by G.S. Ghurye (1969). According to him, urbanisation means migration of people from village to city and the effect of this movement upon the migrants and their families and upon fellowmen in the villages. D.F. Pocock's observation (1961) seems to be quite refreshing. He writes: "... the Indian city, old or modern, is Indian just as an American city is American. Nothing is gained by imagining that the word 'city' automatically implies certain comparable features." Thus, the Indian urban situation needs to be explored in its specific context and historicity. R.K. Mukherjee (1957) rejects the notion of dichotomy between rural and urban, and also the view that urbanisation is an independent variable. He refers to the notion of "degree of urbanisation" as a useful conceptual tool for understanding rural urban relations. Hence, he also prefers the concept of "rural-urban continuum". K.L. Sharma and Dipankar Gupta based on some case studies have suggested the country-town nexus as a useful analytical tool to understand rural-urban ties historically and contextually.

The concept of urbanisation needs to be distinguished from the concepts of urbanity and urbanism. Urbanisation refers to the process of change in values, attitudes, and styles of life of those people who migrate to cities from villages and the impact of these people on those who are left behind in the villages. Urbanity is a state of people living in urban areas distinct from those living in the countryside. Urbanity refers to a pattern of life in terms of work situation, food habits, stress patterns and worldview of the people living in urban centres. Urbanism can be characterised as a system of values, norms and attitudes towards interpersonal relations in terms of formalism, individualism and anonymity.

Urban Social Structure and Stratification

A number of criteria have been used to understand urban social structure and stratification. The most important ones are the extent of closure or openness and the nature of deprivations and gratifications. These apply to specific groups and collectivities as some of them have opportunities for betterment of their social standing whereas others remain deprived of the same. The individual is the basis in regard to motivational structure, utilisation of available opportunities and use of means of communication for realising one's aspirations. Thus, theoretically speaking, urban social structure can be characterised in terms of having openness, attributional criteria (occupation, education, income, etc.), mobility and individual ranking.

Victor S. D'Souza (1974) has analysed kinship, caste, class, religion and displaced or non-placed conditions in his study of the city of Chandigarh. Internal differentiation among different groupings has been analysed on the basis of education, occupational prestige and income. The assumption is that if the groupings of a particular type are alike in respect of education, occupation and income, then, the principle on which they are formed is not an important basis of social organisation. For it to be called important, the members of each grouping should tend to be homogeneous and the different groupings should be heterogeneous.

D'Souza finds that the educational, occupational and income hierarchies are significantly correlated with each other. However, the correlation of each of them with the operational caste hierarchy is not significant. Social class position (occupational status) is positively correlated with education and family income. For the Chandigarh people social status is a fundamental value, which is based on education, occupational prestige and family income.

D'Souza writes: "A social class may be defined as a category of persons having more or less equal prestige or social status." D'Souza considers occupational prestige the most reliable indicator of class position. He has also taken into account self-identification by different categories of respondents. The objective criteria have a correlation with the subjective class identification. The main classes are: (1) upper class, (2) middle class, (3) working class, and (4) lower class. D'Souza also identifies seven occupational grades which are differentially associated with different classes, depending upon the ranks of individuals within these grades.

Cities consist of a variety of professional classes. They perform specialised functions, such as teaching, medical, legal, etc. A study of the social origins of professionals may offer significant insights into the process of social stratification and mobility. Compared to other Asian countries, the professional classes in India constitute a very small proportion of all workers. For every 10,000 workers in India, there are 171 professional workers. In Japan, the figure is 489, in China 349, in Sri Lanka 446, in Malaysia 314 and 294 in the Philippines. Unevenness in the growth of professions comes to light clearly. It is revealed that the recruitment to professions is heavily in favour of the upper castes and urban people.

Thus, the upper, upper-middle and middle classes dominate most of the opportunities and positions in the professions. The upper and upper-middle caste and class background of most of the top-level political elite conforms to this general pattern. This is true of political parties of all hues with some exception of individual members. However, in recent years, the rural rich are replacing the urban rich in the field of politics to a large extent. Some change is also visible in the recruitment to various civil services and medical and engineering professions. More than 70 per cent of the employees in registered factories live in urban areas. The mass of white-collar workers also live in towns and cities.

The social structure of towns and cities comprises (1) top level businessmen, industrialists and bureaucrats, (2) higher income professionals, scientists, technicians, professional managers in industry and large merchants, (3) clerks and minor officials in government offices and private firms, school teachers, working journalists, struggling professionals, petty shopkeepers and small-scale entrepreneurs, and (4) members of the working class, such as operators, artisans, household industry workers, service-workers, hawkers, peddlers, construction workers and unskilled labourers.

We may conclude our discussion on urban life by saying that urbanisation refers to the movement of people from rural to urban areas. The rate of urbanisation during the twenty-first century will be more rapid than in the past. There has been an uneven degree of urbanisation and urban growth. This has had serious repercussions on the socio-economic development of India in general and of specific regions in particular. The location of towns in a given region becomes an important factor in the economic development of the area. Along with spacing, the size of a city also assumes importance. Both hierarchy (size) and location of towns determine, to a large extent, the nature of the rural-urban interaction, including migration, supply of goods to urban markets and purchase of consumer goods from cities.

CONCLUSION

In this chapter, we have analysed the structure of villages and urban communities in India. Our analysis of the village community focuses on the nature of village life in ancient, medieval and modern India. The Indian village has been a very vital part of social life. It was a system, not only of social and cultural ties, but also of economic and administrative functions. British ethnographers and administrators characterised the Indian village community as a 'little republic', a society unchanged and self-sufficient. However, we have found that it was changing, and had ties with wider society and with other villages and towns. The *jajmani* system was a mechanism through which various caste groups interacted with each other. Migration, village exogamy, *jajmani* system, dependence upon towns for a market, division of labour, and visits to religious places speak of the fact that the Indian village was not an isolated whole. The British themselves created several new patterns of social and economic relations by introducing the zamindari and raiyatwari systems of land tenure. With the abolition of these systems and with initiation of several new plans and programmes, we witness new social relations in post-independent India. However, in spite of these changes, the village community in India has an ethos of social life, different from that of towns and cities. There are some aspects of village social life which have not changed much.

Urbanisation is a worldwide phenomenon. India has also witnessed an increased growth of urbanisation and industrialisation in the post-independence period. Urban growth in India is particularly due to large-scale migration from villages to towns and cities, as the latter offer better facilities for education and training and more and better avenues for employment. Besides structure and composition of towns and cities, we have discussed the concept of urbanisation, urbanisation in India, and urban social structure and stratification. Our main focus has been on understanding the causes of uneven urban growth. Towns and cities are an important factor in the development of the region in which they are located. The development of towns and cities depends upon the support villages in the vicinity extend to them in terms of migration, supply of farm produce to the cities, and purchase of consumer goods from them.

Exercises

1. Give a brief account of village life in ancient India.
2. How was village social life different in medieval India as compared to the one in ancient India?
3. Write short notes on the following
   (i) Kautilya
   (ii) Megasthenes
   (iii) Metcalfe
4. Explain the *jajmani* system. Describe the factors which have weakened this system.
5. Is the village an 'isolable' unit?
6. In what way has the caste system been a major social institution in the Indian village community?
7. Explain the *zamindari* and *raiyatwari* systems of land tenure.

8. Discuss the following:
    (i) Joint family
    (ii) Rules of marriage
    (iii) Caste panchayats
    (iv) Caste dominance
    (v) Untouchability
9. Differentiate between the city and the village.
10. Describe the features of the following types of towns:
    (i) Pilgrim centres
    (ii) Capital towns
    (iii) Centres of trade and commerce
    (iv) Towns having universities and institutions of academic learning
    (v) Industrial towns
11. Define urbanisation. Distinguish it from urbanism and urbanity.
12. Explain the following:
    (i) Industrialisation
    (ii) Westernisation
    (iii) Rural-urban continuum
    (iv) Social class
13. Describe the urban social structure. Bring out class-based distinctions in urban India.
14. Explain the role of the professional classes in urban India.

Select References

Chauhan, B.R., "Rural Studies", a trend report, in *A Survey of Research in Sociology and Social Anthropology*, Vol. I, Bombay: Popular Prakashan, 1974.

Desai, A.R. (ed.), *Rural Sociology in India*, Bombay: Popular Prakashan, 1969.

D'Souza, Victor S., "Urban Studies", a trend report, in *A Survey of Research in Sociology and Social Anthropology*, Vol. I, Bombay: Popular Prakashan, 1974, see also Volumes II and III.

Dumont, Louis, *The Caste System and its Implications*, London: Paladin, 1972.

Foster, G.M., "What is folk culture?", *American Anthropologist*, Vol. 55, April-June 1953.

Ghurye, G.S., *Caste and Race in India*, Bombay: Popular Prakashan, 1969.

Mandelbaum, David G., *Society in India*, Bombay: Popular Prakashan, 1972.

Mukherjee, Ram Krishna, *The Dynamics of a Rural Society*, Berlin: Akademic, Verlag, 1957.

Pocock, D.F., *Social Anthropology*, London, 1961.

Rao, M.S.A. (ed.), *Urban Sociology in India*, New Delhi: Orient Longman Ltd., 1974.

Redfield, Robert, *Little Community, Peasant Society and Culture*, Chicago: The University of Chicago Press, 1956.

Rosen, George, *Democracy and Economic Change in India*, Berkeley: The University of California Press, 1966.

Sharma, K.L. and Gupta, Dipankar, "Introduction", in K.L. Sharma and Dipankar Gupta (eds.), *Country-Town Nexus: Studies in Social Transformation in Contemporary India*, Jaipur: Rawat Publications, 1991.

Sharma, Surendra, *Sociology in India: A Perspective from Sociology of Knowledge*, Jaipur: Rawat Publications, 1985.

Singer, Milton, *When a Great Tradition Modernises*, New York: Praeger Publishers, 1972.

Sjoberg, G., *The Pre-industrial City: Past and Present*, New York: The Free Press, 1960.

Srinivas, M.N., "Social Structure", in *The Gazetteer of India*, Vol. I, Government of India, 1973, see also Volume III.

Unnithan, T.K.N., Deva, Indra and Singh, Yogendra, *Towards a Sociology of Culture* (ed.), New Delhi: Prentice-Hall of India, 1965.

7 Kinship, Marriage and Family

No society can exist without having institutions of kinship, marriage and family. Despite varying modes of relations based on these institutions, there are certain universal elements emanating from the fact that there is no 'kinshipless society' and no 'kinlessman'. It is the family which puts together husband and wife, children and other kin under the same roof. Both from normative and structural points of view, kinship, marriage and family become the central foci of all societies irrespective of their socio-economic and political development. Normatively, kinship and marriage refer to rules and regulations regarding hierarchy, avoidance and inheritance of property. Structurally, nature and type of family, kin groups, clans, castes, etc., can be explained as collectivities and groupings in terms of their interconnections and interdependence. Thus, the study of kinship, marriage and family brings out not only issues of socio-cultural nature, but also the ones related to rights, claims, obligations, contract, agnation and cooperation.

KINSHIP

The system of kinship, that is, the way in which relations between individuals and groups are organised, occupies a central place in all human societies. Radcliffe-Brown (1964) insisted on the study of a kinship system as a field of rights and obligations and saw it as part of the social structure. Evans-Pritchard's study of the Nuer of the southern Sudan (1951) focussed on kinship groups, particularly groups based on descent in the male line from known ancestor. Morgan called them *gens* (clans). However, Morgan's view, along with that of McLennan and Sir Henry Maine, that the kinship systems should be equated with evolutionary law, is not favoured today. Kinship systems are not subject to cumulative evolution as the evolution of technology is. Kinship systems cannot be ranked as better or worse, higher or lower. They simply represent alternative ways of doing things, namely, in terms of acknowledged rules and regulations regarding succession, inheritance and marriage.

Evans-Pritchard showed how gens functioned as political groups in Nuer society. He emphasised on the recruitment, perpetuation and functioning of such groups in Africa. Emphasis on interpersonal relations between individuals and groups is found in the study of kinship by Meyer Fortes. Thus, we can look at the total society and ask how it forms its kinship groups, and how they function. We can look at the network of the relationships that bind individuals to each other in the 'web' of kinship. Kinship systems are also seen as methods of organising marriage relations between groups. Through marriage, Levi-Strauss (1969) observes, members are recruited to kinship groups. A female is recruited as a wife, as a daughter-in-law and so on through her marriage to another group; and a male through his marriage is recruited as husband, son-in-law of his wife's parents. Thus, kinship group alliances are transacted through marriage.

Robin Fox (1967) writes: "The study of kinship is the study of what he (man) does and why he does it, and the consequences of the adoption of one alternative rather than another". Fox further says: "The study of kinship is the study of what man does with these basic facts of life such as mating, gestation, parenthood, socialisation, siblingship, etc." Four basic principles outlined by Fox regarding kinship are as follows:

1. The women have children.
2. The men impregnate the women.

3. The men usually exercise control.
4. Primary kins do not mate with each other.

In its commonest definition, kinship is simply the relations between 'kin', i.e., persons related by real, putative or fictive consanguinity as stated by Fox. However, it is difficult to define and find the 'real' consanguinity. Generally, we remember people up to two to three generations. Thus, a consanguine is one who is defined by the society as a person related by real or supposed blood ties. However, blood relationship in a genetic sense has not necessarily anything to do with it. We draw a distinction between 'pater' or legal father from the 'genitor' or actual biological father. In case of adoption also a child is treated as consanguine. A female becomes a consanguine after her marriage as soon as she bears a child. Consanguinity is thus a socially defined quality. Affines are married to consanguines, for example, in the case of levirate.

John Beattie (1974) provides an adequate explanation of kinship. According to him, the basic categories of biological relationship are available as a means of identifying and ordering social relations. Kinship provides categories for distinguishing between the people. Hence, kinship categories are more social than jural or economic. The categories of kinship are used to define social relationships – distinct types of social behaviour and particular patterns of expectations, beliefs and values. These social relations may be of authority and subordination, of economic exchange, of domestic cooperation, of ritual or ceremonial nature, and they may be enacted in many different ways. In this way, kinship refers to the ways and means by which social ordering takes place. But kinship is also a principle of succession, inheritance of property, bifurcation and divisions. A couple of studies have revealed that 'factions' in Indian villages are found corresponding to castes, sub-castes, clans and even lineages. Kinship encompasses, therefore, a whole way of life. It is necessary to know language, values and behaviour of people in a given society to understand its kinship system. Kinship provides a guide to a very great many of the social relationships in which a person is involved in his life. It provides a way of transmitting status and property from one generation to the next. This is true about all societies irrespective of the levels of their technological and industrial advancement. Based on kinship we also find effective social groups even in modern democratic societies. Thus, realising kinship as a complex and elaborate system, Malinowski (1954) referred it as 'kinship algebra'.

Kinship Terminology

Murdock (1949), while analysing the interrelation between kinship terminology and kinship behaviour, mentions two categories of kinship terms: (1) terms of address, and (2) terms of reference. Terms of address form an integral part of the culturally patterned relationships between kinsmen. Terms of reference are linguistic symbols denoting one of the two statuses involved in each such relationship. Since any status is defined in terms of the culturally expected behaviour, there are apriori reasons for assuming a close functional congruity between the terms of reference and the relationship in which the denoted kinsmen interact. A close correlation has been found between the terminological classification of kindred or relatives and the social classification. But, the congruity between kinship terms and behaviour patterns is not absolute. The gap between the two is due to the application of a single classificatory term to a variety of different relatives – for example, 'mother' to all the wives of the father. The kinship terms like 'uncle' and 'aunt' are unable to explain the proper relations unless they are specified in contextual terms. 'Uncle' can be referred to denote father's brother, mother's brother, father's sister's husband and so on. Kinship terminology is determined by several factors such as historical influences, differences in language, psychological processes, rules of marriage, etc. Some of the important kinship terms defined by Lucy Mair (1984) are as follows:

Kindred: Kindred are a body of persons, who are genealogically linked to the ego. They may have common obligations to the ego.

Cognates: All the people who are related by 'blood' in any way to an individual are known as cognates.

Affines:	Those who are related to a person by marriage are affines.
Corporate groups:	These are continuing property holding groups. Corporate groups are recruited by descent – patrilineal or agnatic and matrilineal or uterine kin.
Lineage:	A corporate group recruited by descent is called a lineage. There may be several lineages in a given clan.
Lateral:	It indicates the 'side' of the kinship group.
Lineal:	It refers to the 'line' of the kinship group.

Kinship in India

Kinship in India can be analysed within family and beyond family separately as well as in terms of the nexus between the two. Kinship within family would include 'primary relatives' with the focus on intra-family relationships, which include husband and wife, father and son, mother and daughter, mother and son, father and daughter, elder and younger brother, elder and younger sister and brother and sister. These relationships are part of the same nuclear family, which is also referred as 'family of procreation'. Kinship beyond family comprises of 'secondary' and 'tertiary' relatives. Murdock (1949) refers to eight 'primary' and 33 'secondary' relatives. Each secondary relative has primary relatives. The tertiary relatives number 151 possible kins, and there are also 'distant' relatives who are beyond the tertiary relatives.

In India, we have, generally speaking, 'clan exogamy' and 'caste endogamy'. A given caste has several clans, and a given clan has several lineages. The common ancestor of lineage members is usually an actual, remembered person, but the common ancestor of a clan is typically a legendary, supernatural entity. The members of a clan are spread over a given area, and hence they find themselves unable to have common interests or joint action. A clan, however, provides generally a basis for corporate activity, common worship. On the basis of clan, eligibility for marriage within a given caste is determined. In many ways, more than clan-based primordiality, there is caste-ethnocentrism in regard to observance of rituals, performance of economic activities, mutual aid, etc. 'Feminal kin' and 'fictive kin' too provide basis for commonality of interests and allegiance.

We have noted earlier that kinship is certainly a major basis for social organisation, but at the same time it is also a basis for division and dissension in regard to succession and inheritance of property. Hostility at times supersedes lineage unity. Fights between sons and grandsons, brothers and cousins have been experienced quite often. Sibling rivalry has also been observed.

Karve's Study of Kinship Organisation in India

Iravati Karve (1953) undertakes a comparative analysis of four cultural zones with a view to trace out something like a regional pattern of social behaviour. A region may show various local patterns. There are variations between castes because of hierarchy and caste-based isolation and separation. Karve analyses the process of acculturation and accommodation in the context of kinship. She has adopted a historical perspective covering a span of 3,000 years based on ethno-sources, observations and folk-literature along with Sanskritic texts. Karve's comparative study takes the following points into consideration:

1. Lists of kinship terms in Indian languages,
2. Their linguistic contexts and corresponding behaviour and attitudes,
3. Rules of descent and inheritance,
4. Patterns of marriage and family, and
5. Difference between the Sanskritic north and the Dravidian south.

Karve spells out the configuration of the linguistic regions, the institution of caste and family organisation as the most vital bases for understanding of the patterns of kinship in India. She divides the whole country into northern, central, southern and eastern zones keeping in view the linguistic, caste and family organisation.

The kinship organisation follows roughly the linguistic pattern, but in some respects language and kinship do not go hand in hand. For example, Maharashtra has Dravidian impact, and the impact of northern neighbours speaking Sanskritic languages could be seen on the Dravidian kinship system. Despite variations based on these factors, there are two common points: (1) marriage is always within a caste or tribe, and (2) marriage between parents and children and between siblings is forbidden.

Kinship in North India

In north India, there are (1) terms for blood relations, and (2) terms for affinal relations. There are primary terms for three generations of immediate relations and the terms for one generation are not exchangeable for those of another generation. All the other terms are derived from the primary terms. The northern zone consists the areas of the Sindhi, Punjabi, Hindi (and Pahari), Bihari, Bengali, Asami and Nepali. In these areas, caste endogamy, clan exogamy and incest taboos regarding sexual relations between primary kins are strictly observed. The rule of *sasan* is key to all marriage alliances, that is, a person must not marry in his patri-family and must avoid marriage with *sapindra* kin. *Gotras* in the old Brahmanic sense of the word are exogamous units. Sometimes a caste is also divided into endogamous *gotras* or exogamous *gotras* as also *gotras* which do not seem to have any function in marriage regulations. There is village exogamy. Thus, there are at least four basic features of kinship in north India: (1) territoriality, (2) genealogy, (3) incest taboos, and (4) local exogamy. Considerations of caste status tend to restrict the area of endogamy. Marriage prohibitions tend to bar marriage over a wide area in terms of kinship as well as space. Cognatic prohibitions and local exogamy are strictly adhered to in marriage alliances. Four-*gotra* (*sasan*) rule, that is, avoidance of the *gotras* of father, mother, grandmother and maternal grandmother is generally practised among Brahmanas and other upper castes in north India. However, some intermediate and most of the lower castes avoid two *gotras*, namely, that of father and mother.

Kinship in Central India

The central zone comprises the linguistic regions of Rajasthan, Madhya Pradesh (now Chhatisgarh also), Gujarat and Kathiawad, Maharashtra and Orissa with their respective languages, namely, Rajasthani, Hindi, Gujarati and Kathiawadi, Marathi and Oriya. All these languages are of Sanskritic origin, and therefore, they have affinity to the northern zone. But there are pockets of Dravidian languages in this zone. There is also some impact of the eastern zone. Tribal people have their unique and somewhat different situation compared to other people in the region. In regard to the central zone the following points may be noted:

1. Cross-cousin marriages are prevalent which are not witnessed in the north zone. Cross-cousins are children of siblings of opposite sex, parallel cousins are children of the siblings of the same sex.
2. Many castes are divided into exogamous clans like the north zone.
3. In some castes exogamous clans are arranged in a hypergamous hierarchy.

However, none of these features are found all over the zone. In Rajasthan, for example, Jats follow two-*gotra* exogamy along with village exogamy; Banias practise four-*gotra* rule; and Rajputs have hypergamous clans, and feudal status is an important consideration in marriage alliances. Rajputs are not a homogeneous caste. They put a lot of emphasis on purity and nobility of descent. The fact of being a hero and a ruler has been a major consideration. Symbolic marriages (marriage with sword) were quite a practice. Status of mother on either side is also a factor in marriage alliances.

In Kathiawad and Gujarat one finds a mix of peculiar local customs and northern practices. Some castes allow cross-cousin marriages, others allowed marriages once a year, and some others permitted once every four, five, nine or twelve years. When the marriage year arrives, it is announced from village to village and there is a rush to perform marriages. The practice of 'Nantra' (levirate) exists even today. Brahmanas, Banias, Kunbis and higher artisan castes follow the northern pattern of kinship organisation, but some practices of southern region are also observed. Cross-cousin marriage among the Kathi, Ahir, Ghadava Charan and Garasia castes is quite common. Kolis and Dheds and Bhils (tribe), allow both types of cross-cousin marriages. Thus, Rajasthan and Gujarat largely follow northern pattern. The terminology is Sanskritic in origin and some kinship terms have central Asiatic derivation.

Karve observes that Maharashtra is an area where Sanskritic northern traits and the Dravidian southern traits almost hold a balance with perhaps a slight dominance of the former. Northern languages spoken are like Gujarati, Rajasthani, Himachali and Hindi. The tribals in the area speak Mundari. The Dravidian languages are mixed up with the Sanskritic languages. Maharashtra kinship structure is a little different from both southern and northern zones. The Marathas and Kunbis together form about 40 per cent of the population; Marathas are supposed to be higher in status but a rich Kunbi can reach the status of a Maratha. The two groups call themselves Kshatriyas. Maratha-Kunbi complex has been a ruling clan. Even today headman or *patil* is a Maratha in a village.

Kunbis are divided into exogamous clans. Some practise levirate; other consider cross-cousin marriages as a taboo; but some others do not prohibit such marriages. In central Maharashtra hypergamy and clan exogamy exist. In southern Maharashtra there are instances of both types of marriages, namely, cross-cousin and uncle-niece. The clan organisation of the Marathas has some similarity with that of the Rajputs. For example, mythological origin comparable with Rajputs is also claimed by the Marathas. Their names are also similar to that of Rajputs. The rule of exogamy is, however, not dependent on the clan name but on the symbol connected with the clan. The symbol is called *devaka*. No two people having the same *devaka* can marry. The clans and the *devaka* both play a significant role in marriage. Status of a clan is important in hypergamous marriage alliances.

Marathas have as many as 96 clans. Among these, there are concentric circles of mobility and status. Ethnically, there is no homogeneity. There are *panchkula*, a cluster of five clans, then there are 'seven clans', and all are hypergamous divisions. No taboo is attached to bilateral kinship like north zone. No parallel-cousin marriages are allowed. There is also taboo on paternal-cousin marriages. Generally, preference for a man's marriage is with his maternal cross-cousin. Sisters can and do marry the same man. Brothers generally avoid marrying two sisters. Levirate is practised among the northern Kunbis. However, exchange marriages are avoided.

The tribal people in Orissa like Gonds, Oraons and Konds speak Dravidian languages, and their kinship system can be equated with that of the Dravidian-speaking people. The Munda, the Bondo and some of the Saora speak Mundari languages. The Oriya-speaking people have the same type of caste divisions as are found in northern regions with slightly different names. Brahmanas in Orissa seem to be immigrants from Uttar Pradesh, Bihar and Madhya Pradesh. Aranyaka Brahmanas and Karans (Kayasthas) do not allow cross-cousin marriages. Some agricultural castes allow cousin-marriages, but others prohibit. Junior levirate is found among the poorer classes.

Kinship in South India

There are five regions in the southern zone consisting of Karnataka, Andhra Pradesh, Tamil Nadu, Kerala and the regions of mixed languages and people. The southern zone presents a very complicated pattern of kinship system and family organisation. Here, patrilineal and patrilocal systems dominate. However, some sections have matrilineal and matrilocal systems, and they possess features of both types of kinship organisation. Some castes allow polygamy, whereas some have both polygyny and polyandry. In Karnataka, Andhra Pradesh, Tamil Nadu, and among some castes of Malabar, patrilineal and patrilocal joint family dominates as in the northern zone.

The Nayars, the Tiyans, some Moplas in Malabar region and the Bants in Kanara district have matrilineal and matrilocal family, and it is called *tharawad*. It consists of a woman, her brothers and sisters, her own and her sister's sons and daughters. No affinal relation lives in the *tharawad*. Some consanguines are excluded (children of the males). There is no husband-wife, father-children relationship in a *tharawad*.

In the southern zone there is the system of caste endogamy and clan exogamy similar to the northern system. It is called as 'Bedagu' or 'Bedaga' or 'Bali' in Karnataka. The Kotas of Nilgiris call it 'Keri', the Kottai Vellals call it 'Kilai', the Koyas name it 'Gotta' and the Kurubas call it 'Gunpu'. Some Telugu people call it 'Inti-peru', and the Malayalis mention it 'Illom'. In Travancore, it is referred to as 'Veli'. The word 'Gotra' is also widely used. The main symbols used for clans are of silver, gold, axe, elephant, snake, jasmine, stone, etc.

In northern zone village exogamy is a widely accepted norm. But, in southern zone, there are inter-marrying clans in the same village. Gonds do not observe village exogamy. The only principle is that of exogamy or *illom* or *veli*. A given caste is divided like northern castes into exogamous clans. Inter-clan marriages do not cover all clans. Within an endogamous caste, there are smaller circles of endogamous units made up of a few families giving and receiving daughters in marriage.

The southern zone has its peculiar features which are quite different from that of the northern part of India. Preferential marriages with elder sister's daughter, father's sister's daughter, and with mother's brother's daughter are particularly prevalent in the southern zone. The main thrust of such a system of preferential marriages lies in maintaining unity and solidarity of the 'clan' and upholding of the principle of return (exchange) of daughters in the same generation. However, there are taboos on marrying of younger sister's daughter, levirate, and mother's sister's daughter. Maternal uncle and niece marriages and cross-cousin marriages result in double relationships. A cousin is also a wife, and after marriage a cousin is more of a wife than a cousin.

Comparing the southern kinship system with the northern one we can mention that there is no distinction between the family of birth and the family of marriage in the south whereas such a distinction is clear in the northern India. In the north, terms for blood relatives and affinal ones are clear, whereas in the south many terms do not indicate this distinction clearly. For example, Phupha-Phuphi for father's sister's husband and father's sister and Mama-Mami for mother's brother and his wife are used in the north, whereas in the south Attai is used for both Phuphi and Mami. Mama is used for both Phupha and Mama. In the north, there are the 'extended family of birth' and the 'extended family of marriage'. There is no such distinction in the south. No special terms are used for affinal relatives in the south. Same relatives appear in two successive generations in the south.

Thus, southern and northern kinship systems differ in the context of relations by marriage and relations by birth and more particularly in regard to the arrangement of kin in different generations. There does not seem to be any clear-cut classification of kin on the principle of generation at all in the southern terminology. In south zone all the relatives are arranged according to whether they are older or younger than ego (self) without any reference to generation. There are no words for brothers and sisters in the Dravidian languages. However, there are words for 'younger' and 'older' brothers and sisters. A number of terms are used in common for (1) father and elder brother (Anna, Ayya), (2) mother and elder sister, (3) younger brother and son (Pirkal), and (4) younger sister and daughter (Pinnawal). These terms denote respectability to the elders and not to the actual blood relationships. The point of reference is the ego – and the persons older and younger than the ego are ranked based on their age.

Age, and not generation, is the main consideration in the southern kinship system. Marriage is outside the exogamous kin group called Balli or Begadu or Kilai. Exchange of daughters is favoured and marriage among the close kin is also preferred. The rules of marriage are: one must marry a member of one's own clan, and a girl must marry a person who belongs to the group older than self, and also to the younger than the parents. Older cross-cousins and also younger brother of girl's mother are preferred. A person can marry any of his younger female cross-cousins and also a daughter of any of his elder sisters. Consequently, we find reciprocal relations and kinship terms referred to this reciprocity. Louis Dumont highlights the following points about the southern kinship system:

1. Principle of immediate exchange,
2. A policy of social consolidation,
3. A clustering of kin group in a narrow area,
4. No sharp distinction between kin by blood and kin by marriage, and
5. Greater freedom for women in society.

Kinship in Eastern India

The eastern zone is not compact and geographically it is not contiguous like other zones. Besides northern languages, Mundari and Monkhmer languages are also spoken. The main communities are Korku, Annamese, Saka, Semang and Khasi. The other languages are Mon, Khmer and Chain. The area consists of a number of Austro-Asiatic tribes.

All the people speaking Mundari languages have patrilineal and patrilocal families. The Ho and Santhal have the practice of cross-cousin marriage. But till the father's sister or the mother's brother are alive, they cannot marry their daughters. This condition makes cross-cousin marriage a rare phenomenon. The Bondo people, for example, do not have taboo on cross-cousin marriage, but one does not find an example of cross-cousin marriage among them, as reported by Elwin. The Ho and Munda have separate dormitories for bachelors and maidens and they indulge in pre-marital sexual relationships. Sometimes these relationships result into marriages but quite often the marriage mate is different from the mate of the dormitory days. All these people are divided into exogamous totemistic clans. A person must marry outside of the clan and also outside of the circle of near relations like first cousins.

Money is given for procuring a bride. Service by the would-be-husband in girl's father's house is also considered as brideprice. After marriage one establishes his separate household, but may keep his younger brother and widowed mother, etc., along with him in his newly established house. The Mundari people thus differ from the rest of India in not having joint family. People maintain patriclan relations by common worship of ancestors and residence. They extend help to each other but live independent life.

The Khasi of Assam speak Monkhmer language, and they are a matrilineal people like Nayars, but are quite different from them. The Nayars have a matrilineal joint family and husbands are only occasional visitors. The Khasis have joint family with common worship and common graveyard, but the husband and wife live together in a small house of their own. After death the property goes to mother or youngest daughter. If there are no female relatives, widow gets half of the property if she opts not to remarry. A man's position is like that of a Hindu bride in the patri-family. But there is difference because the Hindu bride is incorporated as a member of her husband's family whereas a Khasi husband is considered as a stranger. A woman enjoys a great amount of freedom. After divorce children are handed over to her. The Khasis have clan exogamy. Marriages of parallel cousins are not allowed. Cross-cousin marriage is also quite rare.

Though we have drawn a sketchy view of the kinship organisation in India, we come to know that both rigidity and flexibility exist side by side in regard to values and norms related to the kinship systems. These are reflected in regard to divorce, widow remarriage, incest taboos, caste endogamy, clan exogamy, rule of avoidance, family structure, systems of lineage and residence, authority system, succession and inheritance of property etc. However, kinship continues to be a basic principle of social organisation and mobilisation on the one hand and division and dissension on the other. It is a complex phenomenon, and its role can be sensed even in modern organisations. Migration, mobility and education have weakened the kinship systems and rules of clan organisation because members of a caste/sub-caste or of a clan do not live at the same place. Matriliny in Kerala has almost withered away. In north-east also it has become weak.

MARRIAGE

Right at the outset, we have stated that kinship, marriage and family are inextricably interwoven with each other. In our discussion on kinship we have in fact discussed about marriage and family. In almost all societies marriage is an institutionalised social relationship of crucial significance. It is generally associated with a number of other important social relationships. There are different types of marital unions. These have implications for population composition, property relations, inheritance, etc. Further, there are various regulations and prohibitions associated with marriage and sexual relations.

Marriage is more than simply a legalised sexual union between a man and woman; it is socially acknowledged and approved relationship. In India, people generally believe that marriage is not between two individuals, but it is between two families in terms of bonds that it creates between them. It is also a sacrament, certainly marriage provides recognition or legitimacy to children; it confers acknowledged social status on the offsprings, and this is important in terms of inheritance and succession.

Types of Marriage

There are two broad types of marriage, namely, monogamy and polygamy. Monogamy refers to marriage of one man with one woman, and this is in general the ideal form of marriage. Polygamy refers to both polygyny and polyandry. The former refers to marriage of more than one woman to one man, and the latter is marriage of one woman with more than one man. There is also sororal polygyny under which a man is married to two sisters. On the contrary, under adelphic polyandry a woman is married to two brothers. Besides these types, there are also institutions of levirate and sororate marriages. Under levirate a man marries his deceased brother's wife even if he is already married or when he has become a widower. In most societies junior levirate is preferred. Such a system is prevalent in the societies in which unilineal descent in the male line is found as the central principle of social organisation. Levirate is also known as *Nata* or *Nantra,* that is, binding by widow remarriage. Sororate refers to marriage of a widowed man with his deceased wife's unmarried younger sister. This is enacted to ensure continuity of social ties between two families. Levirate is practised in northern India among intermediate and lower castes and communities, but it is forbidden among the upper castes. Some castes believe this as a socially degrading institution, and prefer widowhood for their daughters and daughters-in-law imitating notion of purity from the *dwij* castes. However, sororate is preferred even by the upper castes as it involves only the widowers and not the widows. Thus, marriage is always seen in terms of prescriptions, preferences and proscriptions and taboos.

Rules of Marriage and Mate Selection

K.M. Kapadia's study (1964) of marriage and family in India continues to be an important source for the understanding of these two most vital institutions of India's social structure. According to Kapadia, the question of selection in marriage may be considered from three points of view, namely, the field of selection, the party to selection, and the criteria of selection. Preferential code, prohibiting restrictions, endogamy and exogamy explain the field, the party and the criteria in selection of mates for marital alliance. Besides these rules which limit the field of selection in marriage, caste exercises a tremendous control over its members by imposing penalties and ostracization of the defaulting members. With a view to grant freedom to a person in selection of the marriage partner outside one's caste, the Special Marriage Act was passed in 1872. The Act was amended in 1923 to make it more effective. Subsequently, various Acts were passed in 1938, 1946 and 1949 with a view to widen the scope of selection of mates. Despite these legal enactments, exclusivity of caste groups remains a hard fact even today.

The endogamous character of caste persists despite new economic, emotional and psychological functions acquired by the caste in post-independence India. However, in some quarters, inter-caste marriages have received encouragement due to occupational mobility, migration, education and common place of work for both men and women in offices and factories. The Hindu Marriage Act of 1955 defines the degrees of prohibited relationships, which completely ignore rules of caste endogamy and clan exogamy. However, the local customs of various communities related to marriage among cross-cousins have been held valid. Among Muslims, for example, marriage with a father's brother's daughter is more or less preferred. At the same time, Muslims also recognise endogamous rules. The Sunnis and the Shias do not inter-marry. Further, the sub-groups, such as Saiyed, Shaikh, Mughal, Pathan, etc., marry within their own communities. Dowry and social prestige of a family are other important considerations in marriage alliance.

The most common belief even today is that the father should marry off his daughter while she is still *nagnika* (literally naked), the age before attaining puberty. Certainly, such a belief has resulted into child marriage, and pre-puberty marriage was considered pious, and it became a part of Brahmanical cultural ethos. Virginity of a girl became the central concern of both sides. Pre-puberty marriage thus received elitist acclaim and social honour. Another contributory factor, as observed by K.M. Kapadia, is the theory of *samskara*. The whole life of both man and woman is full of *samskara*, beginning from pregnancy till death. A good number of these rites refer to purification and a girl prior to attainment of puberty is considered pious and worthy of marriage. The social ideal of monogamy also contributed to early marriage. Hypergamy was no less a factor favouring child marriage. The lower castes have not been quite seriously concerned about notion of pre-menstruation, yet they have imitated the ideal of child marriage from the upper castes considering it as a Sanskritic act and indicator of social prestige. Raja Ram Mohan Roy, Ishwar Chandra Vidyasagar and Malabari all saw infant marriages not only bad but also opined that it led to the wretchedness of widowhood.

Today, age at marriage has gone up. It is realised that pre-puberty marriage is harmful on health grounds and also results into higher rate of widowhood. Education and employment are considered more or less as valuable for girls as for boys. Hypergamy and concomitant constrain of dowry also contribute to increase in age at marriage. Girls themselves have been coming forward in selection of their mates. Thus, change in the outlook, values, and increased awakening as cultural factors, and education, occupation, migration and dowry as structural factors, have all contributed to higher age at marriage.

Family cycle and marriage are closely related to each other. Birth of the first child marks the second stage in the cycle, and death and formal partition of family property and assets are other important events. In an Indian family, marriages of the children are significant as they indicate status of the two families. David G. Mandelbaum (1970) observes: "A marriage mobilizes the family's social sources. Through marriage the members renew kin ties or establish new bonds of kinship." Giving gifts, performing services and just participation in marriage explain structural aspect of marriage in terms of both kin alliances and networks with non-kin. Today, in middle class families, it is quite common to get biodata of the girl in particular. The following example can help explain the status of the girl's family:

> Name: Rani Gupta
>
> Age: 22 years
>
> Height: 155 cms, weight 45 kg, slim but sound health, very fair complexion and beautiful, brilliant, well-versed in household work, including cooking, sewing, embroidery, progressive outlook.
>
> Throughout first division with M.A. in Economics, doing Ph.D.
>
> Match preferred from the same community, but caste no bar for persons of high status
>
> Family background : Father leading advocate, elder brother executive engineer, two sisters married and working as doctors, sons-in-law also reputed professionals. Own house in the town, decent marriage.

Thus, in marriage alliance, a family's status is tested, and all possible efforts are made particularly by the girl's family to come upto the expectations of the boy's family, kinsmen, neighbours and friends. Certainly, a family's status goes up, if it is able to have marriage alliance with a family of high repute in the region.

Hindu Marriage as a Sacrament

Considering these factors can we say that Hindu marriage is a sacrament? The aims of Hindu marriage are said to be *dharma* (duty), *praja* (progeny) and *rati* (pleasure). Sex is given third place in regard to the functions of marriage. *Dharma* is the first and the highest aim of marriage. Procreation is given the second place. Marriage also aims at begetting a son to save the father from going to hell. A son is required to offer *pinda* (offering) to his father on his death. On marriage the sacred fire is enkindled to offer *Panchamahayagyas*. A man with his wife is supposed to offer *puja* throughout his life. Thus, marriage is primarily for the fulfilment of duties of his *dharma*.

Kapadia (1964) points out that performance of *homa*, or offering in the sacred fire, *panigrahana*, or taking the hand of the bride, and *saptapadi*, or the bride and the bridegroom going seven steps together – are important rites for completion of a marriage. All these rites are performed with Vedic *mantras* in the presence of the sacred fire. Thus, Hindu marriage is a sacrament because it is said to be completed only on the performance of the sacred rites and the sacred formulae. Hindu marriage is a sacrament in another sense because marriage is considered essential for woman and she is required to perform rites with her husband throughout her life. Hindu marriage is sacred because it is irrevocable as the parties to the marriage cannot dissolve it at will. Since marriage is considered indissoluble, the husband and wife try to adjust their tastes and temper, ideals and interests, by making sacrifices for each other. Hindu marriage is not an ordinary event, it is an institution of life-long compromise and adjustment.

Marriage is also a social duty towards the family and the community, and as such there is little individual interest. Husband and wife are not individual persons, but they are part of extended family and caste (community). However, the husband and wife have never been equal in regard to their obligations and privileges. The wife is required to follow the ideal of *pativratya* devoted to her husband alone. The institution of *sati* (self-immolation after husband's death) has received encouragement and widow remarriage gets discouraged.

Today, the situation has undergone sea-change. The Hindu Marriage Act of 1955, socio-cultural awakening, education and urban employment, etc., have weakened the sacred ethos of Hindu marriage. Divorce is becoming quite acceptable. The incidence of widow remarriage has also increased. Rules of marriage are not adhered due to inter-caste and inter-religious marriages. Feminism has also created feelings of equality among women with men. Women are claiming status equal to men. Despite these changes, religiosity remains attached to marriage to a large extent, particularly in the villages.

Marriage among Muslims

It is said that marriage among Muslims is more of a contract rather than a sacrament like Hindus. There are two types of marriage among Muslims: (1) *nikah*, and (2) *muta*. Under the *nikah* marriage, a woman comes to live with her husband and the children belong to her husband's clan. Divorce becomes the sole privilege of the husband in Islam, woman can also seek separation ('Khula') from her husband. *Muta* is a separation brought about by the mutual consent of the parties concerned. The contract is stipulated for a specific period, and woman has no right to divorce her husband during the period of the contract. The *nikah* marriage is certainly a preferred one. There are no elaborate rituals attached to Muslim marriage as we find in the case of Hindu marriage.

Islam disapproves of *muta* considering it an anachronism as it amounts to greater freedom for a woman in her personal life. *Muta* also contributes to instability of marriage. Kapadia (1964) writes: "it (Muslim marriage) was a contract which took place in the presence of a *wali*, often with his consent, and attested by two witnesses. Muta marriage, being a personal contract, required neither a *wali* nor a witness. Islam gives the right of divorce only to the male, and this is taken as a part of the Personal Law. Marriage among Muslims is contracted by paying *mahr*, bride-price. It is paid to the wife. *Mahr* clearly symbolises control of the husband over his wife, and his right to *talaq* (divorce)." Muslim women are longing for equality with their menfolk due to their education and economic independence. The orthodox Muslim clergy is being challenged by the young educated Muslims. It is not quite easy for a Muslim male today to abandon or divorce his wife in a whimsical way as he used to do. There is greater emphasis today on stability of marriage and equality of the sexes than before. Patriarchy of the husband and other male members in Muslim society has become a controversial issue. Many women are questioning their hegemony and control over them. Equality with men and woman as a person are the demands of the day among Muslim women.

FAMILY

Family in India has remained a vital institution and a foremost primary group because it is the sheet-anchor of the patriarchal authority on the one hand, and a protector and defender of individual member's (including woman) right to property, on the other. Despite several wide-ranging changes in Indian society, because of synthesis between collectivism and individualism, the Hindu family continues to be joint, partly structurally and mainly functionally; and it has not disintegrated into individual families like the western countries. Several studies on family have revealed that industrialisation, urbanisation, education and migration have not necessarily resulted into nuclearisation of family in India. A nuclear family in India is not simply a conjugal family. A real change in family must refer to changed pattern of kinship relations, obligations of members towards each other, individualisation, etc. In other words, not only change is seen in the composition or structure of family, but also its functions must change.

The word 'family' is used in several different ways. A.M. Shah (1988) outlines at least four interrelated social situations of family life in India. These are as follows:

1. The body of persons who live in one house or under one head, including parents, children, servants, etc.,
2. The group consisting of parents and their children whether living together or not,
3. In wide sense, all those who are nearly related by blood and affinity, and
4. Those descended or claiming descent from a common ancestor – a house, kindred, lineage.

Generally, a family consists of a man, his wife and their children. This is known as an elementary family. Such a family could be an independent unit; it could also be a part of a joint or extended family, without necessarily residing together. An elementary family includes members of two generations – that of ego and his offspring. Such a family may share property in common with other such units of the ego's brothers' families. According to Shah, an elementary family could be both a complete one and an incomplete one. A complete elementary family consists of husband, wife and their unmarried children. In an incomplete family some and not all persons are found.

Joint Family in India

There has been a lot of debate about nature of joint family in India. What is a joint family? The definition given by Iravati Karve (1953) can be taken as a starting point for analysing changes in family in India. Karve writes: "A joint family is a group of people who generally live under one roof, who eat food cooked in one kitchen, who hold property in common, participate in common family worship and are related to one another as some particular type of kindred." Karve's definition of joint family refers to an ideal situation of family life in terms of its corporate character. In any case, in structural terms, joint family implies living together of members of two or more elementary families both lineally and laterally. When a joint family consists of grandparents, parents and grandsons and daughters, it is called a lineal joint family. When married brothers along with their wives and offspring live together, it is known as lateral joint family. Besides patrilineal joint family, there is also matrilineal joint family.

Structural and Functional Aspects of Family

I.P. Desai (1988) asks the question: What is happening to the family in Mahuva? Mahuva is a small town in Gujarat which Desai studied in early sixties. Desai, based on the data collected from Mahuva, examines the question of jointness in terms of religion, occupational relations, property, education, urbanisation, kinship obligations and household composition. According to Desai, jointness is a process, a part of household cycle. A family becomes joint from its nuclear position when one or more sons get married and live with the parents or when parents continue to stay with their married sons. When married sons establish their independent households and live with their unmarried children, they become nuclear families. This is only a structural dimension of family. Desai outlines structure of family as follows:

1. Husband and wife
2. Uni-member households
3. Husband, wife and married sons without children and other unmarried children
4. The above group with other relatives who do not add to generation depth
5. Three generation groups of lineal descendants
6. Four or more than four generations of lineal descendants

In this classification emphasis is on the understanding of structure or composition of households based on generation and lineage combination. House is the unit of the above classification.

There may be several reasons for change in the structure of family. According to Desai, there are two types of reasons:

(1) natural, and (2) circumstantial. Jointness itself could be a cause for a change in family. For example, married brothers or parents and married children staying together separate due to ongoing quarrels in the family. Married and unmarried brothers or parents and unmarried children staying together separate due to unmarried brother's or son's marriage. Brothers separate after parent's death. Separation also takes place because of unwieldy size of the parental family or due to shortage of space in the household. The circumstantial reasons for separation are due to contingent situations in man's life. These are: (1) men staying with relatives such as the maternal uncle later on establish one's own household; (2) other relatives staying with the head, die or go away; and (3) head of the family goes away alone for business purposes.

Besides the structural aspects of family, Desai also examines the types of jointness based on degree, intensity, and orientation in regard to functions and obligations, which people perform for each other through living separately and at times at different places. Desai finds the following five types of degrees of jointness:

1. Households with zero degree of jointness.
2. Households of low degree of jointness (joint by way of the fulfilment of mutual obligations).
3. Households with high degree of jointness (jointness by way of common ownership of property).
4. Households with higher degree of jointness (marginally joint families).
5. Households of highest degree of jointness (traditional joint families).

Desai concludes that today family is structurally nuclear and functionally joint based on the fact that 61 per cent are nuclear and 39 per cent are joint in Mahuva with varying degrees as indicated above. Of the 423 respondents in Desai's study, only 5 per cent are not joint at all. There are 27 per cent families with low degree of jointness, 17 per cent with high degree, 30 per cent with higher and 21 per cent with highest degree. Desai also reports that 220 respondents believe in jointness unconditionally, 24 have faith in nuclearity unconditionally, 51 believe in jointness conditionally and

58 express their faith in nuclear family with certain conditions. It is undoubtedly clear that people have belief in joint family system, though it is another thing that they are constrained to live apart from their parents and brothers and other kin due to structural conditions on which they do not have any control.

Family is an interactional unit with diverse and dynamic intra-family relationships based on age, sex, kinship status, education, occupational status, place of work, office or power, status of in-laws, etc. One cannot understand such a complex situation by looking at family from a legalistic point of view. An extended joint family is a miniature world, and as such it reflects the ethos of wider social system of which it is a constituent unit. Besides the diverse and dynamic relationships within the family, family composition, basic norms of deference and etiquette, authority of the head of the family and rights and duties of members, performance of common and particular tasks, etc., are some other points to be noted in the functioning of family in India. There are also regional variations in proportions of joint families. Higher education does not weaken joint family system and since higher education is found more among the upper and upper-middle castes, joint family is more among them than the lower caste and class people. In functional terms, jointness is nothing but a structure of obligations among the closest kinsmen.

Industrialisation and Family Change

It has been hypothesised that industrialisation would tend to change the structure of family to a particular type more suited to its functioning in a given society. Further, it is said that in an industrialising society where there are different types of family, certain types of family would facilitate industrialisation more than certain others. It has been opined that many Indians are now living in isolated conjugal families and that many more young couples are desiring to do so for the new industrial economy allows ambitious young men to remain independently of their relatives. It is also said that a fast moving industrial economy cannot develop within a society whose hardened social barriers force every son to follow his father's occupation. But this is not true as there is no occupational homogeneity among the members of a caste. Even members of a family pursue different occupations. Today, certainly, emphasis is mainly on income and status and one derives it by doing a particular economic activity. People have been migrating in large numbers to cities, they are becoming urbanised in outlook and individualistic in their orientation.

Richard D. Lambert (1963), based on his study of some factory workers in Poona, concludes that factory does not produce fragmented families. The workers just by living away from their kin do not change themselves into nuclear families. The average size of the family among the factory workers was found to be 5.2 members whereas it was 4.5 for Poona. It was noted that the workers had a heavy pressure of dependents and mainly due to the fact that they were the main earners with regular cash income. Lambert also observes that even where spouses are employed, the familial pattern does not follow the western pattern. Thus, the joint family is not functionally adaptive only to an agricultural society, it is equally functional to an industrial society. The change is towards greater 'jointness'.

Is the joint family breaking down? It is now clearly viewed that there is no linear transformation of joint family into a nuclear family under the impact of industrialisation, urbanisation, education and migration. There are points as given below worth consideration based on the findings of some studies:

1. Large joint families are more prevalent in urban than rural areas and vary in prevalence with region and caste.
2. Nuclear households are prevalent in villages as well as in cities.
3. Such rural-urban distinctions might have been common in the past.
4. Nuclear families in both villages and cities may grow into joint households and decline with separations and deaths into nuclear families again.

Thus, jointness has become complex and multi-dimensional. Today, joint family is a social structure comprising of a network of social relations among persons related in specific ways. It is viewed as a system of mutual obligations and appropriate norms of behaviour for each relative. The presence or absence of joint residence, joint property, particular group of kin is relevant only as a part of the total structure of obligations. The presence of any particular feature does not mean prevalence of joint family, and its absence does not mean otherwise. It is difficult to find joint families on a considerable scale in terms of commonality of residence, property, worship, etc., as it is incompatible with modern urban living and large-scale migration of people from villages to towns and cities. Milton Singer (1972), in his study of families of industrialists, has found that move to the city has not destroyed large family households. The move into industry has been accompanied by a carryover and adaptation of traditional joint family principles into the sphere of industrial organisation. The companies studied by Singer are family firms. He is of the view that Indian joint families have adopted the principles and practices of household management to industrial organisation. Singer writes: "The relationship of the manager of a joint family to the coparceners and other family members is analogous to the relationship of the managing director of a company to its board of directors and stockholders."

We may conclude by stating that there is no positive relationship between nuclear family and industrialisation. Family as an institution has been increasingly adaptive and has proved itself quite effective to meet the requirements of modern industry and urban life. In many cases joint family has proved quite useful in terms of trustworthy manpower, capital and mutual aid and cooperation. The future of the joint family in India depends upon the congruities between macro-structural changes and their effects on the institution and practices at the local level. The way conflicts, strains and stresses and bickerings are resolved in the family will determine family's future. The young people have their own ideas and expectations, and the way they find expression in the family will also determine future of joint family. Joint family has transformed itself from time to time, but it has survived generally with changed adaptive capabilities. This process of change in the family is far greater reality than asking the questions whether joint family in India is disintegrating or what future joint family can see for itself in the face of rapid macro-structural and ideological changes. The future family will also decide the patterns of kinship structure and relations and adherence to rules of marriage.

Exercises

1. Define kinship. Explain its main functions.
2. Draw a sketch of your kin at primary, secondary and tertiary levels.
3. Write a note on kinship terminology.
4. Give a brief description of kinship in India.
5. Highlight similarities and differences between kinship systems of north and south India.
6. What is caste endogamy and clan exogamy?
7. Explain the meaning of cross-cousin marriages.
8. Explain the following:
   (i) *Gotra*
   (ii) Descent
   (iii) Lineage
   (iv) Incest taboo
9. Discuss the types of marriage.
10. What are the main rules of marriage among Hindus?
11. Is Hindu marriage a sacrament?
12. Is Muslim marriage a contract?
13. Define family. Explain its main functions
14. Give a brief account of changes in family in India.
15. Discuss structural and functional aspects of family.
16. Has industrialisation brought about family change?
17. Explain the future of joint family in India.

Select References

Beattie, John, *Other Cultures*, London: Routledge & Kegan Paul, 1974.
Dube, Leela, *Sociology of Kinship*, Bombay: Popular Prakashan, 1974.

Evans-Pritchard, E.E., 1951, *Kinship and Marriage Among the Nuer*, Oxford: Clarendon Press.

Fox, Robin, *Kinship and Marriage*, Baltimore: Penguin Books, 1967.

Kapadia, K.M., *Marriage and Family in India*, Calcutta: Oxford University Press, 1964.

Karve, Iravati, *Kinship Organisation in India*, Poona: Asia Publishing House, 1953.

Lambert, Richard D., *Workers, Factories and Social Change in India*, Bombay: Oxford University Press, 1963.

Levi-Strauss, C., *The Elementary Structures of Kinship*, Oxford: Alden Press (English Edition), 1969.

Mair, Lucy, *An Introduction to Social Anthropology*, Delhi: Oxford University Press, 1984.

Malinowski, Bronislaw, *Magic Science and Religion and Other Essays*, New York: Doubleday, 1954.

Mandelbaum, David G., *Society in India*, Bombay: Popular Prakashan, 1970.

Meyer Fortes, *Kinship and the Social Order*, London: Routledge & Kegan Paul, Chapters I & II. Also for views of Lewis Henry Morgan and A.R. Radcliffe-Brown, 1969.

Murdock, G.P., *Social Structure*, New York: Macmillan, 1949.

Radcliffe-Brown, A.R., *The Andaman Islanders*, New York: Free Press, 1964.

Shah, A.M. and Desai, I.P. (eds.), *Division and Hierarchy: An Overview of Caste in Gujarat*, Delhi: Hindustan Publishing Corp., 1988.

Singer, Milton, *When a Great Tradition Modernizes*, New York: Praeger Publishers, 1972.

8 The Caste System

Caste is known as *jati* in common parlance. Caste as a system of social relations has been a central point in Hindu society for several centuries. A lot of conjectures, controversies and explanations have come up about its origin, nature and role in Indian society. It has been claimed that it is an all-encompassing system, an ideology, which would govern all other relations. Its central notion is hierarchy based on the ideas of pollution and purity. In this chapter, we will give a brief account of the caste system, its evolution, role and significance in contemporary India.

A caste is an endogamous group, that is, its members marry within the caste. A man is born in a caste and remains in that for ever. Members of a caste used to have a particular occupation on a hereditary basis. A given caste occupies a particular rank in the hierarchy of castes, hence some are superior to it and some are inferior. At the top are Brahmanas and at the bottom are the 'untouchable castes'. There are certain rules regarding eating, drinking and social interaction, which are to be followed by all castes. Caste panchayats used to regulate the behaviour of its members by implementing these rules. Caste is a dynamic institution; it has changed a great deal in accordance with changes in the wider society. In the following paragraphs, besides discussing the caste system in ancient, medieval and British periods, we will also discuss problems related to definition of caste, caste dynamics, caste as an ideology, caste and class, and changes in the caste system.

Caste System in the Ancient Period

The Vedic Period

The origin of the caste system dates back to the age of the RgVeda. There is a reference to the word *varna* (colour) in the RgVeda. *Arya* is referred to as fair and *Dasa* as dark. However, there is no reference to Brahmana or Kshatriya. People of the two *varnas* (fair and dark complexioned) differed not only in their skin colour but also in their worship and speech. Thus, the differences were both racial and cultural. Brahmanas, Rajanyas (Kshatriyas) and Vaishyas constituted the Arya *varna*, whereas the non-Aryans made up the Dasa *varna*.

The Purusha-sukta, a part of the RgVeda, states that the Brahmanas, Rajanyas, Vaishyas and Shudras sprang up from the mouth, arms, thighs and feet of the Purusa (God). Later on, these became castes. However, there is no reference to the classes becoming hereditary. Classes were merely functional. The priest and the warrior occupied positions above the Vaishya and the Shudra, but they were neither hereditary positions nor exclusive ones. There was interchange of duties and also inter-class marriage prevailed. The ban on eating food cooked by Shudras did not exist. There was no trace of untouchability.

The Later Vedic Civilisation

The later Vedic civilisation consists of Samhitas – Atharva, Yaju and Sama and the Brahmanas and Sutras. The notion of sacrifice gained prominence in this period. The doctrines of Karma, Maya, transmigration, identity of the individual soul with the Universal Soul, and Mukti as main tenets of Hinduism find their first expression in the Upanishads. The performers of *yajnas* came to be known as Brahmanas. They became a distinct class and were highly respected because they performed religious duties. The Aryans who moved to the east and south had to fight with the original inhabitants, and they formed another group known as the Kshatriyas. They were required to protect the conquered territories. The remaining Aryans became a separate class and were named as Vaishyas. The non-Aryans became the fourth class and were known as Shudras. Initially, these classes were not rigid divisions; but gradually restrictions were imposed on change of duties. Further sub-divisions occurred. Birth became the sole criterion of class (caste) determination. These four groups were *varnas* and not castes. Today, castes are identified as endogamous groups, locally known as *jatis*, and they number more than three thousand in India. Brahmana, for example, is not one single caste. In fact, there are hundreds of castes and sub-castes among Brahmanas. So is the case with Kshatriyas and Vaishyas. As *varnas*, Brahmanas, Kshatriyas and Vaishyas are only one each in the entire country.

The power and privilege of the priestly caste (Brahmanas) increased, but the Kshatriyas challenged this from time to time. In course of time, these two castes, namely, Brahmanas and Kshatriyas, enjoyed special privileges, and Vaishyas and Shudras were denied the same status. A system of nomenclature to address the members of these castes emerged. Occupational differentiation also became a necessity, with sub-divisions within these four caste groups. Change of caste, though very unusual, was not as yet impossible. The higher castes could marry into the lower castes, but marriage with Shudras was not approved. Shudras were denied the right to touch. The idea of pollution by touch found expression. Inter-dining was still allowed. The caste system was not yet rigid.

The four ashramas, namely, *Brahmcharya, Grahastha, Vanaprastha and Sanyasa* (the student, the householder, the forest hermit, and the recluse) are mentioned in the Jabala Upanishad. These stages of man's life-cycle were later on closely associated with the caste system. Mention is found about *Chaturvarnya,* and the supremacy of Brahmanas and Kshatriyas. Instances of marriages between these two are also reported. A reference is also found to *Saptavarnas* (seven castes), signifying differentiation (particularly, sub-divisions) among the Vaishyas.

The Smriti Period

Dharma or a code of duties for harmonious functioning of the various divisions of society became an accepted procedure. Dharma Shastra or Smritis laid down rules for every caste and vocation, for every relation in society, king and subjects, husband and wife, teacher and pupil. The rules were not rigid and were revised from time to time to meet new developments. Sometimes, the law-givers and the priestly class introduced their own ideas and laid down strictures and taboos. However, from the time of the Imperial Guptas, the castes and sub-castes were rigidly separated. Inter-caste relations were defined in regard to dining, marriage, touch and ritual observances. The category of 'outcastes' had emerged. Women faced degradation. The corporate bodies like *gana* (oligarchic states), *shreni* (craft guilds) and *sangha* (monastic orders), which were formed in the early Vedic period, disintegrated. India became an insular and stagnant society. Women did not enjoy social status equal to men. Widow remarriage was not permitted; the right to property was denied to women; and the institution of *sati* was flourished.

Thus, from the state of monolithic character or tribal herd emerged two groups, viz., Arya and Dasa. Further, from these groups emerged the four castes (*varnas*). There was possibility of interchange of caste and occupation. Up to this stage, the caste system was conceived with a recognition of variations in human nature and as a plan to fit these variations in a graded structure according to the needs of society. This was a scheme of cooperation and synthesis to ensure progress. Given sufficient flexibility this was an excellent solution of the dichotomy of the individual and the community. Thus, one finds this functional view of the caste system up to the time when caste rank was not necessarily determined by birth. A functional view of the caste system refers to advantages and merits which society derived from the distribution of work and duties to various groups known initially as *varnas* and later on as castes and sub-castes.

Inflexibility in the Caste System

The caste system became inflexible when birth became the basis of caste rank. Restrictions on marriage and social relations were also imposed. The codes of Gautama, Bodhayana and Apastamba have references regarding heredity, connubiality and commensality in the context of the caste system. Thus, the four *varnas* were separated from and related to each other by a set of laws based on two cardinal principles: division of labour and synthesis. A number of sub-castes and mixed castes emerged with the rise of new crafts and vocations. Thus, with increased occupational differentiation, the caste system became more diversified. Inter-caste marriage, abduction and rape contributed to the weakening of the monolithic nature of the caste system. The Smritis, such as Manu, Vishnu, Yajnavalkya, Brahaspati and Narada, report cases of mixing of castes and numerous violations of Shastric canons and injunctions.

Economic distinctions did not necessarily coincide with caste distinctions. The economic pyramid consisted of four layers. At the top came the high officials, merchants, bankers and landlords (Amatya, Shastri and Gramabhojaka). Below them came small freeholders, artisans and ordinary officials. Next was labour without right and property, and at the bottom was despised and segregated labour. The third and the fourth classes coincided with the Shudras and the *Malechha*, respectively. The first and the second classes would not fit into the caste hierarchy. The Brahmanas and the Kshatriyas, who were faithful to their callings, enjoyed high esteem and influence, even if they were not well off economically.

Thus, the *varnas* (castes) were not mere economic classes. When a Brahmana or a Kshatriya adopted trade and commerce, he still retained his precedence over the Vaishya. Caste also overlapped with class as we see particularly in the case of the Vaishyas and the Shudras. One view is that property and privilege were separate. Brahmanas enjoyed privilege. The Vaishyas had property but were treated as a commoner. The Shudras were allowed the Vaishya callings of agriculture, crafts and trade, but were not allowed the privileges of Vedic studies and *upanayana* (regeneration). A functional view and the dynamic and adaptive nature of caste system can be seen in the following statement: "The caste system was devised to solve the differences in society, to reduce competition and to maintain a balance of interests". It was from time to time adjusted to new developments. Thus, up to the Smriti period, caste was projected as a positive and useful system of social relations.

The Aryan society, as a result of the glorified functionality of the caste system, became static and immobile. Buddhism attacked the organic character of the caste system, but the Brahmanas tried to retain the organic nature. *Varnashrama Dharma* (division of society into the *varnas* and *ashramas*) was accepted as instrument of retaining socio-cultural distinctions and division of labour. The organic character of the system refers to interdependence of different caste groups upon each other, as we find in the interdependence of different parts of the human body.

Caste System in the Medieval Period

Class or occupational distinctions crystallised in the early phase of the medieval period. Artisans, servants, priests and moneylenders were the main groups. The caste panchayats had become very strong instruments for regulating the behaviour of its members. The Turks placed a premium on high lineage in matters of appointment. The nobles and officers were graded into *Khans, Maliks, Amirs, Sipahsalars* and *Sar Khails*, according to their military status. There was also a class of slaves.

The Turkish rulers had a preference for luxurious city life. The lower classes of Muslims mainly consisted of converts from Hindus. They retained a Hindu identity even after conversion to Islam, and continued to work as artisans, shopkeepers and clerks. Many worked as workers and slaves in the royal palace and in the households of the nobles and the rich. In social matters, they were treated as inferiors by the ruling group.

The Mughal rule did not adversely affect the socio-cultural aspects of the caste system. The Brahmanas looked after the temples, directed religious ceremonies, worked as teachers, administered Hindu personal laws and served the Hindu society in various other ways. The Kshatriyas were rajas, rais and zamindars, although they lost a large part of their dominion in the north. They were a war-like people, and fought against the foreign invaders to protect their interests, position and prestige. The Vaishyas were quite prosperous, as they were engaged in banking, commerce, transport and crafts. They generally served the royal families and the rich. The plight of the Shudras was the same as before because they continued to suffer from social disabilities.

Numerous castes, sub-castes and sub-sub-castes arose based on occupational and regional differences. The Kayasthas came into limelight as government servants, and continued to be so until India became independent. The Khatris proved to be successful financiers and administrators. The Nagars, the Brahmanas and the Chettiyars became influential as they performed administrative and financial responsibilities. However, the Bhakti movement, by recognising spiritual equality of all persons, reduced the rigidity of the caste system in day-to-day social relations.

The caste system is known for its adaptive capacity. It has adapted to innumerable difficult situations, forces and pressures. I have written elsewhere: "Because of its (caste) adaptability, caste has evolved simultaneously in several directions and adjusted with ideologically antagonistic systems, adjusting its principles whenever necessary. It has never paved the way to the emergence of an alternate system of stratification and social relations, though the contents of its functions and other paraphernalia changed from time to time" (Sharma, 1980).

Caste System in the British Period

The various views on caste are based either on impressionistic understanding or on the scriptural texts. Lines of distinction between *varna* and caste, and caste and class, have not been clearly drawn. Extreme views have been expressed about the caste system. One such view is that caste is an undesirable and harmful institution because it serves the interests of the entrenched and dominant caste groups. Contrary to this is the view that caste is a functional institution as it ensures division of labour, orderliness and regulation of behaviour of its members through endogamy and caste panchayats. The caste system has also been considered as a coercive system. It compels members of a caste to follow certain rules of marriage and interpersonal relations. The freedom of the individual is curtailed by the corporate strength of the caste system. Due to these divergent views, it is difficult to arrive at a precise definition of caste.

Max Muller, a German indologist, writes: "The whole caste system, as it has come down to us, bears unmistakable evidence of Brahmanical origin." The Brahmanas, according to Muller, have been the strongest advocates of the caste system. They have created the vast divisions in Hindu society. They cruelly punished those who questioned the caste system and their supremacy. The principle of exclusion/inclusion or seclusion/rejection based on birth and endogamy resulted in diversification of caste groups, occupational roles and rituals.

However, caste has never been a static system. The prevalence of thousands of castes and sub-castes and many more clans and sub-clans within these castes is a proof of diversification, differentiation and change in the caste system. Inter-caste or mixed marriages, migration, change in occupations, the Buddhist movement, the impact of Islam, the impact of the British, and several other factors have made caste not only an adaptive but also a living system of social relations.

A number of books written, particularly in the pre-independence period, refer to the advantages and disadvantages of the caste system. The advantages are: division of labour, measures of protection, cleanliness, respect for authority and moral restraint. The disadvantages are: physical degeneracy, national poverty, hindrance to intellectual progress, hostility to social reform, curbs on individual liberty, hindrance to the growth of nationality, discord between classes, human suffering, exploitation and cruelty, the pride and arrogance of Brahmanas, moral gradation and blasphemous falsehood, etc. Caste was and is considered to be a tyrannical system. For the Brahmanas the caste system itself became a religion under the pretext of maintaining the unity and wholesomeness of Hindu society.

The British Raj encouraged the continuity of the caste system by favouring some caste groups with higher status and by granting them titles and land. The system was basically inegalitarian, and the British never discouraged caste-based inequalities, injustices and discriminations. On the contrary, British administrators and ethnographers defined caste in terms of its 'functionality' to society and culture in India. They have emphasised inter-caste and intra-caste harmony and discipline with the implicit objective of keeping people divided into castes and sub-castes so that they did not unite against British colonial rule in India.

Defining the Caste System

According to some scholars, the main features of caste are: (1) a common name, (2) a common descent, (3) professing the same hereditary calling, and (4) forming a single homogeneous community. S.V. Ketkar considers hereditary membership and endogamy as the basis of caste as an organic structure of relations. The organic nature of caste refers to harmony of relations between different caste groups. Emile Senart writes: "A caste system is one whereby a society is divided into a number of self-contained and completely segregated units (castes), the mutual relations between them are ritually determined in a graded scale."

J.H. Hutton (1946) takes a functional view of the caste system. He speaks of three types of functions of the caste system: (1) functions for individual members, (2) community functions, and (3) functions for the state, for society as a whole. G.S. Ghurye (1950) gives a comprehensive definition of caste. According to him, the six main features of the caste system are: (1) segmental division of society, (2) hierarchy of groups, (3) restrictions of feeding and social intercourse, (4) allied and religious disabilities and privileges of the different sections, (5) lack of the unrestricted choice of occupation, and (6) restrictions on marriage. Endogamy is the stable feature of the caste system. However, in recent years, inter-caste and inter-religious marriages have been taking place, particularly in towns and cities.

Several other views on caste are: (1) Karl Marx's belief is that the Asiatic mode of production was related to the stability of the caste system in India. (2) H.J.S. Maine's view is that caste is an example of a non-contractual 'status society'. (3) Senart's focus is on the purity of descent and purity of occupations. (4) Louis Dumont's view refers to pollution-purity as the ideological basis of Hindu society reflected through the caste system. (5) Hocart's belief is that the performance of certain rituals and ritual services to the deity and the feudal lords was the basis of the caste system. (6) Max Weber's view is that caste is based on the other-worldly doctrines of Hinduism. (7) C. Bougle's view of the caste system emphasises on hereditary specialisation, hierarchy and mutual repulsion (social distance).

Caste as an All-encompassing System

Caste has been treated as a comprehensive system of social relations. One could even say that it has been equated with the Hindu society itself. Surjit Sinha (1974), in a trend report on caste, prepared for the Indian Council of Social Science Research, lists the studies on caste as follows: village studies, caste and politics; caste, economic organisation and economic development; caste and land tenure; caste, class and social inequality; caste ranking; social mobility in the caste system; social structure of caste; caste and the changing legal system; demography of caste; caste in the urban setting; caste among the non-Hindus in India and Pakistan; caste across civilisations; caste and the Indian civilisation; tribe-caste continuum; caste and personality structure; and caste and social dialect. Further, Sinha lists the following trends in the studies of the caste system:

1. Speculative theories about the origin of the caste system have been given up. The fact of the matter is that today we do not

talk of origin, but refer to levels of its evolution in the Indian society.

2. The bulk of the work on caste is done by the methods of social anthropology and sociology on the basis of studies of multicaste villages.
3. In these studies, considerable interest is shown in understanding the adaptability of the caste system to new situations and forces of change.
4. The study of inter-ethnic status-ranking is done through analysis of data.
5. The study of social mobility in the caste system refers to both structural (vertical) and positional (horizontal) changes.
6. The concept of hierarchy based on the 'binary opposition' of purity and pollution has received considerable attention. Binary opposition refers to Dumont's view that everything in the caste system can be seen in terms of pure and impure. The pure encompasses the impure. In other words, 'pure' is higher and superior and 'impure' is lower and inferior. As such pure and impure are opposed to each other, but at the same time the 'pure' is found in the 'impure' and vice versa as they are parts of the same value system.
7. Inter-regional comparisons within India and comparisons of castes beyond the Indian civilisation have also been done.

In addition to these points, there is a need to reflect upon the caste and class nexus, the caste, class and power approach to social stratification, and caste as a cultural aspect or a structural phenomenon in Indian society. What we need is to examine the theory or ideology of the caste system, the structure of caste groups, and processes of change affecting the caste structure.

Caste, Varna and Class

Varna is an all-India frame of reference frame by which Hindu society is supposedly divided into four categories, namely, Brahmanas, Kshatriyas, Vaishyas and Shudras. Caste, as a system, is an Indian phenomenon, but specific caste groups are found as local or sub-regional entities. A given village or a number of villages in a given area consist of several caste groups (*jatis*). It is this group which becomes an effective interactional entity, a localised phenomenon, a source of strength or a basis for formation of factions in a given village. Such *jatis* living in a village or town observe commensal and connubial rules in social intercourse and marital relations.

Caste as a system has become an overarching ideology which pervades all aspects of Hindu life in particular. All social relations emanate from the ideology of caste, that is, from the notions of hierarchy, pollution-purity and inclusion-exclusion. Caste is both a normative system and a system of actual social relations.

Thus, the question is: What do we mean by caste? An answer to this question is not easy. Members of a caste compete with each other, they are also found cooperating with each other. Today, intra-caste class-based distinctions are found in a pronounced form. Major ramifications of India's class structure may be found in the economic distinctions among members of a given caste in a village. While observing rules of marriage, members of various castes may place a premium on class or status considerations in matrimonial alliances.

Caste as an Ideology

Louis Dumont (1970) considers inequality of the caste system a special type of inequality. "Ideas and values" are basic for knowing actual and observable behaviour of people. For Dumont the idea of pure and impure is basic to caste hierarchy. Hierarchy is a "universal necessity". Society in India, according to Dumont, has remained static. Change has occurred *in* society; but change *of* society is absent. Caste, as an empirical reality, can be located in the form of *jatis* in a specific rural/urban context. Caste is seen as a specific status group in these contexts. However, caste is also a means of identity at a macro-level. At the macro-level, it is not a functioning reality of informal, day-to-day relations. Caste does not become, at this broad level, a basis of marriage; for example, between a Tamil Brahmana and Kanyakubja Brahmana from Uttar Pradesh.

However, both a Tamil and a Kanyakubja Brahmana may have a sense of belonging to the same social stock and may even cooperate for common good particularly in situations of crisis.

Another question is: Is caste an interest group? Caste is certainly a 'resource' in psychological as well as social terms. However, this quality varies from caste to caste depending upon the status of a given caste in a given region or sub-region. Members of a caste articulate their concerns at various levels in the form of interests – economic, social and political.

'Caste Model' of Indian Society

Louis Dumont (1970) thinks of Indian society as a 'caste society'. As such caste is thought to be a logical opposite of the class system. Andre Beteille (1965) outlines the main features of the 'caste model' of Indian society formulated by Dumont as follows:

1. It is based primarily on the ideas held or expressed by certain sections of society and not on the observed behaviour of people. There is always a difference between the 'ideal' and the 'actual'.
2. It attaches a sort of primary and universal significance to caste as this has been conceived in the scriptural texts, but the fact is that caste has changed a lot and acquired new dimensions and roles to perform in the changed situations.
3. The entire system is viewed as being governed by certain more or less explicitly formulated principles or "rules of the game".
4. Different castes are seen as fulfilling complimentary functions and their mutual relations as being 'non-antagonistic'. The reference here is to the *jajmani* system, that is, performance of functions assigned to the members of different caste groups on hereditary basis.

Beteille is of the view that this model, as a general scheme, does not tell much about specific properties of any society. Secondly, the model in its specific form does not take into account certain crucial features of economic and political life. Thus, the model is essentially concerned with ideas and values, hence useful in the interpretation of systems of religious beliefs. The 'caste model' leaves the study of interests, political and economic problems, and inter-group relations incomplete. Acceptance of this model limits the understanding of caste as a cultural system.

The structural aspect of caste does not receive due attention when caste is seen as a cultural or ideological system. Relations between upper and lower castes, between the landowning and the landless castes, between the *Jajman* and the *Kamin* castes, etc., would demand a study of caste from the structural point of view. Domination/subjugation, surplus/exploitation, privileges/deprivations, for example, become the points of reference in the structural perspective. The cultural perspective, however, puts emphasis on ideas and values, namely, pollution-purity, rules of marriage and rules relating to intercaste relations (including physical contact).

Cultural and Structural Aspects of Caste

Undoubtedly, due to multidimensionality and complexity of the caste system, one encounters numerous difficulties in giving a precise definition to caste. We have already stated that there are two prominent views about caste: (1) the structural aspect of caste, which is explained by accepting it as a general principle of stratification; and (2) caste as a cultural system, which is understood in terms of prominence of ideas of pollution-purity and notions of hierarchy, segregation and corporateness. The structural view explains that stratification is a universal reality, and caste is, therefore, an aspect of this reality. The culturological view perceives caste as a distinct phenomenon found in Indian society in particular.

Some scholars view caste as a 'closed system' of social stratification. Others consider it both 'closed' and 'open'. As a closed system, caste has an 'organic' character, that is, different castes depend upon each other for fulfilment of various socio-cultural and economic needs. Caste, as an open system, has segmentary character, that is, different castes become somewhat independent of each other because of the emergence of 'differentiated structures' in India. Such analytic variations hinder a common definition of caste. These, however, indicate that caste is like all other systems of stratification in some ways, while it is quite unique in some other respects.

Caste is not really a very flexible system, but history shows that 'caste mobility movements' have taken place right from the ancient period till today. The process of sanskritisation, as defined by M.N. Srinivas (1972), explains that lower caste people imitate the styles of life, rituals and practices of the upper castes, with a view to improve their status. Such a process of mobility in the caste system has brought about horizontal distinctions or what Srinivas refers to as 'positional' changes. Positional change does not change the caste system; change is within the system. 'Structural' change, however, is a change in the vertical arrangement of the social order. It is ultimately a change of the system. Structural change has been, no doubt, at both the macro and micro levels, but it has been more in the form than in the substance of the social system.

As an entity, a given caste is guided by norms of the caste system, barring those aspects of the caste system which have undergone change and where new mechanisms have evolved to perform the functions earlier performed by those aspects. At the same time, a given caste enjoys its autonomy in regard to observance of its practices, rituals and protection of its rights vis-a-vis other castes. Thus, the fact of the matter is that caste has adapted itself to hostile and adverse situations and has found alternatives to make up for the loss of certain functions or norms. Even today, the caste system demands a certain kind of cooperation from different castes living in a village on social occasions and in agricultural activities. But, such a demand remains unattended. The fact is that the caste system has diminished its significance, however, caste as a discrete entity remains. Caste persists without intercaste relations.

Thus, the view that castes cooperate with each other is a misconception. Non-antagonism and hierarchy are both nomological categories. In reality, defiance and conflict or clash of interests between different caste groups are common. The view that cooperation refers to caste and a competition (or conflict) refers to class is naive and unrealistic. If it is true that the upper castes compete with each other to extend patronage to the lower castes for maintaining their dominance, it is also true that the lower castes compete with each other to seek favours from the dominant castes. The lower castes are not strong enough to oppose the upper castes. A 'dominant caste' is defined in terms of its numerical preponderance, landholding, high ritual status and social and political networks. One or a combination of these attributes may decisively determine dominance of a particular caste at a particular point of time.

The competition which we have mentioned above is not really a new phenomenon. Feuds were quite common between the Brahmanas and the Kshatriyas for seeking power over a territory in ancient and medieval India. Besides the inter-caste conflicts, revolts by the lower castes against the upper castes have been a part of the historicity of the caste system itself.

Caste among the Non-Hindus

It has been stated that caste is an exclusively Hindu institution, but there are studies which have found castes among Muslims, Sikhs and Christians also. The Census Commissioners of the pre-independence era reported the existence of caste-like endogamous strata among non-Hindus in India. Among the Muslims of Kolkata and Uttar Pradesh and among the Sikhs, Jains and Jews, the modes of socio-economic relationship are patterned on caste system. These communities have hereditary occupational groups as endogamously ranked sub-groups. A number of lower caste Hindus converted to Islam in the hope that they would improve their status as Islam did not approve of caste-like distinctions. Since, they were not successful in improving their status, they retained many of their caste traits in the changed set-up. Muslims in India are divided into groups closely parallel to the caste system. Also notions of pollution and untouchability are found among Muslims, despite the fact that Islam rejects hierarchy and inequality.

Muslims in India are distinguished as Ashrafs and non-Ashrafs. The Ashrafs are believed to be of superior origin and live mainly in towns, whereas the non-Ashrafs are supposedly converts from Hinduism and live mainly in villages. There are also ritual distinctions among Muslims based on occupation. There are sweepers, landowners, barbers, washermen and artisans of various kinds as ranked groups among Muslims. Functional castes with some degree of pollution and untouchability are found among Sikhs and other communities.

Caste groups are found even in Sri Lanka, where Buddhism has been the religion of the Sinhalese people. Examples of similar caste systems are also reported from Burma, Japan and some other countries. The blacks of the United States of America have been compared with the 'untouchables' of India. However, the way in which caste has become an ideology pervading over the entire Hindu society is not found elsewhere. It is a culturally specific and unique system.

Are Castes the Opposite of Classes?

Caste and class are polar opposites, as understood by the western scholars, and in particular by the British administrators and ethnographers. They observe that caste and class are different forms of social stratification. The units ranked in the class system are individuals, and those ranked in the caste system are groups. According to this view, change is taking place from caste to class, hierarchy to stratification, closed to open, and from an organic to segmentary system. Such a distinction between caste and class is more of a heuristic nature.

A narrow view of class is taken by considering it a result of objective rating of positions based on certain attributes. To think of class as a case of fluidity and of caste as a case of rigidity is too simplistic and unrealistic – a depiction of these two systems of social stratification. Acceptance of such a distinction would obviously mean defining caste through the concepts of status – rigidity, organic solidarity, functional interdependence, homo hierarchicus and pollution-purity. Obviously, class is described by the ideology of individualism, competition and equality. Such constructs of caste and class are grossly erroneous. Caste-class nexus has always been a historical fact. Continuity and change of this nexus needs to be seen both as a historical reality and a contextual phenomenon.

Caste, as a system of social stratification, represents a semblance of both rigidity and fluidity, cooperation and competition, holism and individualism, organic and segmentary divisions, interdependence and autonomy, and inequality and equality. The genesis of these polar characteristics of caste and class lies in the notion of the imagined superiority of the non-caste western society. These distinctions between caste and class are analytic and not historic and experiential. Ascription and patronage are as much part of the western society as they are found in Indian society.

The distinction that caste is a real phenomenon and class is a category, an attributional construction, is untenable. Both caste and class are real and empiric. Both are interactional and hierarchical and caste inheres elements of class, and class inheres elements of caste. Another fallacy is that class has only the Marxian meaning for the Indian society. What about unity and harmony among the patrons and clients, landlords and tenants, the upper caste 'haves' and the lower caste 'have nots'? At the same time, these polarities refer to contradictions and resultant conflicts between the powerful and the weaker sections. Power is not a zero-sum reality in the Indian context. There are people who are not just at the top and at the bottom. It is a multi-layered and intricate social formation. Thus, caste does not have an air of finality and completeness. It has been dynamic and full of contradictions. Violation of caste norms does not lead to removal of caste as a principle of social stratification. The lower castes demanded for fair wages and gifts from their patrons whenever justice was not done to them. Sometimes, they even decided not to render services to the patrons. In most cases, their demands were acceded to by the *jajmans*.

Since caste incorporates class and class incorporates caste, neither the 'caste view' alone nor the 'class view' alone can explain the entire gamut of India's social reality. The fact is that a perfect congruence between caste class and power never existed in pre-British India. Mobility and migration were normal activities, particularly resulting from warfare for acquiring power. There were also revolts against the excesses and atrocities committed against the lower castes. In recent years, land reforms, adult franchise and certain constitutional provisions have brought about some incongruities in the 'summation of statuses'.

We have earlier discussed caste relations in ancient, medieval and British periods. Material and cultural traditions existed in a congruent form, and class transformation was a vital fact in the form of new kingdoms, settled agriculture, trade, cities and banking and guild organisations. A.R. Desai (1975) observes that caste inheres an underdeveloped but potentially explosive class character. He considers the Indian state 'capitalistic' in its essence and reality, as the state holds economic power, and uses political power for granting or denying economic power to the people.

Thus, both caste and class are real dimensions of India's social formation, and seem to be inseparable from each other. Class is not simply a conceptual abstraction, a construct based on certain attributes or operational indices; it is a concrete reality. Classes of landowners, landless labourers, traders and moneylenders are structural components of Indian society. Interactional ties between them refer to their life-situations.

The caste and class nexus is highlighted by Kathleen Gough (1980) in her analysis of the mode of production as a social formation in which she finds interconnections between caste, kinship, family and marriage on the one hand and forces of production and production relations, on the other. Class relationships are taken as the main assumption in the treatment of caste and kinship in India. Even, the *varna* and *jajmani* systems have been explained by some scholars in terms of class relations and the mode of production.

Caste and class represent, to a large extent, the same structural reality. Yogendra Singh's comments on the caste and class nexus are quite pertinent: "The situation corresponds to a 'prismatic' model of change where traditional sentiments of caste and kinship undergo adaptive transformation without completely being 'diffracted' into classes or corporate groups. Classes operate within the framework of caste" (1968). Caste conflicts are also class conflicts as the upper and the lower castes correspond to the high and the low classes, respectively, in terms of their social placement. Castes also function as classes because they function as interest groups. Caste associations undertake several economic and political activities for their members. Joan Mencher (1974) finds that caste is used as a very effective system of economic exploitation of the lower castes. The upper castes have not allowed the emergence of a class consciousness among the lower castes (classes), as the former feared a threat to their entrenched status.

Changes in Caste and Class Relations

How should one analyse India's class structure? The orthodox Marxists, for example, observe only two classes in Indian agriculture: (1) the class of big landlords; and (2) the class of agricultural labourers. The other view is that today class differentiation in terms of agricultural labourers, poor peasants, middle peasants, rich peasants, landlords, etc., exists and has also existed in the past. The Marxist scholars consider relations between these classes as 'capitalistic', hence the 'haves' and the 'have nots'. A.R. Desai's view is that the state in India has assumed the property norms of a capitalist society as the axis of developmental strategy. Economic determinism, implicit in the orthodox Marxism, is countered by those who emphasise the use of indigenous concepts for understanding of the specific social reality of Indian society.

While examining the nature of class and class conflict in Indian society, five major classes are listed by V.M. Dandekar (1978). These are: (1) pre-capitalist workforce (cultivators, agricultural labourers and household industry), (2) independent workers in capitalist society, (3) employees, (4) white-collar employees, and

(5) blue-collar workers. The main classes can also be referred as: (1) the agrarian classes, (2) the industrial classes, (3) the professional classes, and (4) the business and mercantile classes.

Dandekar expresses his doubts about the application of the Marxian approach to India's class structure. Large-scale industry and monopoly capitalism have different implications in India compared to western countries. The role of trade unions and collective bargaining of workers have been undermined. Along with class antagonism, class harmony is also a fact of life. The multiplicity of classes in between the 'haves' and the 'have nots' cannot escape our attention. The emergence of the new middle classes in India during the British period and more so after India's independence does not support a simple two-class theory in regard to the Indian situation. The proletariat is propertyless but he does have a chance for embourgeoisiement. The categorisation as 'wage earners' is a loose one, as it comprises those earning Rs. 200 to Rs. 2,000 per month. Thus, like the 'haves', the 'have nots' are also a heterogeneous lot. A large number of workers are not 'organised'. Today, salaries and wages have gone up enormously, and particularly as a result of 'globalisation'.

Further, the Indian state, being a 'welfare state', is the largest employer today. Can a democratic welfare state be as oppressive or exploitative as the monopoly capitalists could be? In India, only one-ninth of the total workers are organised through trade unions. Thus, like caste, class is also a complex phenomenon in Indian society. It overlaps with caste, occupation, factions and pressure groups. Instead of the classes at the top and at the bottom of the class pyramid, the middle classes and the mixed classes have emerged as crucial phenomena in contemporary India. The emergence of an upper-middle class during the past decade and half has also set in a new trend of social mobility, particularly among the highly qualified people in the fields of science and technology.

The resurgence of caste, with its multiple facets, is a new phenomenon in the post-independence period. Those who have analysed class relations as a dominant causality, they explain caste and other cultural aspects in Indian society as a part of class analysis. Class alone is not a result of the new forces of change. Changes are in the traditional caste and class relations and not in caste alone paving the way to the emergence of class relations. Thus, classes are found as a part of a system of social stratification in the same way as castes are rooted in Indian society. Class, class relations and class conflicts are not monolithic. There are objective criteria of class identification, and class is also a concrete unit of interaction vis-a-vis other units.

Caste inheres numerous problems related to economic domination and subjugation, privileges and deprivations, and conspicuous waste and bare survival. Class relationships are treated as background assumptions in the treatment of caste and kinship in India. The *jajmani* system can be explained in terms of class relations and the mode of production. Division of labour and patron client relationships refer to the economic dimensions of the *jajmani* system.

Caste riots are frequent in areas where economic deprivations have been reported. The upper castes have waged a class war against Harijans. Dalits/Harijans have been attacked and murdered, their womenfolk raped and put to indignities by the upper caste landlord families. The intermediate castes have ascended in the class hierarchy, but they are struggling against the upper castes socially and culturally. These castes have been benefited by land reforms and adult franchise more than other caste groups. The Brahmanas have lost their traditional dominance mainly because of the emergence of the numerically preponderant middle castes.

The caste system is used as an effective method of economic exploitation. The dominant class (caste) also acquires political power and social prestige with which it further perpetuates and consolidates caste hierarchy. Thus, caste hierarchy reflects ownership of land, and economic hierarchy is closely linked with social hierarchy. Caste determines a definite relation to the means of production and subsistence, specially in rural areas. Caste riots reflect conflict of class interests. Ambedkar rightly observed that the caste system was not merely a division of labour, but also "a division of labourers". However, caste prevents labourers from becoming a class-by-itself, hence caste is an ideology. Caste has persisted as a religious and feudal ideology. However, today, the caste system is not strong because of disappearance of inter-caste relations. Castes are discrete groups, and hence segmentary entities. Depending upon a given situation, members of caste behave or do not behave like a caste group. Caste is no more an everyday life phenomenon.

Incongruities between caste, class and power are indicative of social mobility in the caste system. The corporate character of caste is under attack; the dominant castes do not enjoy hegemony of power. Sanskritisation, as a process of change, affects dominance of the upper castes, and creates an awareness among the lower castes about their rights. However, it has been noted that castes are not dominant; only families and individuals enjoy dominance and power. Corporate mobility (sanskritisation) is generally not feasible in economic and political spheres. Mobility in the caste system, therefore, takes place at three levels: (1) individual, (2) family, and (3) group. Individual is present in both family and caste, and family is considered significant in caste, and both family and caste become sources of identity and support for individual. Intra-caste differentiation can be explained in terms of the status and honour of the members and the families of a given caste.

Castes function as interest groups because they strive for new patterns of distributive justice and equality. Caste associations, caste panchayats and caste-run magazines have strengthened caste ideology. Caste lobbies in parliament, state assemblies and in zila parishads, panchayat samitis and village panchayats have become a fact of today's political life.

Elections have been fought very much on caste lines. Caste and politics have come to stay together. Caste is very much a source of power for its members. Corporateness has acquired new dimension. From ritual activities it has shifted to elections, jobs and employment opportunities. However, castes have not become classes simply in economic or psychological terms. Caste continues to retain the ethos of the system in terms of organising intra-caste and inter-caste relations in certain spheres. Untouchability, pollution-purity, norms regarding dining, etc., have weakened, but expression of caste solidarity in social and political spheres has acquired a new character.

Conclusion

In this chapter, we discussed evolution of the caste system in ancient, medieval, British and modern India. In the beginning it was a system for division of labour devised for smooth functioning of society, but later on it became a rigid system based on birth and hereditary occupation. Social relations between different caste groups were regulated by certain norms. At this stage *varnas* got transformed into caste groups. *Varnashrama* with further distinctions attained a sort of religious character. Class or occupational distinctions crystallised in the early medieval period. In fact, the ritual aspect of caste became rigid in this period in the face of foreign invasions.

The British rule in India brought about further diversification, differentiation and change in the caste system. In pursuance of their policy of "divide and rule", the British encouraged continuity of the caste system. Though caste could not remain an 'organic' system, yet it continued to remain 'segmentary' in nature. Today, with the decline of the *jajmani* system and other changes, a given caste is a segmental unit. At times, it is an interest group, a source of mobilisation, at the time of elections and other occasions.

Though caste was an all-encompassing system in the past, today, it is more of an instrument to mobilise people for economic and political gains. We have discussed caste in terms of its class dimension and social mobility. To a considerable extent, caste and class represent the same structural reality. Classes operates within the framework of castes, and castes take care of class interests. In caste conflict there is more of class conflict. We find resurgence of caste in very many situations with new facets. The corporateness of the caste system has eroded at the ritual level, but it has emerged at political and economic levels. Use or abuse of caste has become discretionary. It is no more preordained by ascription or dictates of some members of a given caste.

Exercises

1. Explain the *varna* scheme. Discuss its role in ancient India. Was it a functional system?
2. Bring out the relationship between ritual and economic aspects of the caste system in ancient and medieval India.
3. Compare and contrast the caste system in the medieval and the British periods.
4. Attempt a suitable definition of the caste system. Is this phenomenon also found in non-Hindu communities in India?
5. What is a 'caste model' of Indian society? Can the caste system be treated as an ideology?
6. In what respects is caste different from class and *varna*?
7. Caste inheres class and class inheres caste. Elucidate.
8. Explain the cultural and structural aspects of the caste system.
9. Define social mobility. Discuss the nature of caste mobility in India.
10. Prepare notes on the following:
    - (i) Functional view of caste
    - (ii) Hierarchy
    - (iii) Pollution-purity
    - (iv) Politicisation of caste
    - (v) Structural and positional changes

Select References

Beteille, Andre, *Caste, Class and Power*, Bombay: Oxford University Press, 1965.

—, "Ideas and interests: some conceptual problems in the study of social stratification in India", *International Social Science, Journal*, Vol. 21. No. 7, 1969.

Dandekar, V.M., "Nature of class conflict in the, Indian society", *Artha Vijnana*, Vol. 20, No. 2, 1978.

Desai, A.R., *State and Society in India: Essays in Dissent*, Bombay: Popular Prakashan, 1975.

D'Souza, Victor S., "Caste and class: a reinterpretation", *Journal of Asian and African Studies*, Vol. 2, Nos. 3-4, 1967.

Dumont, Louis, *Homo Hierachicus*, London: Paladin, Granada Publishing Ltd., 1970.

Gough, E. Kathleen, "Modes of production in southern India". *Economic and Political Weekly*, Vol. XV, Nos. 5, 6 & 7, 1980.

Ghurye, G.S., *Caste and Class in India*, Bombay: Popular Book Depot, 1950.

Hutton, J.H., *Caste in India*, Oxford: Oxford University Press, 1946.

Ketkar, S.V., *History of Caste in India: Evidence of the Laws of Manu*, Jaipur: Rawat Pulications, 1979.

Mencher, Joan P., "The caste system upside down, the not-so-mysterious east", *Current Anthropology*, Vol. 15, No. 4, 1974.

Muller, F. Max, *Comparative Mythology*, New York: Arno Press, 1977.

Murdoch, J., *Review of Caste in India*, Jaipur: Rawat Publications, 1977.

Senart, Emile, *Caste in India: The Facts and the System*, London: Metheun and Co., 1930.

Sharma, K.L., "New Introduction" in *Review of Caste in India*, ibid.

—, *Essays on Social Stratification*, Jaipur: Rawat Publications, 1980.

Singh, Y., "Caste and class: so me aspects of continuity and, change", *Sociological Bulletin*, Vol. XVII, No. 2, 1968.

Srivinas, M.N., *Caste in Modern India and Other Essays*, Bombay: Asia Publishing House, 1972.

Sinha, Surajit, "Caste in India", *A Survey of Research in Sociology and Social Anthropology*, Vol. 1, Bombay, Popular Prakashan, 1974.

The Gazetteer of India, Vol. 2, Government of India Publication, 1973.

9 The Scheduled Castes

The position of the Scheduled Castes (SCs) has a bearing on the social structure of the 'caste society', that is, division of Hindu society into caste groups. At the top of the caste hierarchy are Brahmanas. 'Untouchables' come at the bottom. There are several caste groups in between. Ritual pollution and purity based on birth in a particular caste group is considered as the basis of high and low caste ranks. The notion of pollution-purity pervades over all aspects of social life, including food, cloth, metals, occupations, etc. Thus, not only are persons and castes pure and impure or less pure or more impure, but everything in Hindu society is seen in terms of purity-pollution. Gold is pure and silver is less pure; silk is pure and cotton is impure, etc.

The notions of 'dharma' and 'karma' are associated with roles and obligations as per the caste hierarchy. The dharma of a Chamar, for example, is to remain at the bottom end of the caste hierarchy, and to adhere to his hereditary occupation and to follow the norms associated with his caste in relation to other caste groups. This applies to all caste groups, but those who are at higher levels of the caste ranking are certainly less subjected to suppression and exploitation.

The theory of 'karma' leads to a person to the belief that his low or high caste position is because of his past bad or good deeds, and therefore, he cannot do anything about his ascribed position. He can improve his future by performing his duties in accordance with what he has been assigned to perform under the caste system. These twin notions of 'dharma' and 'karma' have made the caste system stagnant and regimented. Since Brahmanas were at the top of caste hierarchy, they were the rule-makers and prescribers of norms.

In chapters two and eight, we discussed the evolution of the division of labour and the caste system. Those who occupied the lowest positions pursued defiling occupations. They were at the bottom of the caste hierarchy and were known as 'Chandals' (exterior castes). They lived on the outskirts of towns and villages. These castes remained low and suppressed for ages. Under the Constitution of India, these castes have been listed as the 'Scheduled Castes'.

Social and Economic Problems of the Scheduled Castes

With a view to elevate their position, the 'untouchables', who are now known as 'Scheduled Castes', launched several anti-Brahmana and anti-'twice-born' movements in the past. They also began several reformative and status-emulative movements, which particularly aimed at the imitation of the lifestyles of the upper castes and rejection of their own traditional practices and defiling occupations. The inhuman and exploitative conditions in which these people were forced to live for centuries made them conscious of their deplorable condition in the Hindu society. Besides their own realisation, factors external to the caste system also contributed to the weakening of the caste system.

The Constitution of India has listed the 'untouchable' castes as the 'Scheduled Castes' with a view to provide them protection against discrimination, exploitation and degradation. It provides for their social, economic, political, cultural and educational upliftment. A policy for reservation of jobs, positions, educational facilities, and constituencies for state assemblies and the Lok Sabha and for nomination to local bodies has been adopted by the governments of independent India. Today, 15 per cent reservation is available to the SCs in government jobs and in educational institutions for studies.

Dr. Babasaheb Ambedkar fought for a place of honour and dignity for the SCs during the freedom struggle. The British conceded political representation to the 'untouchables' under its policy of the Communal Award. Gandhi did not agree to this because the Muslims had already made such a demand with a view to quicken the process of separatism and communalisation of social relations. Gandhi undertook a fast unto death against the Communal Award. The Award was withdrawn under the Poona Pact. It was stated that Harijans were part of the Hindu social order, and therefore, their condition had to be ameliorated within the framework of the system. Ambedkar became a Buddhist at the fag end of his life. However, he did his best as Chairman of the Drafting Committee of the Constitution of India to make constitutional provisions for the upliftment of the millions of downtrodden Harijans. The name 'Harijan' was given to the untouchables by Gandhi. The word 'Harijan' means "children of God", and implies that Harijans needed special treatment. Gandhi started a periodical entitled as *Harijan* to highlight the plight of the children of God.

Provisions have been made against social discrimination and untouchability with a view to attain equality of the *SCs* with the caste Hindus. However, ascriptive status cannot be changed simply by constitutional provisions. The processes of social change and modernisation of traditional values alone can bring about a change in due course of time. The Constitution of India makes provisions for the upliftment of the SCs in economic, political and educational fields. Since these provisions have made a tangible impact and have generated a certain level of consciousness among the SCs, the upper and intermediate castes have begun to feel uncomfortable. Clashes between the caste Hindus and the SCs have been frequently reported from different states. The SCs are emerging as a force to reckon with representing secular values, egalitarianism and the quest for equality. However, some sections of the SCs, who have derived considerable benefits from the constitutional provisions, have attained an elite status among them. These sections continue to enjoy the special provisions despite enormous improvement in their socio-economic condition. Such beneficiaries from amongst the SCs are known as 'creamy layer'.

In some areas the SCs are still not allowed access to temples, tea stalls and public wells or water taps. However, today, demands are rarely of a religious and ritual nature. What the Harijans demand today is to be treated as persons. They should not be driven from their land, and no longer be bonded labourers, and should be given fair wages. Their children should be educated and considered equal to children of other communities. They should be allowed to have their say in all democratic institutions. However, the fact remains that the SCs continue to be inferior to the caste Hindus in all secular or mundane matters. The SC leaders are subordinate to the caste leaders. The SC votes have generally been controlled by different political groups and parties. Many of the leaders of these castes do not wish to be identified with the SCs. They, in fact, desire to be identified with the upper caste leadership.

Nearly 90 per cent of the SCs live in villages, and they continue to suffer because they work under the command of the dominant castes and landlords. They continue to be economically dependent on the upper caste and class groups. Constitutional provisions have been availed by the poor SCs in a marginal way. Since they continue to be poor, they are subjected to exploitation.

Social Mobility among the Scheduled Castes

It has been noted that today there is an increasing possibility for upward mobility for the SCs. Mobility is possible through two processes: (1) by corporate mobility; and (2) by competition between castes and within castes. There is inter-caste variability in regard to social mobility; and also there are sacred and secular channels for status emulation. Migration, education and white-collar jobs (like those held by the caste Hindus) have been the main source of social mobility among the SCs. There has been perceptible change among the SCs in regard to social status, patterns of interaction, levels of aspirations, styles of life, employment, position of women and awareness about government policies. They have also used their caste associations for political action in towns and cities.

Despite their pitiable condition, we notice two patterns of social mobility among the SCs: (1) welfare measures have induced a certain level of mobility among some sections; and (2) a certain level of awareness about their own low status has emerged along with an anti-upper caste attitude. One serious consequence of the first pattern is creation of socio-economic unevenness between different SCs and among members of the same SC. The benefits of the constitutional provisions and uniformity to other changes have not reached different SCs and individuals. As a result of the second pattern, 'caste wars' or hostilities of the SCs against the upper castes has also increased.

In general, those sections of the SCs, who have extracted greater benefits, have migrated to urban centres. They are educated and have taken up employment in towns and cities. Those who cannot get these benefits, satisfy themselves with 'sanskritisation' or imitation of the lifestyles of the upper castes. Even sanskritisation does help, though latently, in bringing about tangible social change among the SCs.

It is now accepted that the SCs suffer today not so much because of social and cultural disabilities, the imbalances created by structural differentiation in their ranks have become pronounced. This unevenness is a result of the faulty execution of the policies and plans. The atrocities committed on the SCs and their exploitation by the dominant caste Hindus should be analysed in view of these distinctions and their relations with the caste Hindus.

All the SCs have not uniformly been victims of the atrocities of the landlords, rich peasants and upper castes. To say that conflict between a landlord and an SC person refers to a class war or to say that a conflict between a Brahmana and an SC member refers to a caste war are not correct characterisations of the two situations. In the first case, it is not truly a class war, as the landlord is certainly an upper or upper-middle caste landowner. In the second case, a Brahmana is not so poor as an SC member is; he is certainly economically better off than the SC member. Therefore, a given situation is neither purely a class war not purely a caste war. Both the situations are two sides of the same coin referring to economic and social dimensions of Indian society. However, a class war has a tilt towards economic considerations, and a caste war is an expression of caste dominance.

Untouchability

The rigidity regarding pollution-purity has considerably weakened during the post-independence period. The institution of 'untouchability' is no more functioning in a rigid way. Its pollutional aspect has receded. The caste Hindus do not seriously observe untouchability while dealing with the 'untouchable' castes. The SCs have also changed along with changes in the wider society. The caste Hindus observe untouchability on very few occasions, like birth, marriage and community feasts and festivals. In day-to-day life untouchability is not a consideration in relations between an upper caste man and an SC person. Since caste has become resilient and adaptive, a corresponding change has occurred in the institution of untouchability as well.

It is not that caste has withered away with all its class-like character, and untouchability has been continuing and vice versa. Since caste remains a pivotal force in the grab of class, untouchability refers to a situation of exploitation, suppression and powerlessness of the wretched of the earth. Naturally, the exploiters are well-off caste Hindus, landlords and big peasants. The SCs may not be doing today what they were forced to do a couple of decades ago, but they largely remain under the economic and social hegemony of the upper castes and the landed interests.

Constitutional Provisions

Article 46 of the Constitution of India provides: "The State shall promote with special care the educational and economic interests of the weaker sections of the people, and in particular, of the Scheduled Castes and the Scheduled Tribes, and shall protect them from social injustice and all forms of exploitation." In view of the constitutional obligation, several provisions have been provided, such as the reservation of seats for the SCs in the state assemblies and PRIs, parliament, and reservation of jobs at various levels. Likewise, Article 17 declares: "Untouchability is abolished and its practice in any form is forbidden. The enforcement of any disability arising out of untouchability shall be an offence punishable in accordance with law." In pursuance of these constitutional provisions, several programmes have been undertaken for the welfare of the SCs.

The question is: How close to equality are SCs? Compared to caste Hindus, the SCs are still far behind in regard to landholding, and in economic and social mobility. Urbanisation and education are much less among them. Their per capita income is also low. All the posts in the administration reserved for the SCs are not filled. The same is true in regard to education as not many reach to high professional levels.

Inequalities among the Scheduled Castes

Several studies have shown that new inequalities have crept in among the SCs due to uneven educational attainments. Education has not filtered down as expected. Equal access for unequal groups is not true equality. Even the awareness and acceptance necessary for an optimum use of educational opportunities are not uniformly found among the SCs. Thus, the spread of education among the SCs has created social classes among them parallel to those existing among higher castes.

Facts stated below substantiate the emergence of inequalitarian relations among the SCs. For example, the scheme of post-matric scholarship is neither equitably distributed nor optimally used. Caste patterns within the SCs determine differential distribution and utilisation of scholarships and other amenities. Even independent of the imbalances created by education and other measures for their welfare, there are clear differences among them in terms of social and economic status.

There is a well recognised hierarchy among them based on degrees of defilement and pollution. There are also religious cleavages among the SCs. Each one of the SCs is aware of its separate identity, and at the same time they are conscious of their common status as SCs.

The SCs have elites from within their ranks. The elites are educated, economically better off, and elected members of the state assemblies, parliament, PRIs, etc. It is by and large realised that unevenness among the SCs is inherently prevalent and it has been created by the faulty implementation of policies and programmes designed for their welfare. It is this unevenness that is mainly responsible for their backwardness. Awareness of this unevenness could have a levelling effect on these weaker sections. However, more changes would come only through effective distributive justice and decision-making.

Atrocities and Exploitation of the Scheduled Castes

Because of the unevenness, which we explained above, all SCs are not subjected to the same ill-treatment and atrocities by the landlords, rich peasants and upper castes. The SCs who are not victims of atrocities and exploitation belong to a higher class than their brethren who fall prey to the rich landlords. It is this class of SCs who extract maximum benefits from various policies and programmes. The poor SCs were victims of massacre, loot and rape at many places. The role of caste is detrimental to the progress of the 'untouchables'. While analysing the caste-class tie-up, Ramkrishna Mukherjee (1981) observes that "caste riots are frequent in those areas where the caste-wise social deprivations are manifestly correlated with the class-wise economic deprivations, such as in Bihar, Maharashtra, Tamil Nadu, etc." According to Mukherjee, these caste contradictions are due to inherent class contradictions in the caste system.

Caste system functions both as a system of relations of production and as an ideology. Hence, it is both an economic and a social organisation. It is a source of economic exploitation of the 'untouchables'. Caste system is not merely a division of labour. It is also a division of labourers. Capitalist relations make agricultural and industrial labourers a distinct *class-in-itself*, but the caste system prevents them from being a *class-for-itself*. Caste and religion are used to perpetuate a particular class structure. Caste persists as a part of feudal ideology. Caste has discouraged emergence of class consciousness among the weaker sections of Indian society, and the fact is that caste performs class-like functions and activities related to political power.

It has been observed that literacy, education and employment are the most important indicators of social mobility among the SCs, and the phenomenon of violence is closely related to social mobility. The upwardly mobile SCs have reacted sharply against their exploitation and suppression, hence, they become the target of the fury of the upper castes. Apart from prejudices among the upper castes against the SCs, it is also a fact that rivalry is now between the well-off SCs and the caste Hindus entrenched into or aspiring for lucrative jobs, positions of power and high status. As such, it is a class war behind the apparent caste riots.

The upper castes are demanding merit as the basis for higher education, jobs, promotions, etc. The SCs have been demanding extension of the policies of protective discrimination and reservation to elevate the weaker sections to the level of the caste Hindus. The upper castes are so strong that even today they escape punishment for flouting the Untouchability Offences Act of 1955 and The Scheduled Caste and Scheduled Tribe (Prevention of Atrocities) Act, 1989. Under these Acts, the practice of untouchability is a cognisable offence.

The bulk of the SCs are engaged as agricultural and manual labourers. They are victims of assault, murder, rape and other cruel and inhuman treatment. In case they even slightly react to these indignities, they become the target of social boycott, denial of public facilities and employment on farms by the landlords. Such incidents have taken place in Bihar, Uttar Pradesh, Gujarat, Maharashtra, Madhya Pradesh, Andhra Pradesh, Tamil Nadu, Rajasthan, etc., in the recent past. In May 1977, in Belchi, nine

Harijans were burnt alive. The people were killed not only because they were Harijans, but also because they were working as agricultural labourers and sharecroppers for the rich and dominant landlords. The issues of minimum wages, the occupancy rights of the sharecroppers, and access to public amenities were mainly involved in these incidents. Since such atrocities are not committed on non-Harijans, there is an element of *Harijanness* in the atrocities committed on the Harijans by the caste Hindus. At times the issues of dignity and honour prominently figure in dehumanising the 'untouchables'.

In July 1978, in Maharashtra, riots began due to the renaming of the Marathwada University as Dr. Babasaheb Ambedkar University. The conflict crystallised between the Dalit and the non-Dalit student activists. The movement against the Dalits provoked violence, including the killing of people, molestation and rape of Harijan women, burning of Harijan houses and huts, pillaging their bastis, eviction from their houses and villages, killing of their cattle, denying them drinking water and refusing them work. The upper caste dominants were indignant that how the Marathwada University could be renamed after a Harijan leader. They thought it against their dignity and a step towards lowering their position in the region.

A few cases of Dalits reported above indicate that it was a very different situation two decades ago. Today, Dalits and other groups react quite vehemently on crime against their womenfolk and marginalised groups and families. The glaring example of murder of four members of a Dalit family in Kherlangi village of Bhandara district in Maharashtra by upper castes was committed on 29 September 2006 to carve out forcibly and illegally a passage through the field of a Dalit family. Though the head of the family Bhaiyyalal Bhotmarge escaped the carnage on the fateful day, his wife, daughter and two sons were killed in cold blood. The mother and daughter were stripped and raped for over an hour before being hacked to death as reported in the *Hindustan Times* of 9 November 2006. Bhaiyyalall alleges that the heinous crime was committed by the upper caste Sarpanch and deputy Sarpanch of the village. Since the matter was not seriously taken up by the police, the media (both visual and press) took it up along with several NGOs and Women's organisations. Violent protest brought the government to terms. Chief Minister and Home Minister had to visit the village. Employment and other allurements were turned down by Bhayyalal as he insisted on death penalty for the murderers. The case has been handed over to the CBI for investigation. In the violent protest one person was killed and several injured, including some police personnel. The government had to impose curfew as the Dalits and the *maratas* (a upper caste) came face-to-face to settle scores in the streets of Solapur and some other towns. Such incidences of atrocities on Dalits are being reacted strongly all over the country. The question of *izzat* (honour and dignity) has became a prime concern of Dalit and the institutions/agencies associated with their welfare and progress.

Incidents of atrocities due to land disputes, payment of wages at lower rates, indebtedness, forced labour and denial of access to public places have become a routine matter. In 1977, there were 8,905 cases of atrocities on the SCs, and more than 50 per cent of the cases were reported from Uttar Pradesh.

Awareness about Protection of Civil Rights Act, 1955; SC/ST (Prevention of Atrocities) Act, 1989; and constitutional provisions and safeguards has increased manifold among the SCs and STs. Compared to 2004, in 2005 crime against SCs and STs declined by 2.4 per cent. The states such as Madhya Pradesh (7.3%), Rajasthan (6.2%), and Andhra Pradesh (3.9%) have high incidences of crime compared to the national average of 2.4 per cent. Uttar Pradesh has accounted for about 50 per cent of the total murder cases (323 out of 669).

Today, the SCs are far more advanced than what they were at the time of independence. There is a paradigm shift in their status both in theory and practice. The category known as 'untouchable' was transformed into 'Harijan' by Gandhi. The 'Harijan' of Gandhi was named as the 'Scheduled Caste' in the Constitution of India. The SC is being referred as *Dalit* by the new generation of leadership. Each of these nomenclatures connote a particular status of the 'untouchables' from 'exterior castes' to "children of God" and to 'legal equality' and to assertion of right to equality. In reality, the SCs are there in services, professions and politics, and react quite strongly to injustices done to them.

Conclusion

The SCs have made tangible several efforts to come out of the clutches of the dominant sections of the caste Hindu society. These include sanskritisation, conversion to Buddhism, migration, education, urban employment, etc. Recently, the educated SCs have also shown militancy against their oppressors. The Dalit Literature Movement in Maharashtra has created consciousness among the SCs about their rightful place in Indian society. Dalit writers have written articles on the pitiable condition of the Dalits. Dalit magazines and periodicals have been launched. Seminars and symposia have been organised to propagate Dalit literature. However, the SCs have yet to go a long way to achieve equality with the upper and middle castes. These efforts are more in the nature of a quest for equality rather than actual realisation of equality with the caste Hindus.

Exercises

1. What are the main problems of the Scheduled Castes of India?
2. Discuss the main constitutional provisions made available to the Scheduled Castes.
3. Highlight the contributions of Mahatma Gandhi and Ambedkar to the upliftment of Harijans in India.
4. Bring out the patterns of social mobility among the Scheduled Castes, particularly since independence.
5. Explain the following:
   (i) Pollution-purity
   (ii) Untouchability
   (iii) Atrocities on Harijans

Select References

Ambedkar, B.R., *The Untouchables: Who were they and why they became untouchables?* New Delhi: Amrit Book Co., 1948.

Beteille, Andre, *Caste: Old and New*, Bombay: Asia Publishing House, 1969.

Chitnis, Suma, "Education for equality: Case of scheduled castes", in *Economic and Political Weekly*, Vol. VII, Nos. 31-33, 1972.

Desai, I.P., *Untouchability in Rural Gujarat*, Bombay: Popular Prakashan, 1976.

Ghurye, G.S., *The Scheduled Tribes*, Bombay: Popular Prakashan, 1963.

Issacs, R., *India's Ex-Untouchables*, Bombay: Asia Publishing House, 1965.

Mahar, J. Michael (ed.), *The Untouchables in Contemporary India*, Tuscon: The University of Arizona Press, 1969.

Mukherjee, Ramkrishna, "Realities of Agrarian Relations in India", *Economic and. Political Weekly*, Vol. XVI, No. 4, 1981.

Reports of the Commissioner for Scheduled Castes and Scheduled Tribes, Government of India Publication.

Sachchidananda, *Harijan Elite*, Faridabad, 1977.

Sharma, K.L., "Caste and Class: Factors affecting social mobility among the Scheduled Castes", *The Journal of Sociological Studies*, Vol. 2, January 1983.

10 The Scheduled Tribes

Tribes of India are varied in terms of their socio-economic and political development. Some of them have changed through Hinduisation, and some through conversion to Christianity or other routes. Some tribal people are in the transitional phase, while others are adhering to their old lifestyles. This shows an uneven process of change and development among the tribal people in India. Only a small number of tribal people have been benefited by the policies and programmes meant for their development. According to the 1991 census, the tribal population was 6.78 crore, that is, about 8.08 per cent of the total population of India. Madhya Pradesh, Orissa and Bihar have highest ST population in descending order, respectively. Gujarat and Rajasthan have over 3 million each. Maharashtra has nearly 8 per cent, followed by Assam, West Bengal, and Andhra Pradesh. Lakshadweep islands, Nagaland, Arunachal Pradesh, and Dadra and Nagar Haveli have a little less than 100 per cent tribal population. Uttar Pradesh, Jammu and Kashmir, Punjab, Haryana and Himachal Pradesh have a negligible number of tribal people. According to 1981 census, the percentage of the Scheduled Tribe (ST) population was 7.7 per cent. Madhya Pradesh, Orissa, Gujarat, Rajasthan, Maharashtra and Bihar have the ST population ranging from 22.97 per cent (in Madhya Pradesh) to 8.31 per cent (in Bihar). In the smaller states like Mizoram, Arunachal Pradesh, Nagaland and Meghalaya more than 80 per cent of their population is tribal. According to 1991 census,

STs are 8.08 per cent and as per the 2001 census this increase is just by 0.1 per cent as it is 8.2 per cent.

Noted anthropologist L.P. Vidyarthi (1974) classifies the tribal people into four regions: (1) Himalayan, (2) middle India, (3) western India, and (4) southern India. The tribes, numbering about 450, belong to various racial, linguistic, economic, social and religious categories. There are differences between these tribes because they are at different levels of development and participation in national life. However, in general, the tribals are economically, educationally and politically backward, compared to the non-tribal people. Despite the tribals' proximity to caste groups tribes have their distinct identities. According to the 2001 census, the Scheduled Tribes form 8.20 per cent of the total population, whereas they were 8.08 per cent as per the 1991 census. There are very small tribes as well as very large ones. Variations are also quite prominent among tribes in regard to their economic pursuits. There are nomadic tribes as well as the settled tribes engaged in agriculture and other occupations like the caste Hindus.

Towards a Definition of Tribes

G.S. Ghurye, in his book *The Scheduled Tribes* (1963), writes: "The Scheduled Tribes are neither called the 'Aborigines', nor the 'Adivasis', nor are they treated as a category by themselves. By and large, they are treated together with the Scheduled Castes and further envisaged as one group of the Backward Classes." This is the quintessence of the constitutional provision about the STs. Obviously, Ghurye would like the tribes of India not to be treated as distinct social and cultural entities. However, to club them with the Scheduled Castes (SCs) or other backward classes (OBCs) or to change them would mean that they become part of the wider Hindu or Indian society, and this would do a lot of harm as this precludes their point of view or their need for assimilation.

The Constitution of India, under Article 342, states that the President of India may "by public notification specify the tribes or tribal communities or parts of or groups within tribes or tribal communities which shall for the purposes of this Constitution be deemed to be Scheduled Tribes". The tribes of India, prior to independence, were considered animistic by the census authorities. Distinction was made between those who were Hinduised and those who followed their own religion. However, some scholars have opined that no sharp line of demarcation can be drawn between Hinduism and Animism. There is no uniform pattern of religion among the tribal people of India. The word 'Animism' was wrongly given a communal connotation while distinguishing it from Hinduism. One view is that Hinduism itself is an amalgam of the pre-Aryan beliefs and the religion of the RgVeda.

Variations among the tribes can be seen in terms of the areas they live in, such as the Aravali hills, the Vindhyas, the Satpuras, the Mahadev hills, the Chhotanagpur plateau and several other areas. Numerically, the most preponderant tribes are: Gond, Santhal, Bhil, Oraon, Kond, Munda, Bhuiya, Ho, Savara, Kol, Korku, Maler, Baiga and Meena. Some of these tribal people share Hinduism along with Hindus, and speak the languages spoken by them. They are not exclusive groups in spatial terms. Some scholars consider the tribals as autochthons, the earliest and the aboriginal inhabitants of the country, who were pushed to forests and hills by the invaders. Whatever may be the fact regarding tribal exclusivity, it is accepted that the tribes such as Baiga, Bhil, Gond, Kol, Korku, Meena, Santhal, Bhumia, Binjhwar, Mahato, Korwa, Maria, Kamar, Bharia and Maler have not only adopted Hindu pantheon and rituals, but have also taken up various versions of Hindi, Marathi, Bengali and other languages. Some of these tribes do not accept meals from lower and 'untouchable' Hindu castes.

Thus, a large number of tribes have a Hinduised section, which is evidence of their contact with the Hindus, at least in regard to religion, language and occupation. These Hinduised tribal people look upon themselves as Hindus. V. Elwin (1943) is of the view that with the exception of the North-East, all the aboriginal tribes should be classed as Hindus by religion, but be separated in terms of race. Several ethnographers have distinguished tribes from castes in terms of physical traits. These include Sir Herbert Risley, G.S.

Ghurye, J.H. Hutton and B.S. Guha. Ghurye is, however, of the view that the proper description of tribal people must refer to their place in or near Hindu society and not to their supposed autochthonism. Some are properly integrated into the Hindu society; some are loosely integrated; while some tribes are living isolated in hills and forests. Ghurye prefers to call the Scheduled Tribes as 'Backward Hindus'. Those who refer to a 'tribe-caste continuum' hold the view that a sharp line between tribes and castes cannot be drawn. To call a group a tribe is, therefore, only a legal status granted under the law.

Problems of the Tribal People

The tribes were alienated from their own lands. The landlords and moneylenders of the plains gradually replaced the tribal landowners. There were a number of movements against the British Raj and the Hindu moneylenders and landlords. The tribes were given protection in view of such an oppressive situation. Ghurye lists a number of socio-cultural and economic problems of the tribes of India in view of their distinctions. Some tribes represent aristocracy, landlords and noblemen; others consist of the Hinduised sections of tribesmen; and thirdly, there are tribes and some sections from amongst them who are still largely isolated from the non-tribal population.

Ghurye mentions three ways for solution for the problems of the tribal people: (1) no change and revivalism, (2) isolationism and preservation, and (3) assimilation. No change and revivalism has been supported by Elwin, whereas isolationism has been advocated by Hutton. The famous anthropologist S.C. Roy (1970) was an assimilationist. However, today, a paradoxical situation exists. Protective discrimination isolates the tribal people from the non-tribesmen, but in course of time this very policy would bring the tribals at par with the non-tribals. The dominant thinking today is in favour of assimilation of the tribal people into the national mainstream without any disruption. It is not easy to have both dissolution and assimilation at the same time.

Since tribal people are at different social, political, economic and ecological levels, their problems also differ in degree from each other. These differences can be seen in terms of hill tribes and plainsmen; between those who are engaged in forest-based economic pursuits and the ones who are employed as settled agriculturists; or between those who are Hinduised or converted to Christianity; and those who are adhering to an unadulterated tribal way of life. Despite these distinctions, some common problems of the tribal people are: (1) poverty and exploitation, (2) economic and technological backwardness, (3) socio-cultural handicaps, and (4) problems of their assimilation with the non-tribal population.

S.C. Dube's five-fold classification of the Indian tribes provides a clear picture of the problem of tribes in India. Dube (1982) mentions: (1) aboriginals living in seclusion; (2) tribal groups having an association with the neighbouring non-tribal society and also maintaining their distinctiveness; (3) tribals living in villages along with caste groups, sects and religious groups and maintaining their identity; (4) tribals who have been degraded to the status of untouchables; and (5) tribals who enjoy high social, economic and political status. Such a classification is based on the nature of cultural contacts of tribals with non-tribals. The U.N. Dhebar Commission recommended that an area be declared 'tribal' where more than 50 per cent of the people were tribals. Economic criteria have also been suggested, such as dependence upon forests for food, primitive agriculture, agriculture and forests both as sources of livelihood, and modern occupations, particularly employment in industries. Thus, no uniform solutions of the tribal people can be provided as they do not share common existential conditions and cultural ethos.

The tribal people had a strong sense of community life before the British rulers and Hindu zamindars and moneylenders intruded into their lives. Exchange of goods and transactions at weekly markets and fairs was the basic mode of economic relations. However, the British took over the forests on which they depended for their livelihood. The moneylenders brought them under their control by extending loans at exhorbitant interest rates and then by mortgaging their lands, alienating them from land they cultivated. Indebtedness led to exploitation and pauperisation of the tribal people. Hinduisation has also contributed to indebtedness and exploitation, as the tribals adopted Hindu ways of life and rituals which forced them to spend as the Hindus did. Tribals occupied a very low rank in Hindu society after they copied Hinduism.

At some places, the tribals have been made to serve as bonded labourers. The Doms and Koltas in Uttar Pradesh serve the upper caste families even today. In Rajasthan, the *Sagri* system, in Andhra the *Vetti* system, in Orissa the *Gothi* system, in Karnataka the *Jetha* system and in Chhattisgarh (earlier part of Madhya Pradesh) the *Naukrinama* system are the examples of the bondedness of the tribals. They have borrowed money from the moneylenders, but have not been able to pay back and are therefore bound to work till they return the loan. A situation of emancipation does not arise as the tribal is not able to repay the loan completely and quickly.

K.S. Singh (1992) points out that agrarian issues are basic to tribal development in India. The tribal agrarian problem cannot be treated in isolation. Tribal people have to be treated along with other weaker sections of Indian society. Keeping the situation of Jharkhand (earlier part of Bihar) in view, Singh observes that the concept of aliens (*dikku*) is crucial to the understanding of an agrarian situation where non-tribals outnumber tribals. The class of moneylenders has arisen due to several factors, including the agrarian legislation. Alienation of land has resulted from tribal backwardness and indebtedness. Integrated Tribal Development Blocks (ITDBs) have not produced the desired results in the tribal areas. Famine and drought have become a recurrent feature. The tribal sub-plan has been introduced to combat problems of famine, drought, illiteracy, indebtedness, exploitation, etc., by taking up special schemes for the development of tribal areas.

A study of the impact of the decentralisation of Minor Forest Produce (MFP) trade on the tribals of Jharkhand shows that the dominant causality is economic rather than political and ideological. The study refers to the control of forest produce like bamboo, Kendu leaves, Mahua, Kusum, Karanj and Sal seeds by the government of Jharkhand. The MFP contributes about 35 per cent of the state's revenue from forests. The takeover has adversely affected the institution of *hat* (weekly market), where the tribals carried out economic transactions, and also performed several social and cultural activities. Forests provided a collective life to the tribals, and this was being denied to them as a result of the MFP trade takeover. The tribals have been agitated over this step taken by the government of Jharkhand.

Per capita landholding has decreased among the tribals due to three reasons: (1) alienation of land due to indebtedness and socio-economic backwardness; (2) increase in tribal population; and (3) takeover of tribal lands by the government for establishing industries. Land was alienated much before legislations were passed by the state governments. Today, even after passing such legislations, the tribal elite are alienating the tribals from their lands. The tribals have been displaced in parts of Jharkhand, Orissa and some other states by the taking over of their lands for establishing industries. However, the tribals have not been provided with alternative avenues of employment. The compensation paid to them for their land was quickly spent by them without making any investment in productive and remunerative enterprises.

Some tribals even today are engaged in *jhum* (shifting) cultivation, which is not only uneconomical but also causes deforestation and soil erosion. Since the tribals have no alternative source of livelihood, they continue to use shifting cultivation and cutting of forests for their livelihood. In protest against the government's policy of MFP takeover in Jharkhand, the tribals cut forests on a large scale in the Singhbhum and other districts. Forest cooperatives can do a lot to ameliorate the pitiable plight of the tribals, but unfortunately the benefits from these societies have reached largely to the well off sections of the Bhils, Meenas, Oraons, etc.

However, significant achievements have been made by the SCs and STs in the field of literacy. In 1991 of the total population of the SCs and STs 52.2 per cent were literate, of which 64.1 per cent were males and 39.3 per cent females. As per the Census of

2001, the literacy increased to 64.8 per cent, of which 75.3 per cent were males and 53.1 per cent females.

The dilemma for the tribal people in India is the choice between isolation and contact. Isolation keeps the tribals away from forces of change and development and contact with the wider society creates problems of adjustment, cultural shock and disintegration of tribal social organisation and community living. The intrusion of outsiders into tribal life, for example, has adversely affected the institution of weekly market, dormitory and reciprocal relationships. The institutions of untouchability, pollution-purity and high and low status have also made inroads into tribal life. The tribals have become to a large extent a 'caste' or 'pseudo-caste' by this process of cultural contact. Ignorance, illiteracy, superstition and poverty are the major problems of the tribal people in the Indian sub-continent.

Tribal Social Movements

Social movements among tribes aim at collective action to alter, reconstitute, reinterpret, restore and protect social structure, with a view to improve social, cultural, economic and political conditions of the tribal people. Hinduism, Christianity, British rule, modern education and post-independence legislations have generated a high level of consciousness among the tribals, which has in turn encouraged several movements. Some movements have asserted their tribal identity and political solidarity. Ecological-cultural isolation, economic backwardness and a feeling of frustration have been responsible for these movements. However, those tribals who are either too isolated or too integrated with Hindu society are not involved in these socio-cultural movements. The Unnati Samaj, an organisation established in 1912 for socio-cultural reforms, and the Adivasi Mahasabha established in 1938, aimed at revivalism in the Jharkhand region of Bihar. The Jharkhand movement in 1950 was, however, started to fight land alienation and exploitation and for political solidarity among the tribes of Bihar and the adjoining states of West Bengal, Orissa and Madhya Pradesh. This movement ultimately culminated into a demand for the formation of a separate state for the adivasis of these four states.

Tribal movements encompass a very wide arena. The unique geopolitical situation and historical background need to be taken into consideration while analysing movements in the North-East, including Manipur, Nagaland and Mizoram. Movements in these areas generally refer to cultural and political revivalism. Political autonomy, control over the forests, socio-religious, cultural and linguistic considerations have been the key factors in other tribal movements. For example, in case of the Jharkhand movement in Bihar, West Bengal, Orissa and Madhya Pradesh the main points were related to historicity, ideology, structure, leadership and sub-regional identity. Based on these considerations, Jharkhand was formed as a new state out of Bihar. Along with Jharkhand, Uttranchal was carved out from Uttar Pradesh and Chhatisgarh was created from Madhya Pradesh. Socio-cultural movements have given primacy to status elevation through sanskritisation. The various modes of status elevation for tribes include emphasis on a specific script, language, religion and ethnic identity.

A given region may have a particular type of movement because of its specific geographical and political situation in the wider context. S.M. Dubey (1982) provides a classification of tribal movements in North-East India: (1) religious and social reform movements; (2) state formation movements; (3) insurgent movements; and (4) culturological movements. An all-India tribal movement has not emerged because of the diversity and unevenness among the tribes of India. K.S. Singh (1982) has given detailed accounts of 36 tribal movements in India, of which 14 were in the North-East region alone. Singh classifies the various movements into: (1) movements for political autonomy; (2) agrarian and forest based movements; (3) sanskritisation process; and (4) cultural movements.

The questions which still remain inadequately answered are: (1) Why have the tribals been pressing for cultural revivalism, autonomy and restoration of aboriginality? (2) Why have some tribes been making efforts for cultural, ethnic and linguistic revivalism? (3) Why have some others been raising their voice for the formation of a separate state and for a greater share in educational institutions, jobs and other opportunities? Exploitation of the adivasis by outsiders, non-adivasis and dominant elements from among the tribals is a stark fact of life.

Integration of the Tribals with the Non-Tribals

In their own interest the British pursued a policy of isolation of the tribals from the mainstream. The British retained under their control the tribal chiefs with curtailed powers. Today, integration of the tribals with the non-tribals is the cornerstone of the policy of the Government of India. The constitutional provisions are as follows: (1) Article 46: "The state shall promote with special care the educational and economic interests of the weaker sections of the people, and in particular, of the Scheduled Castes and Scheduled Tribes, and shall protect them from social injustice and all forms of exploitation." (2) Article 244: "Empowers the President to declare any areas, where there is a substantial population of tribal people as Scheduled Area under the 5th Schedule or in Assam as a tribal area under the 6th Schedule." (3) Article 275: "There shall be paid out of the Consolidated Fund of India as grants-in-aid of the revenues of a state such capital and recurring sums as may be necessary to enable that state to meet the costs of such schemes of development as may be undertaken by the state with the approval of the Government of India for the purpose of promoting the welfare of the Scheduled Tribes in that state or raising the level of administration of the Scheduled Areas therein to that of the administration of the rest of that state."

The Governors of states have been given powers to reserve seats in educational institutions and jobs in government departments and public sector undertakings. A sum of Rs. 19.83 crores was spent in the First Five-Year Plan for the welfare of the Scheduled Tribes. This was raised to Rs. 43 crores and Rs. 60.43 crores in the second and the third plans, respectively. This was a really meagre allocation for the welfare of the tribal people. The Fifth Five-Year Plan made a separate sub-plan for the tribals to promote integrated tribal development. ITDBs have been entrusted the responsibility of tribal welfare in Rajasthan, Bihar (Jharkhand), Madhya Pradesh (Chhatisgarh) and other states. These provisions have certainly created social and political consciousness among the tribals and have also improved social and economic positions of some sections of the tribal population.

The tribals have largely come under the impact of the dominant cultural stream of India. New divisions have been created among the tribals due to cultural change in their ranks. Tana Bhagats in Jharkhand are the Hinduised tribals, whereas there are others who claim to remain custodians of their aboriginality. The latter have made efforts to rectify the distortions of their culture by launching restoration movements. The Bhils in Rajasthan are divided into Bhagats and non-Bhagats. The Bhagats are further divided into the Kabirpanthis and the Shambu Dal. The non-Bhagats strive to maintain their traditional way of life. The Bhagats have adopted a Brahmanical way of life, including vegetarianism and teetotalism. The Bhagats consider themselves superior to the non-Bhagats and the Kabirpanthis consider themselves superior to the Shambu Dal. The notions of untouchability, pollution-purity and the rules of marriage such as caste endogamy, clan exogamy, hypergamy, etc., have been adopted by the Bhagats. The tribals, who have converted to Christianity, are generally ahead of the non-converts in regard to education, white-collar employment and economic status.

Thus, stratification in tribal society in India has its roots in British policy, unevenness due to the impact of economic development, and varied cultural contact with wider society. In fact, there are levels of integration as there are layers of tribals in India. Industrialisation in the tribal areas of Jharkhand, West Bengal, Orissa and Chhatisgarh has apparently reduced the gap between the tribals and the non-tribals, but it has also created new problems. The tribals, who have been uprooted from their lands, have not been absorbed in the new system. Hence, they are facing a new form of pauperisation without a traditional support base. The Narmada Sarovar Project has displaced a large number of villagers. Such a displacement has been caused in other parts of India as well by establishment of industries and construction of dams, etc.

Conclusion

Tribes in India are not a monolithic people. They have differences in terms of their historical background, socio-economic and cultural problems and level of advancement. Some tribes live in forests and on hill tops, whereas others live in the plains. Some are settled agriculturists whereas others depend upon forest produce. Some have been in close contact with wider society and have adopted the lifestyles of Hindus, Christians and other communities. As a result of these variations, tribes are not found at the same level of socio-political awakening and economic standing. However, in general, all tribes are a weaker section of the society (with the exception of their power elite and economic dominants).

The Constitution of India declares Scheduled Tribes as a weaker section of society. Several provisions have been made for their overall upliftment. Efforts have been made to bring about socio-economic change to make them a part of the mainstream by putting checks on land alienation, exploitation, indebtedness, and by ensuring their increased participation in the socio-economic and political life of India. A tribal sub-plan was introduced in the Fifth Five-Year Plan with a view to develop tribal areas and to bring them at par with non-tribal areas.

Tribals themselves have started a number of social movements to bring about socio-cultural, economic and political change. Tribal identity has been asserted for revival of tribal cultures, scripts and languages. Demands for control on forests and forest produce, for the formation of states for tribal people, and for the exclusion of non-tribals from tribal areas are some of the issues taken up by leaders of various tribal movements. These movements have certainly resulted in an increased cultural and political consciousness among the tribes in various parts of India. However, to make these movements more effective, it is necessary to reduce intra-tribal economic distinctions. The constitutional provisions have not been equally shared. Distributive justice has not been the end result of these provisions and other efforts.

Exercises

1. Define Scheduled Tribes. How are they different from Scheduled Castes and Other Backward Classes?
2. Give a brief account of the tribal map of India.
3. What constitutional provisions have been made for the Scheduled Tribes? Are they adequate enough for their upliftment?
4. Explain the term 'conversion'. What do you understand by conversion of tribal people to Christianity and Hinduism?
5. What are the main problems of the tribes of India?
6. Explain the possible solutions to the problems of tribal people.
7. Discuss intra-tribal stratification. What are its reasons?
8. In what way are agrarian issues basic to tribal development in India?
9. Explain the following:
   (i) Cultural revivalism
   (ii) Land alienation
   (iii) Tribal elite
   (iv) Bhagat movement
   (v) Jharkhand movement
10. What are the main features of tribal social movements in India?
11. In what way have tribals come closer to non-tribals in contemporary India?

Select References

Dube, S.C., "Inaugural Address", in K.S. Singh (ed.) op. cit., 1972.

—, *Tradition and Development*, Delhi: Vikas Publishing House, 1990.

Dubey, S.M., "Inter-Ethnic Alliance, Tribal Movements and Interpretation in North-East India", in K.S. Singh (ed.), *Tribal Movements*, Vol. I, New Delhi: Manohar, 1982.

Fuchs, Stephen, *At the Bottom of Indian Society*, Delhi: Munshiram Manoharlal Publishers, 1981.

Furer-Haimendorf, Christoph Von, *Tribes of India*, Delhi: Oxford University Press, 1982.

Ghurye, G.S., *The Scheduled Tribes* (3rd edn.), Bombay: Popular Prakashan, 1963.

Government of India, "Statewise Information on SCs and STs", Ministry of Education, New Delhi, 1985.

Roy, S.C., *The Mundas and their Country* (reprint), Bombay: Asia Publishing House, 1970.

Singh, K.S. (ed.), *Tribal Situation in India*, Simla: Indian Institute of Advanced Study, 1972, See also, K.S. Singh (ed.), *Tribal Movements in India*, Vols. I and II, New Delhi: Manohar Publications, 1982.

Singh, Parmanand, *Equality, Reservation and Discrimination in India*, New Delhi: Deep and Deep Publications, 1982.

Verrier, Elwin, *The Aboriginals*, London: Oxford University Press, 1943.

—, *Tribal World of Verrier Elvwin*, Oxford University Press, 1964.

Vidyarthi, L.P., "Tribal Ethnography in India", in *A Survey of Research in Sociology and Social Anthropology*, Vol. III, Bombay: Popular Prakashan, 1974.

Vyas, N.N. and Mann, R.S., *Indian Tribes in Transition*, Jaipur: Rawat Publications, 1980.

11 Other Backward Classes

The Scheduled Castes (SCs), the Scheduled Tribes (STs) and the Other Backward Classes (OBCs) together are considered backward and form more than two-third of the total population of India. The OBCs are entitled to special provisions in education and employment. Unlike the SCs and the STs, they are not given the privilege of political representation through reserved constituencies. How do we define the category 'backward classes'? Castes and occupations are two structural criteria which we may use to define the term 'backward classes'.

In terms of caste, rank and occupation, the backward classes were higher than the SCs in the caste hierarchy. In terms of caste hierarchy, the backward classes would have intermediate agricultural and functionary (clean) castes.

Andre Beteille (1965) considers peasant castes as the core of the backward classes. The backward classes have certainly been far behind the upper castes in education, professions and government jobs. They are also at a lower rung in the caste hierarchy. One view is that those who belonged to the Shudra *varna* could be considered as the backward classes. Ritually also, the backward classes have been considered inferior to the 'twice-born' castes. The name 'backward classes' implies that there are also 'forward classes', and this is why in Bihar people are identified as 'backward' and 'forward'. The 'forwards' look down upon the 'backwards'. The Backward Classes Movement in Bihar gained currency in the late

1970s, particularly in 1977 when the Janata Party formed government at the Centre and in various states. Karpoori Thakur, who belonged to a backward caste, was Bihar's chief minister in 1977.

Caste and agriculture are closely related in India. The higher castes have traditionally large landholdings. The lower castes work as landless agricultural labourers. The intermediate castes are the principal agricultural castes in terms of actual cultivation. The OBCs are highly differentiated in terms of caste and economic status. The well-off OBCs are known as 'upper backward', and the poor ones are named as 'lower/most backward'. Thus, the OBCs are not homogeneous in terms of both caste and agricultural pursuits. However, the situation has changed considerably since independence in regard to both the criteria, namely, caste and occupation. Caste-based distinctions do not have a place in the Constitution of India. Segregation based on caste is an offence. Land reforms have given an opportunity to the backward classes to make a claim of ownership of the land which they cultivated as tenants. Adult franchise has generated consciousness for political mobilisation and participation. The fact, however, is that the backward classes are still culturally, socially and economically backward, and therefore, they have started movements for their upliftment and for a greater share in education, employment and decision-making.

Defining the Backward Classes

The term 'backward classes' has been used for the weaker sections of society, particularly the SCs, the STs and the OBCs. The term has also been used to designate any other backward classes. In the beginning, after India's independence, the term 'backward classes' had a less fixed and definite reference. It has had a variety of referents. Earlier, the term 'depressed classes' was used for the 'untouchables' and other backward groups. It is certainly a fact that the backward classes are above the ex-untouchable groups and below the twice-born castes. They need special protection and help for their economic and social upliftment. We find references to this term in 1917-18, but it was more specifically used in 1930-31. In 1937, the State of Travancore used the term 'backward communities' to include all educationally and economically backward communities. But, in the Madras Presidency, the term 'backward classes' was used to refer to the strata above the untouchables. In 1934, the Madras Provincial Backward Classes League was founded. The 'backward classes' in Madras Presidency included more than a hundred communities, and comprised of 50 per cent of the total population. Thus, the term 'backward classes' had no uniform meaning at the national level. There was no all-India organisation of the backward classes.

In 1948, it was visualised that a Backward Classes Commission be appointed to go through the whole of the country to find out which castes of Hindus, Muslims, etc., were really backward according to certain standards – educational, social, economic, etc. The Commission was supposed to find out the difficulties under which they worked and to make recommendations as to the steps that should be taken by the Union or any state to remove such difficulties and improve their condition. The Commission was actually appointed in 1953.

The University Education Commission (1948-49) also recommended reservation of a certain proportion of seats for students belonging to the backward communities. In 1947, the Bihar government made provisions for other backward classes in post-matriculation studies. In 1951, the Government of Bihar announced a list of backward classes. The list contained the names of various castes, which constituted 60 per cent of the state's population. In 1948, the Government of Uttar Pradesh gave educational concessions to other backward classes. A list of 56 castes was prepared, which covered 65 per cent of the population. Thus, even before the implementation of the Constitution, the notion of backward classes existed referring to the groups between the top and the bottom strata of society based on their economic and educational backwardness.

Several backward classes' organisations emerged in late 1940s. The Bihar State Backward Classes Federation was founded in 1947. In 1954, there were 88 organisations working for the backward classes in 15 states. Seventy-four of these were named after specific castes and fourteen functioned, in general, on a regional or local basis. The All India Backward Classes Federation was formed in 1950. A national federation was also formed. Lists of backward classes were prepared by the state governments. The list in Karnataka included Muslims, Christians, Jains and several groups other than Brahmanas. However, the lists in Tamil Nadu and Maharashtra did not include the higher non-Brahmana castes.

Backwardness is considered as an attribute of a group and not of an individual. Membership of these backward classes is determined by birth like all other caste groups. In common parlance, backward classes may include some individuals who are educationally and economically well off. Since some castes have been designated as 'backward' by the government, they are entitled to get certain benefits and facilities. The backward classes are, thus, a large and complex constellation of groups and individuals.

Since we are here concerned with the backward classes who are, in effect, intermediate castes in between the SCs and the upper castes, we do not refer to the term 'backward classes' in a broad sense. The backward classes are backward because they have been lagging behind in education, government services, professions, business, etc. However, in the recent years, they have advanced in economic and political fields. Generally, the OBCs are small landowners depending mainly on agriculture for their livelihood. Numerically, they are preponderant, but they are not a monolithic group – socially, culturally and economically. According to the Mandal Commission, the OBCs constitute nearly 52 per cent of India's population. The Mandal Commission was formed in 1978 by the Janata Party government under the chairmanship of B.P. Mandal.

The Constitution of India mentions the backward classes as being "socially and educationally backward classes of citizens". Article 340 authorises the President of India to appoint a

Commission to investigate and report on the conditions of the backward classes in different parts of the country. The state governments also, under Articles 15(4) and 161, can appoint commissions to look into the social and educational problems of different backward castes, and can also make reservations in educational institutions and government services based on the findings of such commissions. The criteria of backwardness differ from state to state as no all-India index of backwardness exists.

The Kaka Kalelkar Commission

A Backward Classes Commission was appointed by the President of India on 29 January 1953 with Kaka Kalelkar as its chairman. The Commission was directed to determine the criteria to be adopted in considering whether any section of people should be treated as socially and educationally backward. It was also to prepare a list of such classes. The Commission was also directed to investigate the conditions of all such socially and educationally backward classes and the difficulties which they encountered in carrying out their work. It was asked to make recommendations on the following matters: (1) as to the steps that should be taken by the Union or any state to remove such difficulties or to improve their conditions; and (2) as to the grants that should be made available.

The Commission took two years to complete its work, and prepared a list of 2,399 castes and communities and suggested several measures for their social and economic development. About 70 per cent of India's population was considered backward. The following criteria were suggested for determining backwardness:

1. Low social position in the caste hierarchy,
2. Lack of educational progress,
3. Inadequate representation in government service, and
4. Inadequate representation in the fields of trade, commerce and industry.

Caste was taken as the key factor in making a list of backward classes. The Commission thought that the problems of a caste-ridden society could be minimised by promotion of the socially and educationally backward classes. Though the Commission did not have adequate data on castes, yet it proposed reservation of at least 25 per cent in Class I, 33.5 per cent in Class II, and 40 per cent in Class III and IV services for the castes listed as backward. It recommended 70 per cent reservation in the fields of medical, scientific and technical education. The Commission also recommended the formation of a separate ministry for the welfare of backward classes.

Thus, caste was used as the sole criterion and unit for determining backwardness and for the classification of backward classes. The position of a caste as higher and lower or superior and inferior was made as the basis. No attempt was made to know the 'backward individuals' of a caste group. A caste as a whole was considered backward. The Commission believed that real social equality could be achieved in India only by eliminating caste distinctions and social discrimination. The evils of the caste system could be attacked only by taking caste into account. However, the other view is that individual and family should have been treated as the basis of backwardness.

The Commission was aware of the fact that backwardness could be assessed by poverty, residence and occupation in addition to the criterion of caste. It was felt that those members of the backward classes, who had reached a certain level of economic and educational advancement, should be declassified. Individual and family would be the best units for judging backwardness because the criterion of caste was somewhat vague and was also against the principles of democracy as it further promoted caste and class distinctions.

The Government of India rejected the recommendation of the Commission that caste be the basis for identifying economic and educational backwardness. The Centre asked the state governments to conduct surveys to identify members of the backward classes, and then to extend them all reasonable facilities. In 1961, the Centre decided not to draw up any list of the OBCs. The states were advised to draw up their own lists using economic tests rather than going by caste. A number of states decided to use the criteria of occupation and income to classify backward groups.

Criteria of Backwardness in States

Only eight states accepted the policy of reservation in the services by 1985. Since the Centre did not come to a conclusion regarding uniform criteria for determining backwardness, the states were left free to evolve their own criteria and lists of backward groups. Sometimes, local, social and political conditions influenced drawing up of the lists of backward classes in different states. Some politically influential groups made efforts to remain classified as backward classes to retain the facilities and concessions extended to them. Even, the economically better off and socially upward mobile groups had a vested interest in continuing to be classified as backward. Several caste groups have demanded from time to time their inclusion in the category of backward classes. The Lingayats and Vokkaligas in Karnataka, the Ezhavas and Nayars in Kerala, the Reddis and Kammas in Andhra, Nadars and Vaniyars in Tamil Nadu, Kurmis, Ahirs and Koris in Uttar Pradesh and Bihar have always exerted pressure for their continued recognition as backward classes. The dominant castes are able to strike a political bargain with those in power for being classified as backward classes. A number of castes like the Jatavas of Agra, who found sanskritisation no longer attractive, decided to politicise themselves to extract greater dividends. After the implementation of the Mandal Commission, the Jats of Delhi and Rajasthan were included in the OBC category by their respective OBC commissions. The Jats were left out in the list of the OBCs prepared by the Mandal Commission.

In 1966, the Government of Andhra Pradesh decided to use 'family' for classifying backward groups instead of caste. However, this was dropped due to legal complications, and in 1970 a list of 92 communities was prepared. Twemty-five per cent of the government jobs are reserved for these castes and communities. The Government of Bihar introduced the policy of job reservation for 128 backward castes and communities in 1978. The decision was based mainly on the suggestions of the Kaka Kalelkar Commission and the Mungeri Lal Commission. The latter was constituted by the Government of Bihar. Ahirs, Kurmis and Koris formed about three-fifths of the total population of backward classes in Bihar. They were, in fact, not so backward and derived maximum benefit from the policy of job reservation. Violent protests were witnessed against this policy in Bihar. It was decided to fix an income ceiling of Rs. 12,000 per annum per family for qualifying as a beneficiary of the scheme. Today, 26 per cent of the jobs are reserved for backward classes in Bihar.

In 1900, the Karnataka government decided to adopt the criteria of income and occupation of a family for determining backwardness, irrespective of caste, religion or race. However, up to 1960, all the castes were treated as backward, except the Brahmanas. In 1972, the Government of Karnataka appointed a Backward Classes Commission with L.G. Havanur as its chairman. After conducting a massive survey, the Commission prepared a list of backward castes and communities. The Commission rejected the criteria of income and occupation as it benefited the Brahmanas, Lingayats and Vokkaligas most, to advance their interests at the cost of the really backward groups. The Commission prepared a list of the backward classes based on the criteria of caste and economic standing. A reservation of 32 per cent of the jobs was recommended for these classes. However, the government decided to include a few more castes in this category and also increased the quota of reservation from 32 to 40 per cent.

The Kerala government appointed a Backward Classes Commission, under the chairmanship of P.D. Nettur, which submitted its report in 1970. The Commission recommended the criteria of educational attainment, economic position, and appropriateness in the appointment to government service and social backwardness. It also made an effort to eliminate the already advantaged families, irrespective of their caste and religion. Despite legal and other difficulties, some success has been achieved in Kerala. Today, 25 per cent of the jobs are reserved for the backward classes in Kerala.

In Maharashtra, 14 per cent, and in Tamil Nadu, 50 per cent of jobs are reserved for the enlisted backward classes. The Uttar

Pradesh government has listed 58 communities and castes as backward and 15 per cent of the jobs are reserved for them. The State of Jammu & Kashmir has reserved 40 per cent of the jobs for the backward communities and castes.

Thus, the states which made reservations by 1985 for the backward classes were Andhra Pradesh, Bihar, Jammu & Kashmir, Karnataka, Kerala, Maharashtra, Tamil Nadu and Uttar Pradesh. Today, all the states have adopted reservation in jobs as per the direction of the Supreme Court of India based on the Mandal Commission. Reservation in jobs was accepted as the principle of compensatory discrimination to counter the inherited caste-based inequalities. However, this principle has been used by dominant political groups and parties to their advantage to considerable extent. Income and occupation, as criteria of determining backwardness, have been upheld, but could not be implemented. Caste continues to be the sole criterion for judging backwardness.

The Mandal Commission

The spirit behind the term 'backward classes' is that the middle strata of the people have suffered and remained ignored. The Janata Party, in its election manifesto in 1977, called for an end to caste inequalities. It promised a "policy of special treatment" in favour of the weaker sections of Indian society. The party promised to reserve between 25 and 33 per cent of all appointments to government services and educational opportunities for the backward classes. The Government of India, headed by the Janata Party, appointed a Backward Classes Commission under the chairmanship of B.P. Mandal, Member of Parliament, with a view to get definite recommendations by which it could implement its election promises. The following were the terms of reference of the Mandal Commission:

1. to determine the criteria for defining the socially and educationally backward classes;
2. to recommend steps to be taken for the advancement of the socially and educationally backward classes of citizens so identified;

3. to examine the desirability or otherwise of making provision for the reservation of appointments or posts in favour of such backward classes of citizens which are not adequately represented in the services of both the central and the state governments/union territory administrations; and
4. to present a report setting out the facts as found by them and making such recommendations as they think proper.

The Commission observed that backwardness was both social and educational. Caste was also a class of people. In case a caste as a whole is found socially and educationally backward, reservation for the entire caste can be allowed. The backward classes, including the non-Hindu castes and excluding the SCs and STs, constitute 52 per cent of India's population, according to the Mandal report. The Commission recommended a reservation of 27 per cent of jobs and educational facilities for this 52 per cent population. It may be stated here that no caste-based census has been conducted after 1931 census. Therefore, no definite data is available about the OBCs. Since the issue of 'reservation' in institutions of higher education has come up (in 2005-06), National Family Health Survey has calculated 32.4 per cent people as OBCs of the total population in 2002, and the NSS mentions approximately 41 per cent people as OBCs. Therefore, in the absence of scientific survey, no definite data are available.

The Commission suggested the following steps:

1. The reservation of 27 per cent jobs be made for those who do not qualify on the basis of merit.
2. The reservation of 27 per cent be made for promotions at all levels.
3 The reserved quota, if unfilled, should be carried forward for a period of three years and de-reserved thereafter.
4. Age relaxation for the backward classes should be the same as it is in the case of the SCs and the STs.
5. A roster system should be prepared for the backward classes on the pattern of the one done for the SCs and the STs.
6. The principle of reservation should be made applicable to all the public sector undertakings, banks, private undertakings

receiving grants from the central and state governments, universities and colleges.

7. The government should make the necessary legal provisions for implementing these recommendations.

The Commission recommended the implementation of an intensive and time-bound programme for adult education, particularly for the backward classes, and the setting up of residential schools for the backward class students. The principle of reservation of 27 per cent was suggested for seats in educational institutions as well as in jobs. Suggestions for the economic upliftment of the backward classes were also made by the Commission with a view to bring about structural changes in Indian society.

The Janata Dal, which was the major constituent of the National Front government at the centre, had promised to implement the recommendation of the Mandal Commission. As a reaction to this commitment of the government, there were large-scale protests in some of the states, particularly in Uttar Pradesh, in December 1989.

After the Janata Dal government announced its decision in August 1990 to reserve 27 per cent of jobs for the OBCs in the government departments and public sector undertakings, large-scale protests erupted throughout the country, particularly in northern and western India culminating into self-immolations, suicides and killings in police actions. One of the social consequences of this was further deepening of the caste divide in Indian society.

Backward Classes Movements

The upper castes dominated in the pre-independent Indian society. The backward classes aimed at capturing political power and socio-economic ascendence, particularly after independence. The backward caste leaders insisted upon caste as the basis of determination of backwardness. The important backward classes movements in the pre-independence India included: (1) Jotiba

Phule's movement in the Bombay Presidency (1870-1930), and (2) the anti-Brahmana Nadar movement in Madras.

Jotiba Phule founded the Satyashodhak Samaj in 1873. The leadership of the Samaj came from the backward classes, namely, the Malis, Telis, Kunbis and Satis. Phule himself was a Mali (gardener). Social service and spread of education among women and lower caste people were the main aims of his movement. Brahmanas opposed the movement as it challenged the Brahmanical supremacy. Phule aimed at the complete abolition of the caste system and socio-economic inequalities. He was against Sanskritic Hinduism. One view is that Phule focussed on cultural and ethnic factors alone ignoring the economic and political ones. It was in essence an anti-Brahmana movement. It was a sort of 'cultural revolution'.

The backward classes movement in South India was in fact an anti-Brahmana movement. E.V. Ramaswamy Naicker was leader of this movement. The 'Dravida Kazhagam' in Tamil means the "organisation of the Dravidians". The DMK was formed by C.N. Annadurai in 1949, and in 1970, M.G. Ramchandran founded the ADMK. These parties have taken an anti-Brahmana stance in politics. The SNDP movement in Kerala was more of a reformist movement, as it emphasised on the upliftment of the backward communities, particularly Ezhavas. Thus, the main goals of the backward classes' movements were either anti-Brahmanism or reformism or both.

Brahmanas have enjoyed not only their superiority over others, but they have also acquired greater power and privileges as a result of the spread of western education. They became, therefore, an object of envy for other castes, particularly for those at the middle rung of caste hierarchy. The Brahmanas were numerically a minority, and they were distrusted by the British because they spearheaded the national movement. On these two counts, the backward classes thought it necessary to weaken the social and political hegemony of the Brahmanas. The western-educated elite from amongst the backward castes took up the leadership of the anti-Brahmana movement. In fact, the backward classes movement expressed the ambitions and frustrations of the educated youth from the intermediate castes.

In the Madras Presidency, though the Brahmanas comprised about 3 per cent of the total population, 71 per cent of the total graduates between 1886 and 1910 were Brahmana. In 1921, the literacy rate among the Brahmanas in Madras State was 28 per cent as against 2 per cent for the Vellalas. In 1913, out of 478 Hindu government officials, 350 were Brahmanas. The Brahmanas were also ahead of other castes in the national movement. In 1918, in Mysore State, all castes except Brahmanas were bracketed as 'backward castes'. In 1925, the State of Bombay declared all communities, other than Brahmanas, Prabhus, Marwaris, Parsis, Banias and Christians, as backward. In 1928, the backward castes were defined as "castes or classes which are educationally backward".

Thus, the backward castes include all castes, except the upper castes, the SCs and the STs. These included peasant castes of various descriptions with a low ritual status. The peasant castes are a dominant force in economic and political life of the countryside. The maximum benefits of the green revolution, rural development schemes and of democratisation and adult franchise have gone to the principal peasant castes.

It has been reported that the status of the Kurmis in Bihar kept rising on account of their benefiting from commercial agriculture. Economic betterment encouraged them to form the All India Kurmi Kashtriya Sabha and also prompted them to adopt more Brahmanical ritual practices. The notion of the Prajapati or Ajgar castes emerged, which signified unity among the major agricultural castes such as Ahir, Jat, Gujar, etc. The Kurmis in Bihar formed a socio-political organisation in association with the Yadavas. This was known as the Triveni Sangam.

It is a fact that the backward classes movement did not meet with as much success in north India as it did in the south. The upper castes reacted more strongly to the backward classes movement in the north than in the south. This was because the upper castes are

20 per cent and 14 per cent in Uttar Pradesh and Bihar, respectively, of the total population, whereas they are only a small percentage in the south. The states of Bihar and Uttar Pradesh witnessed backward classes movement, particularly after the emergence of the Janata Party. After the implementation of the Mandal Commission recommendation for reservation of 27 per cent jobs in the entire country for the OBCs, today demand is being made for reservation of jobs in the private sector as well. The central government is also considering reservation of seats in all central universities and institutions, including Indian Institutes of Technology (IITs) and Indian Institutes of Management (IIMs). Once again debate is on about merit versus reservation. Protests are on against such a move by the union government.

Conclusion

The middle strata of rural society in India are the peasant castes. The abolition of landlordism and the introduction of adult franchise, Panchayati Raj and green revolution have made these castes economically and politically important in Indian society. The emergence of the backward classes movement has received impetus from improvement in their social and economic standing. They do not now suffer from several disabilities.

Compared to the upper castes, however, they still lag behind in social and educational spheres. The upper OBCs have made rapid progress in economic and political fields. Social change among the backward classes has been quite uneven. The most backward castes continue to be non-beneficiary of the reservation policy to a considerable extent.

Excercises

1. Define the main criteria for determining the backwardness of various caste groups other than for the Scheduled Castes and the Scheduled Tribes.
2. Discuss caste as the basis of backwardness in educational and economic fields.

3. Give a brief account of the step taken by state governments for ameliorating the socio-economic condition of the backward classes.
4. Write notes on the following:
   (i) Kaka Kalelkar Commission
   (ii) The Mandal Commission
5. Are backward class movements mainly against the upper castes? Give examples of any two such movements.
6. What are the main patterns of social mobility among the backward castes?

Select References

Beteille, Andre, "The Future of the Backward Classes: The Competing Demands of Status and Power", *Perspective, Supplement to the Indian Journal of Public Administration*, Vol. XI, No. II, 1965.

Dushkin, Lelah, "The Backward Classes", *Economic Weekly*, Vol. 13, Nos. 43, 45 and 46, 1961.

Galanter, Marc, *Competing Equalities Law and the Backward Classes in India*, Delhi: Oxford University Press, 1984.

Hardgrave, Robert, L. (Jr.), *The Dravidian Movement*, Bombay: Popular Prakashan, 1965.

Rao, M.S.A., *Social Movements and Social Transformation: A Study of Two Backward Classes Movements in India*, Delhi: The Macmillan Company of India Ltd., 1979.

Report of the Kaka Kalelkar Commission, 3 Vols., Government of India, 1955.

Report of Backward Classes Commission (Chairman: B.P. Mandal), Government of India Publications, 1981.

Singh, Parmanand, *Equity, Reservations and Discrimination in India*, New Delhi: Deep and Deep Publications, 1982.

12 Status of Women: Quest for Equality

Women have been treated as 'objects' by the male-dominated society in India and elsewhere. However, there is no uniform pattern of social, cultural and economic distinctions between men and women. In contemporary India, gender-based consciousness has its origin in emergence of the middle classes and their problems. Patriarchy is very strong in India despite several movements for the upliftment of women launched by women's organisations during the pre- and the post-independence periods. Sex morals have a direct bearing on hierarchy of caste and class groups.

Four aspects have been studied in detail in the context of the gender-related problems: (1) production, (2). reproduction, (3) sexuality, and (4) socialisation of children. However, in general, the Marxists and the socialists have over-emphasised the first aspect. In India's context, men generally dominate in all the four aspects, though women shoulder major responsibilities in these spheres. Male supremacy emanates from caste, class, patriarchy, and sexuality of the male.

Women are treated as inferior in their own families by parents-in-law and even by their husbands. They are stationed at the receiving end. This is generally true of families belonging to all castes and classes, but it is more often found among those groups who are still under the influence of feudalism or have feudalistic lifestyles and values. Even, the neo-rich in the countryside have put restrictions on women's higher education, migration and jobs. The fact is that women have been made dependent by men and by the social milieu they have created for them. In this chapter we have discussed status of women in ancient, medieval, British and post-independence India, and the role of women's organisations, legislations, social movements and man-woman relations.

Women in History

In the Rig-Vedic civilisation, women enjoyed equal status with men. Women, like men, received education and observed *brahmacharya*, and *upanayana* was also performed for them. Women studied the Vedas, and composed Vedic hymns. Women had access to all branches of knowledge. Women like Ghosha, Apala and Vishvara were composers of outstanding Vedic hymns. In the age of the Upanishads, there were women *rishis* like Gargi and Maitreyi. Women could own property and widows could remarry. They also became teachers. Women were not secluded from men, and they freely participated in public life. Marriage was sacred and indivisible and was not a secular contract. It was a religious bond. Child marriage was unknown. Girls enjoyed great freedom and settled their own marriages. Monogamy was a general rule, but there were cases of polygamy among the rich and the ruling classes. Polyandry and *sati* were non-existent. Wife was given a place of honour and she participated with her husband in religious ceremonies.

The position enjoyed by women in the Rig-Vedic period deteriorated in the later-Vedic period. A daughter began to be regarded as a curse. However, women were granted freedom to participate in public life. They were denied the right of inheritance and ownership of property (like the Shudras). Even, the earnings of women became property of their husbands and sons. However, women continued to have the *upanayana*, received education, and worked as teachers. Inter-marriage between Brahmanas and Kshatriyas was not unknown between A.D. 700 and A.D. 1206.

During the Buddhist period women were not denied learning. They took active part in public life, but did not enjoy the right of

Vedic studies. The position of women really deteriorated in the Gupta Age. Dowry emerged as an institution in this period. Widows could not marry again. They had to spend life in penance and austerity. Women had no right to real property. However, the *purdah* system did not exist. *Sati* had become popular by the seventh century A.D. Some women did receive higher education even in this period. Livavati and Khana were experts in arithmetic and astronomy.

The period between A.D. 1206 and A.D. 1761 witnessed further deterioration in the position of women. In this period, female infanticide, child marriage, *purdah, jauhar, sati* and slavery were the main social evils affecting the position of women. The birth of a daughter was considered a bad omen. Giving freedom to women was thought of as the predecessor of doom. Women were largely uneducated and remained confined to their homes. Conservatism, superstition and belief in magic, sorcery and witchcraft were part of women's life. However, motherhood was respected. A woman's devotion to her husband, children and home was universally accepted as a positive value.

The reform movements and the national movement created social consciousness among women. The All India Women's Conference, established in January 1927, concentrated on educational and social work among women. Mahatma Gandhi brought women into public life. The women of the middle classes came forward to take employment in 1930s and 1940s. However, the British rulers did not want to do anything, which could further women's position in Indian society. On matters of women's inheritance, marriage and rights of married women, the law applied by the British Raj was a mix of ancient Hindu law and British law. For example, Hindu law nowhere did recognise the enforcement of a husband's conjugal rights, but when the principle of 'restitution' was brought up, it was accepted, even though it was taken from Anglo-Saxon law.

The second half of the nineteenth century witnessed several reforms regarding the position of women in Indian society. Raja

Ram Mohan Roy and Ishwar Chandra Vidyasagar started agitation for widow remarriage, and they were successful in getting the Hindu Widows Remarriage Act passed in 1856. In Bombay, a Widow Remarriage Association was formed in 1861. The Arya Samaj gave priority to this programme. Several acts were passed in the first half of the twentieth century regarding inheritance of property and marriage regulations. The most important legislations of the post-Independence periods are: the Special Marriage Act of 1954, the Hindu Marriage Act of 1955, and the Hindu Succession Act of 1956. The Government of India has taken up the problems of divorce, dowry, rape, etc., with a view to find solutions, which will ensure equality of women with men. The latest legislations and actions are not only stringent and effective, but court decisions and police actions are also in favour of the women victims.

Status of Women in the British Period

Sati, infanticide, slavery, child marriage, prohibition of widow remarriage and lack of women's rights were some of the social problems which attracted the attention of the British and social reformers. In the beginning of the nineteenth century, the practice of *sati* was confined to Hooghly, Nadia and Burdwan districts of Bengal, Ghazipur of Uttar Pradesh and Shahabad of Bihar. It was also found in other parts of India, but only as a rare phenomenon. In southern India, it was practised in Ganjam, Masulipatnam and Tanjore districts. In Rajasthan, Punjab and Kashmir, the practice was confined mainly to women of high castes. In Delhi, Charles Metcalfe stopped the practice. Aligarh and Agra seldom had occurrences of *sati*. In Bengal alone three-fourths of the total occurrences of *sati* occurred in British India. It occurred among all castes, but it was more among the Brahmanas and Rajputs. Among the princely families, the sense of pride and heroism elevated the *sati* into a noble act. But, on the whole, the rite was practised by women whose husbands belonged to the middle and lower middle classes. The following factors could be attributed to the practice of *sati*: (1) the position of women in the Hindu system, (2) the institution of polygamy, especially among the *kulin* Brahmanas, (3) the enforced widowhood and austerity, (4) social convention, (5) the sense of salvation attached to the rite, and (6) antiquity and adoration of the practice.

The British had shown interest in the abolition of *sati* in 1813. The persuasive propaganda techniques failed to prevent the occurrence of the practice. The police also did not prove effective. Raja Ram Mohan Roy took it upon himself to eradicate this social evil. He announced that the rite of *sati* was not a part of the Shastras. It was not an integral part of the Hindu religion. A number of religious leaders opposed Ram Mohan Roy's crusade against *sati*. Through the cooperation of the princes, it was virtually stopped in the princely states. But it was not made an illegal act for a long time. Even today, occurrences of *sati* are reported from various parts of the country. And in most of the cases, the police have either reached late or remained ineffective. In Jhunjhunu town of Rajasthan, a huge temple of *sati* – known as Rani Sati Mandir – is a place of worship by all castes and communities. Nearly, two decades ago, in Sikar district of Rajasthan, a young Rajput woman committed self-emolation (*sati*). This particular *sati* occurrence invited protests from all over the state and other parts of India.

Female infanticide was found mainly among the Rajputs of Benaras, Gujarat, Madhya Pradesh and Rajasthan and in parts of Punjab and Sind and among some Sikhs. The institution of female infanticide arose due to (1) the deplorable position of women in Hindu society, (2) the dowry system, (3) hypergamy, and (4) the sense of honour and pride. Marriage of a female is considered compulsory. In 1779, infanticide was declared to be murder by the Bengal Regulation XXI. In 1804, this was extended to other parts of India. However, the practice continued in secret till recently, particularly among the Rajputs in Rajasthan. Dowry is its main cause.

Child marriage is prevalent even today among the rural people, and among the urban illiterate and poor. The institution of child marriage is also the result of hypergamy, dowry, and notion of virginity and chastity. It has resulted in the problems of overpopulation, poverty, unemployment, ill-health, dependence upon parents, etc. The first legislation was passed in 1860 under which the minimum age for consummation of marriage in the case of girls was raised to ten. In 1891, the age of consent for girls was raised to twelve, and in 1925 to thirteen for married girls and fourteen for unmarried ones. In 1929, the Child Marriage Restraint Act (Sharda Bill) was passed. Under this Act, which came into being in 1930, the minimum age of marriage for a girl was fixed at fourteen and for a boy at eighteen. According to the Hindu Marriage Act of 1955, the minimum age for a bride is fifteen, and for a bridegroom it is eighteen. The legislations have not proved effective in this case. Education, economic pressures, and migration to towns and cities from rural areas have certainly contributed to the raising of the age at marriage of both the sexes. However, child marriage persists unchecked. Many a time, even political leaders of repute have enacted child marriages of their wards. No stringent actions are taken for violation of the Hindu Marriage Act of 1955.

Slavery was of two types: (1) domestic, and (2) predial (agricultural). There were also institutions of the *nautch* (dance) girls and prostitutes. The latter was found particularly in the princely states. Predial slavery was found in Bengal, Madras, Assam, Coorg and southern Bombay Presidency (presently in Karnataka and Maharashtra, respectively). The slaves of this category were insolvent debtors. Some of them were migrants from Rajputana. Even slaves were sold out. There was also the practice of entering a contract by a person to work for a specific period of time either to pay the debt or to "have a fresh one". Domestic slavery was confined to females. The foreigners also indulged in the purchase of children in a clandestine manner and exported them overseas. Proclamations were made in Bengal, Madras, Bombay, etc., to prevent the institution of slavery. Today, the institution exists in the form of bonded labour. It is known by different names in different states. The British policy of apparent and selective non-interference in social matters encouraged the institution of slavery and other institutions which supported this evil.

With the efforts of Ram Mohan Roy and Ishwar Chandra Vidyasagar, the Hindu Widows' Remarriage Act was passed in 1856. In 1861, a Widow Marriage Association was formed. The Arya Samaj gave top priority to this programme. The following legislations have enhanced the status of Hindu women in matters of marriage, adoption and inheritance: (1) the Hindu Law of Inheritance (Amendment Act) of 1929, (2) the Hindu Women's Right to Property Act of 1937, (3) the Hindu Marriage Disability Removal Act of 1946, (4) the Special Marriage Act of 1954, (5) the Hindu Marriage Act of 1955, (6) the Hindu Succession Act and the Hindu Adoption and Maintenance Act of 1956, (7) the Dowry Prohibition Act, 1961, (8) the Maternity Benefits Act, 1961, (9) the Equal Remuneration Act, 1976, and (10) the Criminal Law Amendment, 1983.

Today, both sexes have the right to a civil marriage. The age without parents' consent has been increased to 18 for girls and 21 for boys. Thus, monogamy, judicial separation, nullity and divorce are some of the salient features of the post-independence era, which put man and woman on an equal platform. Inheritance, adoption and divorce (even consent) have enhanced women's status in India. These reforms have a long history, and are outcome of the efforts of several reformists through various movements that they launched in the pre-independence period. However, there is no uniform civil code in India. Muslims continue to have their personal laws.

Quest for Equality

Woman's quest for equality with man has become universal. It has given birth to women's movements and activities and associations. All over the world, feminism has its origin in society and unequal man-woman relations. Several constraints, such as inequalities between men and women and discrimination against women, are age-old issues. For a long time women remained within the four walls of their households. Their dependence on menfolk was total. Educated women in particular and the poor ones in general realised the need for taking up employment outside the household. In recent years, the middle class women have taken up the issue of price rise and have launched anti-price rise movements in various cities of India. Within the household, women have demanded equality with men. What exists for men is demanded for women. The demand for equality with men speaks of a notion of man's tyrannical hegemony over woman.

Women have hardly any choice to adopt an independent path for their upliftment. The question is how women can have equality within the framework of the existing highly rigid patriarchal society. Further, why women want to have for themselves the same strategies of change which menfolk have had over the centuries. Women want to follow in the footsteps of men. Our experience shows that even earning women give their earnings to their mothers-in-law and husbands rather than spending independently. This again speaks of the deep-rooted patriarchal normative orientation among women. However, this does not mean that women have always followed men in all respects in their households. Women participated in India's national movement for freedom. Many of them worked with Gandhi in the pre-independence period. Today, women's organisations, women social workers and politicians have taken up the issues of price rise, dowry, rape, exploitation, etc., to seek equal status with men to lead a dignified life. Women have demanded their share of jobs in the police and other such services. Women's organisations have created consciousness for gender equality, particularly in the urban areas. Reservation for women in the PRIs has been made after the recent 73rd and 74th constitutional amendments, which provide statutory status to the local bodies like the state legislatures and parliament.

Consequent upon these urgent social problems connected with women, International Women's Day, International Women's Year, conferences and seminars on women, and women's studies have been instituted in a big way since the late 1960s and 1970s. The provisions made in the Constitution of India regarding equality of women with men have also been widely popularised by these organisations and associations. A notable development was the appointment of the Committee on the Status of Women in 1971 by the Government of India. The committee submitted its report in 1974, which was very widely welcomed. There is also an All-India Association of Women's Studies. Demonstrations, processions and strikes against rape, dowry deaths and murder of women have become a regular feature in Delhi, Mumbai and other cities. Rape is generally committed by upper caste/class landowners, money-lenders, police officials and government functionaries, besides anti-social elements. Dowry has become a sort of market mechanism among the urban middle class, the lower middle class and the upper castes and among the economically well-off rural people. In case of dowry deaths, suicides and extortion, parents of the victims as well as the girls themselves suffer indignities and inhuman treatment.

Andre Beteille (1974) makes some valuable observations about the position of women in peasant families. He asks: "How are we to view families in which men work in the fields but women are by custom debarred from such work?" This is found among the families of the upper castes. Even some families of the intermediate and of the lower castes, who have become economically well-off, have adopted this norm with a view to elevate their social status in the village community. This does not mean that these women, who do not work or have been stopped from working on farms, are given treatment equal to the men in their families. The status of the family within the community is one thing and the status of the individual members within the family is quite another. There is an elaborate sex-based division of labour in rural families. However, this too varies from caste to caste, and also depends upon the economic and social standing of particular families.

Beteille comments upon the process of change in the status of women in the context of manual labour. He very rightly states: "Women are first withdrawn from wage employment on the farms of others. They are then withdrawn from the family farm. Finally, the men either withdraw from work, or change their role from cultivator to supervisor." Thus, withdrawing womenfolk from manual work on farms is a symbol of high status in the countryside.

But this is not true of working women belonging to upper and upper-middle or even to the lower-middle classes in towns and cities. Working unmarried women are considered an asset as they can be married without much difficulty and with less dowry.

Man-Woman Relationship

Can there be an expression of woman's identity independent of man? The answer is: Ideologically yes, and practically no. Meenakshi Mukherjee (1984) rightly observes that social conformity has always been more obligatory for a woman than for a man. Generally, a woman's identity tends to be defined by herself as well as by others in terms of her relationship with men as a daughter, a wife, a mother. This was also true of women in Europe in the nineteenth century. Today, women in China enjoy status almost equal to men. Chairman Mao said: "The day all women in China stand on their feet is the time for victory for the Chinese revolution. Times have changed, and today men and women are equal. Whatever men comrades can accomplish, women comrades can too." Feudal ways of thinking and acting were strongly attacked to elevate women's position in Chinese society. Old beliefs about women's inferiority were discarded. Equal pay for equal work is the practice today in China.

Women's bondage to men and to the social structure is a characteristic feature of capitalism, and emancipation of women from such ties is referred to as a feature of socialism. Employment for women is not a panacea for solving their problems. Women among the lower sections of society are found engaged in several economic activities, and yet they are more enslaved to their menfolk. Similarly, to look at women in terms of literate versus illiterate, rich versus poor and rural versus urban would not give a proper understanding of women's plight in today's India. Women, in fact, cannot be understood independent of men. The family alone has not been enslaving women. The ethos of society is such that women have been treated rather shabbily. Leon Trostsky once remarked: "There are no limits to masculine egotism. In order to understand the world, we must look at it through the eyes of women."

Today, the emphasis in women's studies is not on the status of women, their degradation and social customs, the role of women in the family, community and tradition, but it has shifted to education, economic and legal status of women, political participation, etc. Nowadays, instead of studying their attitudes, roles and status, the causes of women's subordination, work participation, women in movements, patriarchal structure, and women in relation to socio-economic and political structure are being taken up as crucial issues concerning women. Age and sex are not simply biological phenomena; they are social and cultural variables too, and in some societies these are considered as the basis for distribution of rewards and privileges.

It is necessary to have 'empathy' for studying the position of women. For a scientific understanding of their problems, the device of 'role-taking' needs to be adopted. This means placing oneself in the position of women rather than simply expressing sympathy with them. Women working within their own households as dependent members, children and old men by and large constitute a common category against the active and earning male members. Such a situation is found in India where a great deal of concern has been expressed for familial bonds, collective responsibilities and emotional ties for kinship relations.

Women's Struggle against Exploitation and Oppression

In recent years, a number of women's movements have emerged, characterised by theorising, mobilising and acting against suppression and subjugation of women. Are these movements class struggles or are they emancipation movements? Another related question is: How should one link the struggle for the liberation of the working class with that for the emancipation of women? The women's movement, like the students' movement, is more or less middle class oriented. The systems of sexism and male chauvinism are more or less universal in all organisations. Thus, there is a close connection between male dominance and patriarchalism in the family and capitalist exploitation in the larger society.

The women's movement has been organised by white-collar middle class women and women social workers from amongst upper and upper-middle classes. Feminist publications such as Manushi, Bayja, Mahila Andolan Patrika, Feminist Network and several others are run by women's organisations managed by urban middle and upper-middle class women. Women's conferences and seminars in Delhi, Mumbai and Pune have now become a regular means of mobilising working women to achieve equality with men. Intra-household discrimination, women's economic status, work situations, occupational patterns, etc., have become focal themes of these seminars. It has been mentioned in the discussions held in these seminars that women in India receive less consideration and money than what is required to meet their needs and responsibilities within the household and less than their right. One view is that there is economic basis for sexual discrimination within the family. Women can be compared to some extent with the urban proletariat and the poor peasant in terms of their exploitation. Women do a lot of work at home for which they are not paid for. Even working women do not enjoy independent status as they are made to carry the burden of household work actually to be done by their in-laws and husbands.

Some women protagonists have mentioned four major forms of the struggle of women for greater control over their lives. These are: (1) Women have organised (through mass movements) consciousness raising groups, women's centres, etc. These are meant for greater control over their bodies (for example, against rape, for free and safe contraceptives and abortions), for political rights like suffrage, against oppression in the family, against pornography, etc. (2) Women have fought through unions for improvement in their standards of living and in conditions of work. (3) Women have organised themselves for social recognition and remuneration for their work as housewives. (4) Women have also worked for housing, and against political repression, price rise, etc. But all these issues mainly concern the urban women.

Exploitation of women in the countryside has not received proper attention. The question is: Do women have a self and identity in a male-dominated society? Two images of women are found: (1) of the strong and resilient woman, and (2) of the suffering and tolerant woman. Both the images are unrealistic as they do not refer to women as oppressed and suppressed members of the family. Women are seen chiefly as weaker human beings. Women are protesting against forcible sexual contact with men. A woman's willingness is her prerogative. Men do not see these as women's issues of dignity and honour.

Woman's Identity as a Person

Identity of woman is generally defined by her role within the family. She is identified as a daughter, daughter-in-law, mother, mother-in-law, wife, etc., and not as a *person.* She has no independent connections, friends and relatives outside her family. Her only friends, relatives and connections are those of the men-folk of the family, becoming her kith and kin and friends by implication and not by voluntary choice. She has thus a subordinate status in the family. However, there are various degrees of woman's identity, depending upon caste and class background of her family.

Is a woman a person? A woman bows down to her husband's desires even if she is unwilling to do so. She does not have 'gender justice' or equality with man. Whenever a woman has expressed her identity as a person, she has been put to a lot of hardship. Dowry harassment and bride-burning have sprung up as violence against women. The institutions of joint family and hypergamy need a reorientation. The joint family home, for example, is a place where the daughter-in-law is treated as an 'outsider' and a 'servant' of the family. She becomes an object of scolding and ridicule for everyone in the family. Hypergamy demands the marriage of a girl within the framework of caste endogamy and clan exogamy with a boy belonging to a family of higher status. Due to hypergamy and the higher value attached to the boy among the Hindus, dowry has virtually become a price for a boy.

Crime against women has gone up in the recent years. Rape, kidnapping and abduction, homicide for dowry and dowry deaths, torture, molestation, sexual harassment, importation of girls (eve-teasing), etc., have become a frequent feature despite the legal provisions such as Immoral Traffic (Prevention) Act, 1956; Dowry Prohibition Act, 1961; The Child Marriage Restraint (Amendment) Act, 1979; Indecent Representation of Women (Prohibition) Act, 1986; and Commission of Sati (Prevention) Act, 1987. At times even the upper sections of society, including political personalities, are found violating these legal enactments. According to the National Crime Research Bureau (NCR), in 2005, there were 1,55,553 incidents of crime against women. Andhra Pradesh reported 13.4 per cent to total incidents of crime against women, and Uttar Pradesh had 9.6 per cent crimes of total crime, next to Andhra Pradesh. Between 2001 and 2005, the increase in crime against women was by 8.2 per cent. And there are a lot more non-cognizable crimes, and the ones which remain unreported and unrecorded.

Maximum cases of rape in 2005 were reported from Madhya Pradesh. The bureau mentions that incest rape has gone up manifold in the recent years. A large number of rape victims were below 15 years of age, and in many cases family members, close relatives, friends and neighbours were involved in such a serious crime. The highest cases of dowry deaths were reported from Bihar and Madhya Pradesh. Bihar and Bengal had maximum cases of importation of girls. 35 mega cities (over population of one million) reported 20,997 cases of crime in 2005, which were 2.5 per cent more than 2004. Delhi had 3,850 cases accounting for 18.3 per cent, followed by Hyderabad (2,057), 9.8 per cent. Vijayawada and Vishakhapatnam had 60.6 per cent and 55.2 per cent, respectively, as compared to national average of mega cities at 19.5 per cent crime against women. Delhi has accounted for 33.2 per cent of rape case, 37.4 per cent of kidnapping and abduction, 19.1 per cent of dowry deaths and 23.1 per cent of molestation cases. Hyderabad has reported nearly 15 per cent of cruelty cases by husbands and relatives and eve-teasing cases. Bangalore, Hyderabad and Jaipur have booked more cases of crime against women under special laws and local acts.

Several legislations have been passed by the Government of India since independence relating to marriage, inheritance of property, divorce, dowry, rape, etc., in addition to what was incorporated in the Constitution regarding equality and against discrimination based on religion, raw, caste, sex, etc. Social legislations have not been very effective in India. Acts against rape and dowry have been vociferously discussed over the last few years in courts and on public platforms, but both the heinous crimes continue unabated. The victim is generally a poor woman. Recently, the rapists of two German women in Rajasthan were punished severely by the fast track courts at Jodhpur and Alwar. Some cases of rape and murder, such as Priyadarshini Mattoo and Jessica Lal, in Delhi and its neighbourhood have attracted serious attention of media and public. These are now being tried expediteously. In some of them, the court has also given its verdict in favour of the victim. Long delays in disposal of the rape-murder cases are caused because of the involvement of the highly influential individuals and families. Dowry harassment and torture and wife burning and suicides due to torture are continuing unchecked. The victims of dowry harassment and torture are women from amongst the upper castes, middle and lower-middle class families in cities and towns. The institution of *anulom vivah* (hypergamy) has become a deep-seated idea among the upper and some upper-middle caste and class groups. This has created a sort of indirect competition among parents of girls to find a match who belongs to a superior family and whose educational and job status is also high.

Women are in no way inferior to men. They have contributed a lot to India's development. They participated in the freedom struggle against the British. They did a lot of social work in those very difficult days of Indian history. But, they are exploited despite their immense contribution to the national cause. They are generally found in the unorganised sector, hence their oppression and exploitation. Technological advancement has affected women adversely as they have now less control over resources within the family and other sectors of their employment. Advancement in the fields of agriculture, dairy development, fisheries and domestic technology has reduced the economic authority and the general status of women. Men have become less dependent upon women even in domestic affairs. The gap between men and women has further widened. The major areas of hiatus between men and women are, for example, literacy, education and training, women's employment, female mortality, health care and medical services. Female mortality is higher than male mortality. Women are lagging behind men in these areas because of India's social and cultural heritage and strong tradition of patriarchy and male domination.

Conclusion

The problems of women are due to unequal access of men and women to society's resources and their distributive processes. Technological devices, which could have helped women in many ways, have also been adopted by men to their advantage. Can men alone be blamed for these gender-based inequalities? It has been observed that it is women also who obstruct the path of other women even more than men do. For example, mothers-in-law and colleagues at work suppress more the daughters-in-law and junior women workers, respectively. However, all women are not equally exploited or oppressed. Therefore, there is a need to study women as unmarried girls, young wives, mothers, old women, and working and non-working women. Such a scheme of study will provide a comparative picture of the dimensions of women's problems as it covers ramifications and variations in the status of women. Interaction between women in different settings may also provide useful clues for a better understanding of the problem.

Women's struggle for emancipation from social and cultural bondage has been a historical fact in the Indian context. Women have also fought for their right to vote and also against their oppression and exploitation. Women's struggles have challenged the existing system which has made them socially, culturally, economically, and even politically, crippled. To seek 'gender justice' for them (and also for men), it would be proper to understand India's social formation, its layers and levels (including caste and class), male-female images and reality, various views on a woman's place in the family and at the place of work, and the congruence between technological advancement and patriarchy. Scientific and technological devices have not challenged the traditional mechanisms of women's oppression and exploitation. The man-woman relationship continues to be the dominating-dominated relationship. One finds even today a close tie-up between caste, class and man-woman relationship. However, the quest for equality with men has been strongly expressed in recent years. It has made some tangible impact in metropolitan cities and big towns. There is a need for a lot more to be done in this field.

Exercises

1. Give a brief account of the position of women in ancient India.
2. Bring out the factors which led to the deterioration of the position of women in Medieval India.
3. Explain the main problems of women in India during the British rule.
4. What do you understand by women's quest for equality with men?
5. Is family the field of women's oppression?
6. Highlight the role played by legislation in enhancing women's position in Indian society.
7. In what way have women's organisations and social movements contributed to elevation of the status of women?
8. What do you understand by a women's identity as a person?
9. Briefly describe recent steps taken for women's emancipation from exploitation and oppression in India.

Select References

Ahmed, Karuna, "Studies of Educated Working Women in India: Trends and Issues", *Economic and Political Weekly*, Vol. XIV, No. 33, 1979.

Beteille, Andre, *Six Essays in Comparative Sociology*, Delhi: Oxford University Press, 1974.

Gandhi, Nandita, "Women: Introducing Feminist Perspective in Academia", *Economic and Political Weekly*, Vol. XIV, No. 4, 1994.

Mukherjee, Meenakshi, "Reality and Realism: Indian women as protagonists in four nineteenth century novels", *Economic and Political Weekly*, Vol. XIX, No. 2, 1984.

The Gazetteer of India, Volume 2, New Delhi: The Government of India, 1973.

13 Dowry System

In the early days dowry was an institution in which gifts and presents were given to a girl at the time of her marriage when she was required to leave her parents' home and join her husband's household. But, in course of time, it became a crude institution resulting in female infanticide, suicide, bride-burning and other indignities and cruelties. The problem of dowry has become a serious social evil among the upper castes and middle classes both in towns and villages. The rules of marriage, namely, caste endogamy and clan exogamy, and *anuloma* (hypergamy) and *pratiloma* (hypogamy), have been misinterpreted and misused for maintaining the dowry system. These rules restrict the choice of mate selection, as marriage takes place within one's caste and outside one's clan.

Further, a girl needs to be married to a boy who belongs to a family with a status higher than that of her family. This practice of marriage alliance is known as hypergamy or *anuloma*. When a girl is married to a boy whose family status is lower than that of the girl's, it is known as hypogamy or *pratiloma*. Thus, *anuloma* has restricted choice and created a desire to give away a girl through marriage to a superior family. A boy becomes a more valued object than a girl. The net result, therefore, is dowry: the giving of material goods and cash to the parents of the boy at the time of fixing the marriage, at the performance of marriage and even afterwards on several other occasions. This practice has become a serious social problem.

Magnitude of the Problem

In India, and particularly in Delhi and other metropolis, dowry murders and suicides have become a matter of great concern. In Delhi alone, a bride was burnt to death every twelve hours. A total of 162 cases of burning of women were reported in Delhi between 1 April and 30 June 1983. This was an all-time high number of such incidents, and dowry was the most prominent cause of such a phenomenon. The problem of dowry is experienced by all sections of Indian society, but it has become a chronic evil particularly among the educated middle classes engaged in salaried jobs and trade and commerce. Women's organisations, voluntary associations, the intelligentsia and the media have expressed their serious concern for finding legal and reformative remedies to curb the menace of this social evil. Incidences of the dowry-related atrocities and crimes have receded recently as a result of the social awakening created by various groups and organisations.

Dowry is not a 'gift', a 'return gift', an 'exchange' or a 'reciprocal gesture'. It is considered more as an expenditure on the marriage of a girl, which parents are required to incur by force. Parents of a boy of marriageable age, who possesses the qualifications that the parents of a girl are looking for, demand a dowry according to what they think is the 'value' of their son. There are no references to dowry (as we know it today) in the Sanskritic texts. However, there are references to bride-price in the context of the traditional forms of marriage. There are certainly references to ornaments given to the bride. The Smritis also do not mention dowry. Dowry is a phenomenon which emerged in the medieval period. The Rajput princes, thikanedars and jagirdars gave away gifts to their daughters at the time of marriage with a view to exhibit their prosperity and superior status. In course of time the practice filtered down from the rich Rajputs and other twice-born castes to other sections.

Social Dimensions of Dowry

English education and white-collar jobs have accentuated the problem of dowry. A boy with good education and employment becomes much sought after match for a girl. If anything has kept some pace with wider social and economic changes in India, it is the increase in dowry in terms of cash and material goods. Whatever new products come to the market, such as motorcycle, car, music system, DVD player, television, refrigerator, household goods, electrical appliances, clothes, ornaments, furniture, etc., have become a part of dowry. If parents of moderate economic standing cannot meet dowry demands, their daughter remains unmarried; or if they manage to give a dowry, they get into heavy debt. Demands for more dowry after marriage have become a source of conflict between families of the boy and that of the girl. When the demands are not met, brides are harassed, tortured, burnt, or they commit suicide.

Dowry has also become a symbol of prestige for both the dowry-givers and the dowry-takers. It is considered a matter of dignity to give more dowry than one's kinsmen and caste-fellows and others. Parents of a boy boast that their son fetched a very high amount of dowry, including a car, a plot of land or a flat, a video and all other luxury and household goods. Both givers and takers of dowry talk about these things and value them with a feeling of pride.

What is Dowry?

It is not easy to define dowry as it does not refer to cash and material goods alone. It has been defined as a share of a daughter or a sister in parental property, given to her at the time of her marriage. But dowry is not really given as an amount equivalent to a daughter's share vis-a-vis her brothers. Even if there is no substantial family property to be shared, there is a tendency among people to borrow money to meet the expenses of marriage and dowry. The number of people in the marriage party (*barat*), the number and quality of meals, presents to the *baratis*, etc., are all part of the marriage deal along with dowry. Thus, dowry is not simply the giving of cash and material goods.

Another view is that dowry is a gift, a token of love, given to one's daughter or sister at the time of her marriage. Dowry, as a token of love, keeps her attached to the parents' family even after marriage. It has become customary to give dowry. Marriage without dowry has become almost unthinkable. In south India, dowry is called *stridhanam*. In north India, it is considered as a gift or *dahej*. Whatever conception or name is given to dowry, it is certain that dowry is not the right of a girl who leaves her parents' house after getting married. But it is also a fact that since a girl joins her husband's house in Hindu patriarchal society, she is given due compensation in the form of dowry. Dowry is a gift, a *dan*. Even a girl is given as a *dan*. This is called *kanyadan*.

There is also an element of reciprocity because parents of the groom are expected to give gifts and presents, including clothes and ornaments to the bride. However, this is an unequal exchange in two ways: (1) the parents of a groom spend much less on the gifts compared to what the bride's parents spend on dowry; and (2) the gifts given to the bride remain with the groom's family as the bride joins her in-laws' family permanently, and dowry also becomes the property of groom's family. Therefore, there is not really an equal exchange or reciprocity in the system. Today, the fact is that parents want to give their daughter to a family of high repute and to a highly educated boy with a lucrative job or who is likely to get a good job. Dowry is the price for these two attributes. Parents do not think simply in terms of giving gifts at the time of marriage, nor do they think of dowry as their daughter's share in the family property to be given to her at the time of marriage. They try to ensure good future of their daughter, which is entirely dependent upon the qualities of the groom and his parents.

The giving of gifts and help to a daughter was quite a normal activity in ancient India. It was voluntary and not demanded. However, in medieval India, Mughal rulers and *Nawabs* demanded high dowries. The Rajput kings gave dowries to ensure that their daughters lived comfortably after their marriage. Dowry was demanded rather than voluntarily offered. However, the system was confined to the ruling classes, Rajputs and Brahmanas. The lower castes had, on the contrary, a system of bride-price. Among the lower castes, a female member was considered an asset for family useful for agricultural labour and other traditional occupations. Hence, the question of dowry did not arise. In the wake of sanskritisation, the lower castes imitated the practice of dowry. Even, the poor borrowed money to give dowry. The poor Rajputs in Rajasthan started killing newly born female children due to fear of dowry. Bengal also had this evil of dowry in a pronounced form because of the institution of hypergamy.

Social Structure, Social Change and Dowry

The nationalist leaders and social reformers condemned the institution of dowry during the freedom movement. Mahatma Gandhi writes: "Any young man who makes dowry a condition for marriage discredits his education and his country and dishonours womanhood. Young men who soil their fingers with such ill-gotten gold should be excommunicated from society." However, these efforts did not minimise the evil to any noticeable extent. The growth of education, salaried employment, migration to cities and towns, and scientific and industrial advancements not only increased the incidence of dowry but also changed its dimension and magnitude. Educated boys, with administrative and professional jobs, became the most prized prospective husbands. Those who worked in towns and cities were preferred as life was more comfortable in cities than villages. Motorbike, car, music system, television, DVD player, refrigerator, furniture, electrical appliances and household equipments have become a part of the dowry package among the upper sections of society, in addition to cloths, ornaments and cash.

The Hindu Succession Act of 1956 provides girls with the legal right to a share in the parental property, but rarely do girls demand their share nor are they given. The law is redundant. The Dowry Prohibition Act of 1961 has utterly failed to check the growing menace of dowry. The girl does not make a claim for her share in parental property, but the parents spend a lot on her marriage. The

Act of 1961 prohibits dowry. Despite this, the practice of dowry is widespread. It has even spread to the communities, castes and regions which were hitherto unaffected.

Thanks to the efforts of NGOs and government for decline in dowry deaths between 2001-2005. In 2001, there were 6851 cases, whereas in 2002 to 2005, there were 6822, 6208, 7026 and 6787 cases, respectively. Only in 2004, there was slight increase, but again in 2005, the 2001 pattern remerged. Of the total cases in 2005, 23 per cent were from Uttar Pradesh, and 14.9 per cent from Bihar. Madhya Pradesh too was not far behind compared to Bihar.

Dowry varies from caste to caste and from region to region. It varies depending upon urban, rural, caste and family background. Dowry is a socio-structural phenomenon. Variations in social structure, in terms of caste, class, ethnicity, religion, region and culture, result in variations of the system of dowry. There is, however, a clear difference between the bride-givers and the bride-takers because of the rules of marriage practised in most parts of India. The communities in which bride-price exists or where patriliny is weak, dowry has not become a social problem. One who is a bride-giver remains socially inferior to the bride-taker throughout his life, and, in fact, for several generations to come. It is not that the bride-giver gives dowry only once at the time of marriage, but it is a continuous process. The bride receives gifts and presents throughout her life. The quality and amount of these gifts and presents depend upon the status and economic position of the bride-giving family.

Dowry is generally given to the parents of the groom, but in recent years, particularly in the urban areas, dowry is claimed as a 'right' by the couples, particularly in the form of those items which are specifically meant for them and their newly established households. Some parents give dowry in the name of their daughters, fearing its use by the parents of the groom. Several cases of tension and disharmony have come up because of such steps by the bridge-givers.

The problem of dowry is not acute in matrilineal societies and in the societies which are guided by the prescription of cross-cousin marriages. Both are found in south India, and therefore, the problem of dowry is less acute there compared to north India. The Nayars, Tiyyars and the Nangudi Vellalars are traditionally matrilineal societies in south India. The Nayars of Kerala pay neither bride-price nor give dowry. The Nayars are a matrilineal and matrilocal society, with an institution of visiting husbands. The visiting husband occasionally offers nominal gifts, as a token of his love and affection. The Tiyyars have the system of paternal cross-cousin marriage, that is, the girl is married to her father's sister's son. The bride-taker gives some gifts to the bride. In case the girl is married in violation of this rule, the bride's family is required to pay a fine. The Nangudi Vellars also have the same pattern of marriage as that of the Tiyyars. A girl is given a patch of land as a gift at the time of her marriage. These are not really variations of dowry. Matriliny and rules of marriage in south India have not allowed asymmetrical relations to develop between the bride-givers and the bride-takers, as we notice in north India. However, dowry in its modern form has started appearing in south India also. Matrilineal and matrilocal system of family has eroded in modern times. Patriliny is being accepted as a natural way of living. Dowry is also becoming a fact of life in the erstwhile matrilineal societies.

In north India, bride-takers are not only superior in status, but practically dictate terms to the bride-givers. They dictate the items to be given in the dowry and the arrangements to be made at the time of marriage. One often hears in north India: "What can we do, we are on the side of the bride *(ladkiwalas)*." "If a girl is born, you accept your defeat in this world." If anything goes wrong or is against the desire of the groom's parents, it becomes a life-long curse for the bride and her parents. It becomes the cause of her torture by in-laws and, sometimes, even by her husband.

Dowry, therefore, is not considered today as a *dan* (gift) but a unwritten *haq* (right) of a boy and his parents. There are instances of a groom's parents giving accounts of what they have spent on the education and upbringing of their son, and on other things, including the marriage. All this is included in the amount of dowry. Some have even stated that the bride's parents are required to spend a certain amount of money (often a couple of lakhs), and how this is spent would be left to them. Dowry does not include cash and material goods for the bridegroom and groom's parents alone, but it also includes gifts and cash for all the primary kinsmen and some other secondary and remote relatives. The groom's father exhibits the dowry to his kinsmen and fellow-beings with a sense of pride, expressing his superiority and high status. In north India, the girl's parents would not accept water and food at their son-in-law's residence as it would be considered a sin, even after giving an enormous dowry. However, today, enlightened girls and boys insist upon taking water and meals by the parents of girls at their residences.

Why Dowry?

It is difficult to suggest a set of factors responsible for the custom of dowry, but we can think of a tentative list. These include rules of marriage (including hypergamy), caste hierarchy, patriarchy, primogeniture, low status of women, modern education and employment, a false sense of prestige, and economic prosperity of some people. Since dowry has become a complex phenomenon and a social problem, it needs quick and far reaching remedial measures. Only legislation would not be sufficient. Legislation has several lacunae, and it is not easy to overcome them. Some voluntary agencies have started movements against the institution of dowry. These agencies have organised demonstrations against the incidents of dowry homicides, suicides, torture and harassment. Social boycott has also been done in some cases.

What we need today is a crusade against this evil, which has, in fact, ruined several families and has been destroyed lives of thousands of women year after year. There is a need to chalk out a programme having both curative and preventive measures and long-term and short-term devices. The curative and long-term measures would include inculcation of a new ideology and a value system which guarantees a place of honour to women and their parents. Young men of marriageable age do not become marketable commodities sold by their parents to the parents of brides in return for dowry. Egalitarian values are the only substitute for caste-based hypergamous marriages. Inter-caste marriages should be encouraged. Arranged marriages with demands of dowry must go.

The preventive and short-term devices would include immediate action when incidents of dowry deaths, harassment and humiliation occur. The victims of dowry should be provided legal and social protection. Media - both print and electronic – should highlight such incidents with all seriousness to curb the menace in future. Street corner plays should depict such incidents as serious matters of life and not as a source of entertainment. Political leaders, government officials, businessmen and others must not be allowed either to take or give dowry in any form, not even in the form of gifts and presents. It has become a vicious evil. A man who gives dowry to his daughter plans to take more dowry for his son. If such a thing continues, there will be no end to this social evil. Hence, the measures suggested above are the only way out to reduce the magnitude of the problem.

Conclusion

Dowry has become a serious problem, particularly among those sections of society who are constrained to give dowry but do not have adequate resources for savings for dowry. These are generally the salaried groups who have fixed income. We have discussed problems arising out of dowry and efforts being made to cope up with this social evil. Despite all the efforts, the solution to this problem does not seem to be there in near future.

Exercises

1. Define the institution of dowry.
2. Discuss the magnitude of the problem as it exists in present-day India.

3. Bring out die relationship between social structure, social change and dowry.
4. Explain the reasons which have led to the emergence and persistence of dowry.
5. Explain the following:
   (i) Hypergamy
   (ii) *Stridhanam*
   (iii) Bride-price
   (iv) Education and dowry
6. Highlight the role of legislation in curbing the problem of dowry.

Select References

Altekar, A.S., *The Position of Women in Hindu Civilization: From, Prehistoric Times to Present Day*, Delhi: Motilal Banarsidas, 1962.

Goody, Jack and Tambiah, S.J., *Bridewealth and Dowry*, Cambridge University Press, 1973.

Hooja, S.L., *Dowry System in India: A Case Study*, Delhi: Asia Press, 1969.

Kapadia, K.M., *Marriage and Family in India*, Bombay: Oxford University Press, 1966.

Karve, Iravati, *Kinship Organisation in India*, Poona: Deccan College, 1953.

Mandelbaum, David G., *Society in India*, Berkeley: California University Press, 1972.

Prabhu, P.N., *Hindu Social Organization*, Bombay: Popular Book Depot, 1953.

Status of Women in India (ICSSR), New Delhi: Allied Publishers, 1975.

14 Social Deviance

The behaviour of man, which does not conform to accepted norms, is called social deviance. There is no society which can claim a complete conformity to its norms. Also, there is no society where complete violation of norms or normlessness is found. Crime is found in all types of societies. Every society is confronted with the problems of crime, delinquency, prostitution, etc. However, what may be considered a social deviance in one society may be considered normal or not so much a deviant activity in another society. For example, violation of norms related to caste, family, marriage, etc., was considered a deviant activity in the past and it invited punishment and ostracisation. However, today, such violations do not invoke serious punishment and criticism. Thus, social deviance is a relative phenomenon, and changes its form in terms of space and time.

Concept of Crime

Non-conformity to accepted norms implies moral, social and legal violations. In other words, violation of accepted norms amounts to an unmoral, anti-social and anti-legal action. Certain castes and communities had social sanction for committing these anti-social or anti-legal activities. Industrialisation, social and legal reforms, besides their positive effects, have also brought about deviance. Overcrowding, slums, and lack of appropriate means of social control have emanated mainly from industrialisation and urbanisation. Since there are no uniform patterns of change and industrialisation, crime is also a differentiated and ramified occurrence. It is a relative phenomenon.

Crime refers to an overt behaviour supported by an intent to perform the criminal act. A purely accidental act, which amounts to violation of accepted social norms, is not a crime. An act of self-defence also may not be treated as crime. A criminal act resulting from emotional stress makes a person less culpable than the premeditated act. But ignorance cannot always be an excuse. Thus, the act and the motivation are both important considerations in determining whether an act is a crime or not. Since children and insane persons are generally not in a position to premeditate criminal acts, they are excluded from the category of criminals. There are two types of crimes: (1) felonies, and (2) misdemeanours. Felonies are serious offences such as murder, dacoity, rape, smuggling, etc. Misdemeanours are ordinary crimes, which include violation of traffic rules, petty thefts, nuisance in public places, etc.

Sociologically speaking, non-conformity is an important yardstick of criminal behaviour. Conformity refers to behaviour in accordance with accepted values and norms. Values are goals or ends, which are generally non-negotiable. Norms are institutional procedures for realising goals. If a person does not share the accepted values and norms of society, he may be called a criminal or deviant as his activities would be against the expected behaviour vis-a-vis the norms and values. Values and norms are not uniform. They differ from group to group and from situation to situation. Values and norms also vary in terms of rural-urban differences and religious affiliations. However, a violation of religious norms is not punishable by law, but is considered a sin. Some acts are both crime and sin, such as adultery and suicide. There are some acts, which are injurious to the self, such as drunkenness, gambling, use of narcotic drugs, vagrancy, etc. These are considered as vices, but their indulgence in public may be considered as crime.

A sociological view of crime is suggested by Emile Durkheim (1952). According to Durkheim, a differential rate of crime reflects differential degrees of social cohesion and the corresponding social control. The breakdown of social cohesion frees the individual from the pressure of public opinion and of the informal social control, which, in more solitary groups, operate to secure conformity to the norms of conventional behaviour.

Explanation of Crime

There are two types of explanation of crime: (1) 'mechanistic' or 'situational', and (2) 'historical' or 'genetic'. The first explanation refers to geographical, climatic and biological factors in crime. For example, crimes against persons are more prevalent in warm climates and crimes against property are more numerous in cold areas. Crime is caused either by enormous wealth or dire poverty. Thus, crime is committed because of the complexity of an ill-adjusted economic system.

People also commit crime because they want to lead a luxurious life which they cannot afford to have without committing crime. Social and ecological settings also affect the individual's need to commit crime. There are some delinquency-prone areas. We often hear about village and city gangs of offenders. The criminologist Sutherland (1949) talks of the 'differential association theory' of crime, that is, learning about criminality by coming in contact with criminal behaviour patterns.

The genetic explanation states that criminal behaviour is learned, particularly by interaction with other persons. The learning includes: (1) techniques of committing crime, and (2) the specific direction of motives, drives, rationalisations and attitudes. Differential associations may vary in frequency, duration, priority and intensity.

There is also a theory known as a 'systematic theory' of crime. Gangs of criminals operate in specific areas. Such gangs have organisational structures, leaders and specific norms of conduct. Maladjustment with the existing norms and available means is the basis of criminal behaviour. Crime is, in fact, a socially and legally undesirable behaviour, hence, invites punishment. Whatever may be the situations in which a person indulges in criminal acts, there is never one single cause because crime is a complex behaviour and it is caused by a multiplicity of factors.

Classification of Criminals

Several classifications of criminals are available. The famous Italian criminologist, Lombroso (1911) gives a five-fold classification: (1) the born criminal; (2) the insane criminal; (3) the criminal by passion; (4) the habitual criminal; and (5) the occasional criminal. Recent researches show that heredity and insanity or even passion are not causes of crime because they have not stood the test of scientific rigour. The habitual and the occasional types refer to frequencies of crime rather than its causes.

According to another classification, criminals are classed as murderers, violent criminals, criminals lacking in probity and lascivious (lustful) criminals. Even this classification is based on an impressionistic analysis rather than on facts. Some others have classified criminals as professionals, casual and habitual.

Since crime is a social phenomenon, criminals should be classified in terms of their orientation and in accordance with the values and cultural definitions in the social world in which they live. There are two types of criminals from the sociological point of view: (1) the 'social criminal', and (2) the 'individualised criminal'. The first refers to a general category supported by general cultural ends. The second refers to those who commit crime for their diverse personal and private ends. Political crime and crime by terrorist organisations can be included in the first category. Society has some pre-ordained goals to be realised by its members with some means or norms to be followed for realising the goals. Robert K. Merton (1949) calls lack of correspondence between means and ends as a situation of anomie. According to Merton, a situation of deviation arises when there is a lack of fit between culturally accepted goals and institutionalised means of attaining them. The sociological dimension of crime is stated by Durkheim (1952) as follows: "Crime is a social fact and human act. Crime is both normal and functional. No society can be completely exempted from it. Crime is one of the prices we pay for freedom." The modern state has taken up development programmes. The functionaries working in the state bureaucracy often indulge in underhand and unlawful tactics for making money. Bribes, commissions and gifts are accepted in lieu of the favours extended to the people who are otherwise not eligible for benefits from the government. This as known as 'white-collar crime'.

Crime in India

The factors which hinder the adjustment process also explain the causes and consequences of crime. Indian society has its own unique character, and the phenomenon of crime needs to be seen in terms of its peculiar nature. To understand juvenile delinquency, one must analyse the socialisation process, peer group influence, and the structure of delinquent gangs. The crucial variables in delinquency are age, sex and status of the family

India has witnessed rapid socio-economic changes since independence. Various institutions have been created and recreated due to structural and cultural changes over the past six decades. White-collar crime has acquired new dimensions. Political institutions have changed very rapidly and cultural norms have not kept pace with them. Hence, there is a 'cultural lag' in today's India. Aspirations for status elevation have also increased in recent years. A number of people have adopted malpractices to acquire high status. Economic unevenness among different sections of society has been caused partly by the social heritage of the people and partly by the processes of modernisation and change. The status hiatus created by these factors has been responsible for creating situations of crime and delinquency.

Socialisation and crime are correlated. A man learns both positive and negative roles as a member of a society. Dysfunctional roles are imbibed by those members who are subjected to tension, conflict, dissension and defection rather than peace, harmony, cooperation and stability. Attitudes towards one's own life and towards those of others are determined by these factors in the process of socialisation. Power has also become a source of crime for the privileged sections of society. There is a tendency among powerful persons to abuse their influence and authority. Several cases of rape and murder have been reported by wards of influential persons and political heavyweights in the recent past. White-collar crime is a phenomenon found among the educated people engaged in trade, professions and government services.

The Police Research and Development Bureau has reported murder, homicide, adulteration of medicines, abduction, rape, dacoity, loot, burglary, theft, rioting, forgery, embezzlement and breach of trust as the major criminal activities. In 1981-82, about 85 per cent of crimes were related to burglary, dacoity and thievery. A number of crimes also remain unreported in the police records, particularly in the rural areas. Thus, crime in India is mainly against property. This does not mean that all criminals are necessarily at the bottom of social and economic hierarchies. Economic offences and crimes are committed more often by the economically well-off and well-placed people in society. Tax evasion, smuggling and bribery are some of the common crimes committed by members of the upper strata of society. India being a developing country has a new institutional set-up employing lakhs of people. Since the poor are ignorant and weak, the white-collar workers indulge in bribery and corrupt practices. Corruption has become a dangerous threat to both the Indian state and society.

Let us have an idea of the current crime situation in India. As per the National Crime and Research Bureau, the Indian Penal Code (IPC) classifies crimes against property, public order, economic crimes, crimes against women, children, etc. Besides the IPC, the Special Local Laws (SLL) also take cognizance of crime. During 2001-2005, more than 50 lahk cases were registered as cognizable crimes. In 2004, there were 60,28,781 cases, whereas in 2005, the decline in crime was quite marked as there were

50,26,337 cases of cognizable crimes. During 2001-2003, the number varied between 53 and 55 lakh cases.

It may not be possible to discuss minutely the patterns of crime in different states. However, some trends may be reported here. In 2005, there were 698 districts in the country, 13 districts out of them have reported more than 10,000 crimes annually, while 80 districts have reported crimes between 5,001 and 10,000, and a bulk of them (605) have reported less than 5,000 crimes, annually. The following table shows the districts which have above 10,000 crimes in 2005.

	Name of District	*Incidence*
1.	Mumbai	31432
2.	Bangalore	29042
3.	Jaipur	20293
4.	Chennai	20127
5.	Ahmedabad	17468
6.	Hyderabad City	17276
7.	Indore	16026
8.	Sikandarabad	12079
9.	Patna	11840
10.	Pune	11817
11.	North-West District of Delhi	11019
12.	Bhopal	10850
13.	South-West District of Delhi	10529

It is evident that Mumbai has reported the highest incidence of crime during 2005. Data from other districts indicate that Patna recorded the highest number of murder (436), robbery (633) and dacoity (127). Bhatinda in Punjab had the highest cases of culpable homicide (73). The highest incidence of kidnapping and abduction (572) was reported from the North-West District of Delhi. Mumbai city has reported the highest incidence of burglary (3,175), theft (11,903), including auto theft, and criminal breach of trust

(536). Hyderabad recorded the highest cases of cheating (1,880), sexual harassment (348), and cruelty by husbands/relatives (1,309). Rape cases (236) were highest in Mushirabad of West Bengal. Mallapuram in Kerala has reported highest number of incidents of riots (629). Nadia in West Bengal has reported highest incidence of importation of girls (60). The hurt cases were maximum (4,424) in Jabalpur of Madhya Pradesh. Besides these cases under the IPC, there were very large number of cases and incidences of crime (32,03,735) under the SLL in the year 2005. Fluctuation in crime rate has also been noted during 2001-2005.

The following table shows rate of violent crimes during 2001-2005.

S. No.	*Rate of Violent Crimes (IPC)*	*2001*	*2002*	*2003*	*2004*	*2005*
1.	Affecting Life	9.8	9.3	8.3	8.8	8.5
2.	Affecting Property	2.7	2.5	2.4	2.4	2.3
3.	Affecting Public Safety	8.4	7.7	6.2	6.3	5.9
4.	Affecting Women	1.6	1.6	1.5	1.7	1.7
	Total Crimes	22.5	21.1	18.4	19.2	18.4

The table indicates that the rate of total violent crimes has declined during 2001-2003, and increased in 2004, followed by decrease in 2005. Compared to 2004, in 2005 a decrease of 2.9 per cent was recorded.

A glance at the crime data relating to different states indicate that personal vendetta (11.8%) and property disputes (8.6%) were the main two causes of murders. Love intrigues (7.4%), gain (4.5%), dowry (3.2%) and atrocities by terrorists/extremists (3.1%) were the other main reasons. Maharashtra has reported 60.8 per cent murders due to 'class conflict'. 'Casteism' was the cause of murders (42.5%) in Bihar. Political rivalries accounted for 36.3 per cent, property disputes for 23.9 per cent, and gain for 22.5 per cent as the other motives behind violent crimes in Bihar. Terrorism in Jammu & Kashmir, witchcraft and love affairs in Andhra Pradesh, and communalism and lunacy in Chhatisgarh were recorded as the more significant reasons compared to other states. Rape, kidnapping and dacoity have been reported as a macro phenomenon.

Concept of Delinquency

There is no unanimity on the definition of delinquency. Delinquency has both legal and sociological dimensions. In 1960, the Second United Nations Congress on the Prevention of Crime and the Treatment of Offenders recommended that: (1) the meaning of the term 'juvenile delinquency' should be restricted as far as possible to violations of the criminal laws, and (2) a situation should not be created where society penalises the small irregularities or maladjusted behaviour of minors, when it would not prosecute adults for the same irregularities of behaviour A delinquent child is one who deserts his home, who is habitually disobedient or is beyond the control of his parents, who violates the law of the land, or who does not abide by the rules which he is required to follow.

It is stated that human ecology or institutions have an impact on the individual, and he becomes a delinquent due to its stresses and strains. The factory areas, for example, are delinquency prone. Some areas, in fact, become gang lands. Frederic Thrasher (1936) found 1,313 delinquent gangs in Chicago. Many of these gangs were training schools for criminals. Gangs are even formed for adventurous recreation.

There may be several factors responsible for delinquency. Cultural maladjustment, inadequate housing for the poor, overcrowding, low standards of living, low educational standards, incongenial neighbourhood life, and a decline in norms of social behaviour may be listed as major factors. Can delinquency be measured? Since it is not defined in any one way and is subjectively interpreted, it is not easy to make a full measurement of the extent and intensity of delinquency.

The best-known studies of delinquency are: William F. Whyte's *Street Corner Society* (1943) and Albert K. Cohen's s *Delinquent Boys* (1955). Whyte discusses with anthropological insight the nature and structure of delinquent gangs. Cohen rejects the concept of 'delinquency area', because the slum areas have a vast and ramifying network of informal associations. Systematic delinquent behaviour is found primarily among lower groups. Delinquency is fundamentally related to socio-economic conditions of individuals and groups.

Delinquency in India

The Children's Act of 1960 defines a delinquent child as one who has been found to have committed an offence. A child is defined as a boy under the age of 16 years, and a girl under 18 years. The word 'offence' means any act of omission made punishable under the law in force at a given time. There are juvenile courts to deal with delinquent children. Child Welfare Boards deal with neglected and uncontrollable children. In India, even if children commit serious offences like the ones committed by adult criminals, they are dealt by the juvenile courts. This is in consonance with the recommendation of UNO in regard to social defence.

According to police records, in 1971, there were 1,03,419 juvenile delinquents, which included mainly male children. Violence was not much pronounced, but the number of murders was quite noticeable. Drinking of alcohol, gambling and theft were found as the major deviant activities. Of the delinquents, 70 per cent lived with their parents, and the remaining 30 per cent either lived with their guardians or were homeless. More than 80 per cent of the total number of delinquents were in the lower income group. Upper and upper-middle class children were few and also escaped arrests. More than 53 per cent of them were illiterate, 38 per cent had studied below primary, and only 2 per cent were matriculates. Maharashtra and Madhya Pradesh had the maximum rates of delinquency.

Data on juvenile delinquency since 1986 are being gathered as per the Juvenile Justice Act, 1986, whereby the age of juvenile male and female is at par, that is, 18 years, whereas earlier it was 16 years for a boy and 18 years for a girl.

During 1997 to 2000, the share of juvenile delinquency of the total IPC crime was 0.5 per cent. This share increased to 0.9 per cent in 2001, and it further increased to 1 per cent in 2002, but has remained constant during 2003 to 2005. The increase may be attributed to change in law, that is, from 16 years to 18 years for boys. However, juvenile crime has shown a mixed trend since 2000. The maximum share was 1.8 per cent in 2002 and 2004, whereas it was 1.7 per cent in 2003 and 2005, and it was 1.6 per cent in 2001. During 2005, the incidences of crimes were 18,939, and under the SLL crime incidences were 6,662. Madhya Pradesh (4,557), Maharashtra (4,216), Chhatisgarh (1,557), Gujarat (1,390), Rajasthan (1,324), and Andhra Pradesh (1,186) have reported highest incidences of juvenile crimes under the IPC. The six states taken together account for 74.8 per cent of total juvenile delinquency cases. Theft (4,846), hurt (2,979), burglary (2,270) and riots (934) altogether have accounted for 58.2 per cent of total IPC juvenile crimes.

Highest incidence of rape (145) was from Madhya Pradesh, followed by Chhatisgarh (86). Juvenile theft was highest (1251) in Maharashtra, followed by Madhya Pradesh (564) and Andhra Pradesh (517) out of total incidences (4846). The ratio of girls to boys was 1:15 in general among the juvenile delinquents. Out of the total juvenile delinquents 8,660 were illiterate and 12,394 had education up to primary level. These two categories account for 64.4 per cent of the total juveniles in 2005. 91.7 per cent (29,962) juveniles were living with their parents. Only 8.3 per cent (2,719) were homeless delinquents. Out of the total number, 71.2 per cent belonged to poor families, and only 6.8 per cent came from middle income groups. The upper income group delinquents were just 0.16 per cent.

It is not that children commit crime. Crime is also committed against children like crime against women, poor and deprived sections. Children are victims at times of the problems of their parents, relatives and neighbours. Murder/Killing, foeticide, infanticide, abetment to suicide, exposure and abandonment, kidnapping and abduction, procuration of minor girls, selling of girls, buying of girls, etc., are quite common crimes against children. In November 2006, a three year old male child, son of the CEO of ADOBE (an international software company), was kidnapped for ransoms from a posh locality, Sector 15A of Noida, Uttar Pradesh. Wide media and press coverage had taken place. The boy was rescued after payment of ransom amount of rupees fifty lakh as admitted by the father of the kidnapped child. Crime against children occurs despite Immoral Traffic Prevention Act, 1956, Child Marriage Restraint (Amendment) Act, 1978, Child Labour (Prevention and Regulation) Act, 1986, and as amended in 2006, etc. The following table shows crimes against children and variation in 2005 over 2004.

S. No	*Crime Head*	*Year*			*% variation in 2005 over 2004*
		2003	*2004*	*2005*	
1.	Murder	1212	1304	1327	1.8
2.	Infanticide	103	102	108	5.9
3.	Rape	2949	3542	4026	13.7
4.	Kidnapping and Abduction	2571	3196	3518	10.1
5.	Foeticide	57	86	86	0
6.	Abetment of Suicide	25	33	43	30.3
7.	Exposure and Abandonment	722	715	933	30.5
8.	Procuration of Minor Girls	171	205	145	29.3
9.	Buying of Girls for Prostitution	24	21	28	33.3
10.	Selling of Girls for Prostitution	36	19	50	163.0
11.	Child Marriage Restraint Act	63	93	122	31.2
12.	Other Crimes	3700	5107	4697	8.0
	Total	11633	14423	14975	3.8

The Government of India has adopted a therapeutic approach to the problem of juvenile delinquency. Juvenile courts, the Apprentices Act, 1850, the Reformatory School Act, 1897, the Code of Criminal Procedure of 1898 and 1973, the Children's Acts passed by the states since the 1920s, constitutional provisions, the Children's Act of 1960, psychiatric clinics, educational and recreational programmes and community programmes are some of the major steps undertaken by the Government of India in its efforts to treat juvenile delinquents as amateur offenders, who had fallen into bad company or who lived in incongenial homes or neighbourhoods.

Children indulge in delinquency for reasons of recreation and pleasure. Pleasure and survival are their main objectives. Their pleasure-seeking objective compels them to commit economic offences, and their survival-oriented objective forces them to indulge in aggressive and retributive activities. Smoking, homosexuality, at times heterosexual relations, alcoholism, gambling and drug addiction are some of the activities noted by the criminologist K.S. Shukla (1979). Various experts have reported that gangs form the organisational basis of juvenile delinquency.

Reformative Measures

Reforms are required at three levels: (1) police, (2) prison, and (3) rehabilitation. There is a dire need to improve the capabilities of the police and prison personnel to correctly understand and treat the criminals, prisoners and detenues. Instead of a punitive administration, what we require today is a correctional administration. Improved facilities for food, housing, health and recreation should be made available to prisoners. A prison can be treated as a 'country club' rather than a dark cell. A system of trusteeship and self-government is a philosophy and a technique of dealing with prisoners which can bring about their re-socialisation.

Probation

Probation, as a correctional method, has been practised in India for a long time. An offender is put on trial under the supervision of a probation officer. Imposition of punishment is suspended because there is less stigma attached to a suspended sentence. An offender is given time to prove that he could mend his ways. Supervision is of a friendly nature. It is a method of bailing out the prisoners. Probation is an enlightened attempt to cope with crime in some of its aspects. It affords the offender another chance to improve, to continue to live a life that meets with the approval of society. It averts the stigma of a prison sentence.

Probation is beneficial for the community as it helps produce well-adjusted individuals. The system is much less expensive to the state than institutional treatment. The probation officer can provide all the community facilities for rehabilitation. However, political interference, the inadequately trained judges and probation officers, and legal lacunae are some of the factors preventing the proper execution of the scheme. Some offenders, because of the gravity of their offences, cannot be given the benefit of this system. The Probation of Offenders Act, 1958 is the basis of this reform.

Parole

Parole is another important method of reformation of an offender. It is a form of conditional release granted after a prisoner has served a portion of his sentence in a correctional institution. There is a need for careful selection of serving prisoners and for adequate preparation for their release. Some form of supervision is to be maintained. Parole is not outright freedom. It should not be confused with probation and pardon. People are released on parole with a view to eradicate bitterness and hopelessness, particularly in the case of the poor and the accidental criminals. Parole is not leniency or mercy, but it is part of the stipulated law. It is indeterminate sentence. Parole is often looked upon as a right rather than a privilege.

Parole becomes an ineffective mechanism if prisoners are released because of extraneous pressures. It becomes a weak method if supervision is farcical and funds are inadequate. Each case for parole requires a thorough study by psychologists, psychiatrists and social workers. The success of this method depends upon the prudent selection of those who are released on parole.

Prostitution

Prostitution refers to the sexual behaviour of a female outside or without wedlock on a commercial basis. Prostitution is regarded as a vice, a sinful or degrading indulgence of a natural appetite for itself alone. It is a moral problem. Prostitution is forbidden by religious and civic groups. It is also prohibited by law in some societies. A prostitute and her pimp are vatted with a mixture of pity, scorn, fascination and persecution. Prostitution often results into drug addiction, scandal, veneral diseases, AIDS and deterioration of the neighbourhood in which it occurs.

A sociological analysis of prostitution calls for understanding of its persistence and its causes. It is an ubiquitous institution. It is deplorable in the eyes of all. However, in some societies, it has been legitimised, whereas in others it is prohibited, both legally and morally. It involves a high degree of sexual promiscuity that fulfils no publicly recognised societal goal. Prostitution may be defined as "engaging in a primary contact in a secondary relationship". Promiscuity means willingly indulging in sexual contact with numerous persons, and even with strangers. A prostitute sells her sexual favours without any emotional attachment but for economic gain.

Geoffery J. May (1958), in the *Encyclopaedia of the Social Sciences*, defines prostitution as characterised by three elements: (1) payment, usually involving the passing of money, although gifts or pleasures may constitute equivalent consideration, (2) promiscuity, with the possible exercise of choice; and (3) emotional indifference, which may be inferred from payment and promiscuity. The sexual relation between the buyer and the seller is illegitimate, ephemeral and condemned.

The causes of prostitution may be varied, but psychological and sociological factors are important. Sex is used for various ulterior purposes, as is the case when pretty girls are employed in stores and charity drives, and used in advertisements. These factors lead to promiscuous sexual relations. Alfred C. Kinsey (1948) points out that some aspects of prostitution are useful for certain male individuals. However, this does not mean an advocacy or promotion of this age-old institution. It is found both in unorganised and organised forms. Unions of sex workers and dance bar girls are quite strong in Indian metropolises, particularly in Mumbai. Recently, prostitutes have even formed unions in some big cities and towns.

Prostitution in India

It is difficult to find an exact estimate of the incidence of prostitution in India because it is still considered a sin to visit a brothel. There are at least three types of prostitutes: (1) common prostitutes, working openly in brothels; (2) private prostitutes, mistresses or keeps of particular individuals, who work as singers, dancers and *naikins;* and (3) clandestine prostitutes, who work in secrecy, and maintain their respectability and social position. Thus, prostitution is a complex phenomenon. It is directly not clearly visible.

Several years ago, a study of 425 prostitutes was conducted by S.D. Punekar and Kamala Rao (1955) in the city of Bombay (now Mumbai). The findings of this study are quite educative and useful. One-third of the common prostitutes were *devadasis* (temple prostitutes). Backward communities from rural areas sent girls to the city for prostitution. There are reports that some persons allure poor, young rural girls to towns and cities with the promise of getting them a job or of getting them married. Recently, it was reported that nearly 25 girls were sold in a Bihar village bordering Nepal to people in Mumbai with a promise of setting them married and of leading a comfortable life. Poverty of the parents was the main cause for selling the girls. Many girls from Nepal are sold to people in Mumbai. The fact is that *dalals* visit the vulnerable people to effect the deals. It is a 'business'. In fact, they sell them to brothel-keepers either directly or through middlemen. Prostitution is ultimately adopted by them as a profession though they do not intend it to be the source of their livelihood. *Devadasis* pursue prostitution as a profession. They claim to have a right to this profession. Since they claim to have a right to prostitute, they may attract others to involve in prostitution.

In cities like Mumbai, Kolkata and Delhi there are prostitutes from all parts of the country. Foreigners too are said to be a part of this network. Punekar and Rao's study shows that more than half of the prostitutes are from the state of Karnataka, particularly from the Bijapur, South Kanara and Belgaum districts. Eighty-six per cent are Hindus, and half of these are Harijans. Ten per cent of them are literate, and they are of mentally average calibre. A large majority of them are from rural areas, and belong to poor peasant families. The common prostitutes (the lowest class of prostitutes) are from the lowest economic and social strata. However, it cannot be said that poverty is the most important cause of prostitution.

There are some prostitutes who were indifferently brought up by their parents. Defective socialisation, destitution, carelessness of parents and lack of love and affection have been reported as the main causes of prostitution. Out of the non-*devadasis*, two-thirds were married. They are the ones who became widows at an early age. There are also run-away wives. Among the married ones, unhappy married life is mainly responsible for prostitution. The causes of unhappiness included ill-treatment, drunkenness and unfaithfulness of the husband and unequal marriages. More than half of the unmarried girls reported that nobody saw to their settlement.

Less than two-third prostitutes were regularly working as farm labourers and half of them left their jobs with the definite idea of entering into prostitution. Over half of the prostitutes left their homes between the age of 11 and 20 years. The *devadasis* were generally at the age of 13 to 14 years when they joined prostitution. All of them left their homes to join prostitution, but only half of the non-*devadasis* left homes to take up this socially degraded occupation. Nearly 50 per cent of their clients were middle-aged persons, and 70 per cent of them were businessmen. Gujaratis were predominant among them. Two-thirds of them were married, and were satisfied with their routine life. Only 10 per cent of the prostitutes were willing to give up this way of life as they always thought of the difficulties in their rehabilitation.

Thus, prostitution has become a sort of institution which has various forms. It is practised in a hidden way. No law can completely eradicate this social evil. Some tangible improvement can be brought about by effective social reforms and a crusade against this. The upper sections of society encourage prostitution in the form of 'keeps' and 'call girls'. Others visit brothels to meet common prostitutes. The Suppression of Immoral Traffic Act (SITA) has not been very effective so far.

Recently, homosexuality and lesbianism have gained some ground. Though these are not the same as prostitution, because the latter is a commercial activity. Homosexuality between two men or two women is not commercial, and it is by consent of the interacting individuals. However, it is not legal. Some countries have legalised homosexuality. A similar demand has also been made in India.

Conclusion

Social deviance refers to violation of culturally and legally accepted norms and goals. There are no uniform patterns of deviance, as some violations invite serious punishment and ostracisation whereas some involve ordinary crimes, hence light punishment. The motive behind a given offence has been the main criterion in ascertaining the nature and gravity of the crime. There are several causes of crime, but the economic factor is the most compelling one. However, it is not that the poor commit more crimes than the rich. We have discussed various explanations and classifications of crime and criminals and also the nature of crime and delinquency in India.

Social inequalities, socialisation and social circumstances are the most important causes of crime and delinquency in India. About 85 per cent of the total crimes in India are related to property and income. However, a large number of crimes remain unreported due to apathy on the part of the people, and also due to lack of a well-geared administrative machinery to record all criminal activities. Social crimes, like dowry deaths and caste-based discriminations, have acquired alarming proportions in recent years. Legislations to control such crimes have not proved very effective.

Some social welfare organisations have been doing laudable work in making people conscious about their rights and responsibilities. We have discussed the problem of prostitution as a social evil. A number of unlawful and immoral activities have sprung up around this problem.

Exercises

1. Define crime. Distinguish between serious and ordinary crimes. Give suitable examples.
2. What do you understand by a 'criminal gang'? Give a description of the structure and organisation of a criminal gang about whom you have read in newspapers or magazines.
3. Do you think that the economic factor is the most important cause of crime in India?
4. Give the sociological explanation of crime.
5. Define delinquency. Explain the main causes of delinquency in India.
6. Write an essay on crime in India.
7. Write notes on the following:
   (i) Probation
   (ii) Parole
8. Discuss the nature and causes of prostitution. How far have economic factors been responsible for prostitution in India?

Select References

Chandra, Susil, *Sociology of Deviation in India*, New Delhi: Allied Publishers, 1967.

Clinard, Marshall B. and Richard Quinney, *Criminal Behaviour Systems: A Typology*, New York: Holt, Rinehart and Winston, 1967.

Cohen, Albert K., *Delinquent Boys: Culture of the Gang*, New York: The Free Press, 1955.

Durkheim, Emile, *Suicide: A Study in Sociology*, London: Routledge and Kegan Paul, 1952.

Kinsey, Alfred C. et al., *Sexual Behaviour in the Human Male*, Philadelphia: W.B. Saunders, 1948.

—, *Sexual Behaviour in the Human Female*, Philadelphia: W.B. Saunders, 1953.

Lombroso, Cesare, *Crime: Its Causation and Remedies,* Boston: Mass: Little Brown, 1911

Mathur, A.S., and Gupta, R., *Prostitutes and Prostitution,* Agra: Ram Prasad and Sons, 1965.

May, J.M., *The Ecology of Human Disease*, New York: M.D. Publications, 1958.

Merton, Robert K., *Social Theory and Social Structure*, New York: Free Press, 1949.

Punekar, S.D. and Rao, Kamla, *Study of Prostitutes in Bombay,* Bombay: Lalwani Publishers, 1955.

Seth, H., *Juvenile Delinquency in Indian Setting,* Bombay: Popular Prakashan, 1960.

Shukla, K.S., *Adolescent Thieves: A Study in Socio-Cultural Dynamics*, Delhi: Leela Devi Publications, 1979.

Siddique, Ahmad, *Criminology,* Lucknow: Eastern Book Company, 1978.

Sutherland, Edwin H., *Principles of Criminology*, Chicago: Lippincott, 1949.

Throsher, F.M., *The Gang,* Chicago: The University of Chicago Press, 1936.

Whyte, W.F., *Street Corner Society,* Chicago: Chicago University Press, 1943.

15 Population and Society in India

India is the second largest country in terms of size of its population. One-sixth of the world's population lives in India. India is an overpopulated country because the growth of its population is much faster than the rate of its economic development. Unemployment, poverty, migration and slow mobility are mainly due to the lack of balance between population growth and economic development. Though scientific and technological development has brought about significant improvement in life expectancy and health conditions, there has been little success in containing population growth to the required extent. The death rate has come down without a corresponding decrease in the birth rate. Overpopulation has prevented India from attaining the expected level of economic and social development.

A discussion on the theories of population, namely, the ancient, the pre-Malthusian, the Malthusian and the neo-classical and the theory of demographic transition is essential for understanding of the population problem in the developing and less developed countries vis-a-vis in the developed world. The dominant causality in all the theories of population is economic rather than social and cultural. But, in a country like India, social and cultural factors have contributed to overpopulation, despite rampant poverty and unemployment. The national population policy has remained largely ineffective. The enforcement of family planning methods has been sharply criticised and is considered as an interference in personal, social and cultural life. However, the educated and urban middle class people have smaller families than the illiterate, less educated and those people who are engaged in agricultural and blue-collar activities.

Overpopulation and Socio-economic Problems

The problem of overpopulation has created unevenness with regard to migration, employment opportunities, standards of living and styles of life. There has been a noticeable change in the rural-urban ratio. In 1951, the urban population was 17 per cent of the total population, and in 1981 it was 23 per cent. Today, it is nearly 28 per cent. Despite this change, the pressure on agriculture and allied pursuits has not come down. The literacy ratio has been increasing at a slow pace. The sex ratio has decreased from 972 in 1901 to 930 in 1971. It increased slightly to 933 in 2001. This indicates that not only female infant mortality is higher than male infant mortality but also the mortality rate of females in general is higher than that of males. There are some socio-cultural factors which are responsible for providing greater attention and care to male children and male members in a family, particularly among the Hindus. Premium is placed on a male child and the fact is that the male child turns to be the main earning member of the family. However, this myth is being eroded slowly as many girls are taking up jobs and look after their parental families like the male members.

Today, every person is not able to get proper education, medical care, sanitation, health facilities and amenities, social security measures and proper housing. It is also difficult to get gainful employment. There is a lot of unproductive labour in India. There is also a lack of capital-intensive production. Fifty per cent of the net domestic product comes from agriculture and allied economic activities. Only 10 per cent comes from organised industry. However, the process of globalisation has connected the Indian economy with the wider economy. The market in India is changing fast, and its expansion may change both production and export-import trade.

Is India overpopulated? The answer is both yes and no. It is yes because there is a great deal of unemployment and underemployment in India. A sizeable section is below the poverty line. A large number of people do not even get their barest needs fulfilled. There are limited resources and numerous aspirants for them. However, the richer classes and groups do not suffer because of India's overpopulation. They get labour at very low wage rates, and derive even more surpluses. The surpluses are not invested in labour-intensive economic activities.

India is the second largest country in terms of population, but it also has the second largest trained and technically qualified manpower in the world. The developed countries of the world get the maximum advantage of India's scientific manpower. Therefore, there is a 'no' to the question of overpopulation. India has not yet found an effective mechanism of striking a proper balance between population growth and its economic and social development.

Population and Economic Development

Population and development are correlated. It is stated that the size of population, rate of growth and population composition, and its geographical distribution are important factors in determining the requirements of infrastructure, such as education, housing, health services, food supply, etc. Productive health capacity is also determined by the size and growth rate of population. Thus, to make development plans for the present as well as for the future, there is a need to understand the structure and growth of population. A comparison of the developing countries and the more developed countries shows that the birth rate has been high in both categories, but the difference is still quite significant. Table 1 shows the facts in this context.

The developing countries are faced with several contradictions in regard to population growth and economic and social development. For example, the birth rate has largely been static from

1900 to 1970, and the death rate has declined considerably because of the development in scientific and economic fields. Thus, the increase in the population has been phenomenal – almost three times – from 1900 to 1970. The increase in the population of the developed countries has been just nominal. The birth rate has also declined to the extent of nearly 20 per cent. This clearly shows that along with scientific, technological and educational factors, population is a very important variable in economic development.

Table 1

Birth Rates, Death Rates and the Rates of Natural Increase for the Developing and the More Developed Regions of the World, 1900-1970

(rates per 1,000 population)

Period	*Developing Regions*			*More Developed Regions*		
	Birth rate	*Death rate*	*Rate of natural increase*	*Birth rate*	*Death rate*	*Rate of natural increase*
1900-50	41	32	9		19	8
1950-60	43	22	21	22	10	12
1960-70	41	17	24	20	9	11

Source: United Nations, the World Population Situation in 1970 (1971).

Since 1970 we notice a phenomenal change in birth and death rates and rate of natural increase in both developing and more developed countries. In 2002, in the developing countries, birth rate had declined to 24 from 41, and death rate to 8 from 17 per thousand. Natural increase also declined from 24 to 16. The birth rate was also on decline in developing countries as from 20 it slide down to 11. Death rate was nearly stable as it was 9 in 1970 and 10 in 2002. However, natural increase declined to 1 from 10. Thus, the pressure of population is still a vital factor in the developing countries.

Several studies in developing countries have examined correlations between fertility levels in these countries and their social and economic development. These studies indicate that "improving economic and social conditions is not likely to have much impact in bringing down fertility in developing countries until a certain threshold level of development is achieved". Since 1950s, the developing countries have shown their genuine concern for formulating suitable population policies.

Theories of Population

The following theoretical formulations about population have found currency: (1) ancient writings, (2) pre-Malthusian theories, (3) Malthusian theory, (4) neo-classical theories, and (5) theory of demographic transition.

Population problems have been an eternal concern of man. A modern theory of population was proposed by Malthus in the late eighteenth century. His writings generated interests in population and related economic and social issues for the first time. Earlier to the Malthusian view, views about population were more in the nature of conjectures. In the Roman empire, population was considered a source of power. The economic and political advantages of a large population were emphasised in the context of nation-states and mercantile interests. Malthus' theory had its roots in political, economic and social issues which existed during his time. The same can be said of Marxist views on population. The other approaches to population, namely, mathematical, biological, and sociological were formulated in terms of some contemporary interests. The interest in population theories has aroused due to (1) the upsurge of population growth, particularly in the developing countries, and (2) the preoccupation with the problems of development.

Ancient Writings

The ancient Chinese writers observed that mortality increases when food supply is insufficient, that premature marriage makes for high infant mortality rates, that war checks population growth and that costly marriage ceremonies reduce the marriage rate. In China, the doctrines of Confucius regarding family, marriage and procreation were favourable for population increase. The writers of early Greece, especially Plato and Aristotle, referred to the 'optimum' population for city-states. They looked at population mainly in terms of defence, security and government. Plato suggested a population of 5,000 citizens for a city-state as the ideal number. He suggested remedial measures for both underpopulation and overpopulation. The Romans thought of population in terms of the expansion of their empire. They thought of several devices to promote increase in population.

Kautilya, the author of *Arthashastra*, a classic of economics, thought of a large population as a source of political, economic and military power. He thought of a population of 100 to 500 for a village. Traditional Hindu philosophy considered marriage a sacrament. Marriage of a girl before attaining puberty was considered a pious act, hence child marriages have/had been quite common. A girl was given in marriage in the form of *kanyadan*. Procreation was considered a duty, and the birth of a son was considered a necessity for giving *pitradan* to the dead souls. A girl was denied the right of giving *pitradan*, hence, a male child was considered a necessity. Large families were considered an asset for economic pursuits. Later on, joint families were immensely valued in Hindu society.

The Pre-Malthusian Views

Islam inadvertently encouraged population increase by allowing four wives. Child marriage became a part of the Islamic ethos. Even today, Islam does not openly promote measures to check population increase. Only Christianity emphasised celibacy and thought of marriage and reproduction as evils. However, later on, Christianity considered marriage necessary for procreation. Thus, these views were more philosophical, moral and religious rather than the theories of population.

The period of the Renaissance witnessed the emergence of the nation-state, new scientific discoveries, exploration of new territories, rapid growth of trade, dissolution of medieval feudalism, and development of early capitalism, which later on paved a way for Industrial Revolution. The Renaissance contributed to the evolution of economic ideas and thinking on population. These developments took place between the late fifteenth and the late eighteenth centuries. Mercantilism was the dominant school of this period. Population increase was encouraged through large families, early marriage and immigration. It was not a scientific theory of population. This school had two tenets: (1) increase in national wealth by production and export of goods, and (2) rivalry among nations. A sizeable population was required for warfare. Inflation and human exploitation were its two natural consequences. Thus, mercantilism was a policy for obtaining economic and political gains. Because of the overemphasis on population increase, some people foresaw a scarcity of the means of subsistence, and therefore, suggested some checks on population growth.

The Malthusian Theory

Thomas Robert Malthus was the first to develop a consistent and comprehensive theory of population in relation to economic conditions. His first essay on population: "An Essay on the Principle of Population", was published in 1799. Malthus regarded the social institutions of his times as natural and inevitable. He asserted that the pressure of want, the cause of poverty, and the unequal distribution of property were not related to forms of government. He formulated the principle that man could increase his subsistence only in arithmetical progression whereas his numbers tended to increase in geometrical progression. "Population always tended towards the limits set by subsistence, and was contained within those limits by the operation of positive and preventive checks." In the revised version of this essay, Malthus made the following propositions:

1. Population is necessarily limited by the means of subsistence.
2. Population invariably increases where the means of subsistence increase, unless prevented by some very powerful and obvious checks.

3. These and other checks are all resolvable into moral restraint, 'vice', and 'misery'.

Malthus drew two conclusions: (1) with natural increase, population tends to double itself every 25 years, thus increasing in a geometrical progression; and (2) under the most favourable conditions, agricultural production increases each 25 years by an equal quantity, in an arithmetical progression. In general, Malthus assumes diminishing returns from land. There are other checks, which keep population down to the level of subsistence. These checks are the preventive and the positive checks. The preventive checks are voluntary in nature, and include moral restraint, implying deferring of marriage, and 'vice'. The positive checks include epidemics, wars, plague and famine, all manifestations of 'misery'. These checks have operated in all countries with some variations. Only in a few cases population has increased beyond the means of subsistence.

Neo-classical Theories

In the neo-classical period two schools of thought dominated: (1) the classical school of political economy, and (2) the socialists and the Marxists. Both the schools were concerned with the causes and consequences of population changes, particularly with a view to discover the laws related to production, wages, interest, rents and profits. The scholars of this period argued that population growth tended to depress wages and create poverty. J.S. Mill (1830) thought that population control, through flow of goods and services in a given country, would bring down the population pressure. Circumstances checked the growth of population. Technological progress also brought down the population pressure.

The natural or biological theory is that fertility decreases with the increase in density of population. This is known as the theory of optimum population. M.T. Sadler (1830) argued: "The fecundity of human beings under similar circumstances varied inversely as their numbers increase on a given space." By fecundity he meant *the physiological capacity* to conceive and bear living children "A population cannot have high fertility without being highly fecund, but it can be highly fecund without having either a high fertility or a high rate of increase. Thomas Doubleday (1830) observed that "man's increase in numbers was inversely related to his food supply. The better the food supply, the slower the increase in his numbers". Herbert Spencer (1961) thought that with increase in scientific and economic development interest in reproduction tended to decrease.

Karl Marx (1973) observed that when the capitalistic mode of production was replaced by a socialistic mode of production, the population pressure would decrease. The rise in the standard of living would bring down inequalities and result in a decline in both birth and death rates. Moral restraint would also be strong under the new conditions. Marx's view is just opposite to that of Malthus. Marx traces the genesis of the problem of overpopulation to that of the capitalist society.

Alexander Morris Carr-Saunders (1922) felt that man always strived to arrive at an optimum population. He took all the factors including environment, skill and customs into account to attain this number. The optimum number is not fixed for all times. It depends upon the changes that occur in a given country or context. All the methods of putting a check on overpopulation strive at an optimum number that a country can afford.

Theory of Demographic Transition

The theory of demographic transition is based on the historical experience of different societies such as the primitive, the intermediate and the modern. Similar to historical evolution, stages of demographic evolution have also been found. These stages have been ascertained on the basis of different permutations and combinations of birth and death rates. There are, for example: (1) the high stationary stage; (2) the early expanding stage; (3) the late expanding stage; (4) the low stationary stage; and (5) the declining stage. Certain modern forces of development and change are taken into account in understanding of these stages in different countries.

Composition of India's Population

India is the second most populous country in the world, with a population of 1029 million as per the Census of India, 2001. Out of every 100 persons in the world 15 are Indians, that is, every seventh person is an Indian. A total of 16.7 per cent of the world's population lives in India, inhabiting only 2.4 per cent of the total land area of the world. The growth of India's population has been phenomenal compared to that of other countries and particularly in relation to the growth of necessary resources and infrastructure required to meet the pressure of the growing population. From 1971 to 2001, it increased from 548 million to 1029 million. It is two and a half times the population of the whole of Africa. During the decade the growth was equivalent to the half of the population of Canada and the United States. Every year, a whole Malaysia or Australia is added to India's population. Thus, the problem of population growth is really a serious one as the increase in employment opportunities and other resources cannot keep up with increase in population.

Table 2

Growth of Population in India, 1891-2001

Year	*Total population (in millions)*	*Decennial increase during the decade (in millions)*	*Decennial growth rate during the decade (per cent)*
1891	235.9	-	
1901	238.4	2.4	1.0
1911	252.0	13.7	5.7
1921	251.3	-0.7	-0.3
1931	279.0	27.7	11.0
1941	318.7	39.7	14.2
1951	361.1	42.4	13.3
1961	439.2	78.1	21.6
1971	548.2	108.9	24.8
1981	683.3	135.6	24.7
1991	846.3	162.9	23.5
2001	1028.7	182.4	21.5

The Table 2 shows that the growth rate was not so high upto 1921. However, from 1921, there was a steady increase till 1951. From 1951 onwards the growth rate has been increasing at an alarming rate. The pre-1921 period had a high death rate due to plague, malaria, influenza and famine. In post-independence India, health hazards have been considerably curbed, which has resulted in increased population growth. Since 1951, the population of India has nearly tripled. The growth has been higher in the northern zone compared to other areas, particularly the southern states. The density of population has increased from 72 persons per square kilometre in 1901 to 267 persons in 1991 and 325 persons in 2001. The density of population is 13 persons per square kilometre in Arunachal Pradesh, followed by Mizoram. West Bengal had the maximum density, followed by Bihar.

Table 3

Percentage and Growth Rate of Urban and Rural Population

Year	Percentage of distribution		Decadal growth rate	
	Rural	Urban	Rural	Urban
1901	89.2	10.8		
1911	89.7	10.3	6.4	0.3
1921	88.8	11.2	-1.3	8.3
1931	88.0	12.0	9.9	19.1
1941	96.1	13.9	11.8	31.9
1951	82.7	17.3	8.8	41.4
1961	82.0	18.0	20.6	26.4
1971	80.1	19.9	21.8	37.8
1981	76.3	23.7	19.0	46.0
1991	74.3	25.7	20.0	36.5
2001	72.2	27.8	18.1	31.5

It is true that India is predominantly a country of villages (see Table 3). Out of India's total population, 72.2 per cent lived in villages and 27.8 per cent were in urban areas as per 2001 census. This increased to 25.7 per cent in 1991 and further it went up to 27.7 per cent in 2001. However, it is significant to note that the increase in the urban population has been far more than that of rural population. Over 60 per cent of the urban population lived in 216 agglomerations and cities with populations of one lakh and above.

The increase in urban population is mainly due to migration from rural areas, as the cities and towns offer more job opportunities, better amenities and higher standards of living.

Hindus account for 80.5 per cent of the total population and Muslims of 13.4 per cent. Christians are the third major group. Sikhs are mainly concentrated in Punjab. Jains and Buddhists as social groups are more like Hindus. The census provides details based on age, sex, marital status, literacy, occupation, etc.

The sex composition of India's population shows that there are fewer females than males (see Table 4).

Table 4

Sex Ratio

(females per thousand males)

Census year	*Population (in millions)*		*Sex Ratio*
	Males	*Females*	
1901	120.9	117.4	972
1911	128:4	123.7	964
1911	129.5	122.8	955
1931	142.9	135.8	950
1941	163.7	154.7	945
1951	185.5	175.6	946
1961	226.3	212.9	941
1971	284.0	264.1	930
1981	353.3	330.5	935
1991	439.2	407.6	927
2001	532.2	496.5	933

Like the male-female ratio, the age structure of India's population has remained almost stable during the last six decades. The reason is that natural calamities and man-made problems like wars have not affected India's population on any large scale. Nearly 40 per cent of India's population consists of those below 15 years of age and about 5 to 6 per cent of 60 years and above. This shows that nearly half of India's population is dependent upon those who are earners. The dependency of such a large part of the population adversely affects economic and social development. Savings and investments become almost negligible because almost entire income is spent on consumption. Problems of unemployment, migration and mobility are also related to the age composition of India's population.

National Population Policy and Development

India has formulated a system of Five-Year Plans for achieving higher standards of living and better opportunities for its people. With the rapid increase in population, without a corresponding increase in resources, living standards are naturally low. There has not been an effective institutionalised mechanism to reduce birth rate. On the other hand, efforts to bring down death rate have been quite successful. A high rate of population growth is bound to affect adversely the economic progress of the country. Therefore, it is important that government and voluntary agencies take effective measures to check population growth. Family planning measures become immensely important in population growth. Population growth has become a serious problem and a challenge to development in India.

India has adopted family planning measures to bring down birth rate considerably. A Department of Family Planning was created in the Ministry of Health in 1966. Family planning envisages measures motivating people to bring down the birth rate. A comprehensive National Population Policy was evolved in April 1976 and was modified in 1981. The main objective of the policy was to integrate family planning with the planning of socio-economic development of India. Age at marriage was raised from 15 to 18 years for girls and from 18 to 21 years for boys.

The aim of the National Population Policy is to impress upon the people the need for small, planned families for their own good as well as for the well-being of their children. The 20-Point Programme, announced in January 1982, incorporated the Family Welfare Programme. The programme envisages family planning on a voluntary basis as a people's movement. What is needed is inculcation of an awareness among the people through media and oral communication about the significance of a small family norm. Female literacy and education can play a decisive role in bringing down the rate of population growth.

Today, policies of economic development have not been very effective because the increase in production is absorbed by the growth of population. Improvement in conditions of health and hygiene has lowered the death rate. The family planning movement gains national importance in such a situation of imbalance between development and population growth. A strong, purposeful government policy, supported by effective programmes and adequate resources of finance, men and materials, is an essential condition of success.

The following suggestions have been put forward to curb population growth: (1) group acceptance of the small-sized family; (2) personal knowledge about family planning methods; and (3) ready availability of birth control devices and services.

The crux of the population policy is the reduction of the national birth rate irrespective of the social, cultural and economic milieu. Coercing people to adopt family planning methods has not worked. Volition alone, created through awakening, can be an effective measure.

Conclusion

Population and development are correlated in the sense that overpopulation hinders the expected level of development. With limited productive capacity, it is difficult to provide adequate infrastructural facilities for education, housing, health services, food supply, etc. Also, there is bound to be unevenness in a country where there is a lack of fit between the size of its population and its economic development. The formulation and implementation of a suitable population policy has become necessary to control the population upsurge.

A number of social, religious and cultural factors also hinder the implementation of a rational population policy. Since 1951, the population growth in India has been alarming, and this is because the death rate has dropped considerably and the birth rate has not shown a corresponding decline. Family planning devices have been accepted, particularly by the educated white-collar groups. Awareness of the problem of overpopulation is greater among the people with higher education and white-collar employment.

Exercises

1. Bring out the relationship between India's population problem arid its economic development.
2. Is India overpopulated? Discuss.
3. Explain the Malthusian theory of population. Critically examine its relevance for understanding the problem of overpopulation.
4. Briefly discuss the neo-classical themes of population. How far are they an improvement on the Malthusian theory?
5. Write an essay on India's population structure.
6. Analyse India's National Population Policy. Why has it not been as successful in checking population growth as was envisaged by the planners?

Select References

Bose, Ashish Mitra, Ashok Desai, P.B. and Sharma, J.N., *Population in India's Development – 1947-2000*, Delhi: Vikas Publishing House Pvt. Ltd., 1974.

Carr-Saunders, A., *The Population Problem: A Study of Human Evolution*, London: Clarendon, 1922.

Comte, August, *A System of Positive Polity*, J.H. Bridges and F. Harrison (Trans.), 1875-1877, London: Longmans Green.

Davis, Kingsley, *Population of India and Pakistan*, New York: Russell and Russell, 1951.

Hatunen, Hellevi (ed.), *Family and Population*, Helsinki: Publication of Vaestoliito, 1984.

Malthus, Thomas, *An Essay on the Principle of Population*, Penguin Books, 1986.

Marx, Karl, *Grundrisse*, Penguin Books, 1973.

—, *Capital*, Vol. I, London: Lawrence and Wishart, 1970.

Marx, Karl and Engles, Friedrich, *The Holy Family*, Moscow: Foreign Language Publishing House, 1956.

—, *Manifesto of the Communist Party*, New York: International Publishers, 1948.

—, *The German Ideology*, New York: International Publishers, 1970.

Mill, J.S., *August Comte and Positivism*, Ann Arbor: University of Michigan Press, 1961.

Pettersen, William (ed.), *Readings in Population*, Now York: The Macmillan Co. Inc. 1972.

Premi, M.K., Ramanamma, A. and Bambawale, Usha, *An Introduction to Social Demography*, New Delhi: Vikas Publishing House, 1983.

Sadler, M.T., *The Law of Population*, London: John Murray, 1830.

Spencer, Herbert, *The Study of Sociology*, Ann Arbor: The University of Michigan Press, 1961.

Status of Women in India, A Synopsis of the Report of the National Committee, Indian Council of Social Science Research, New Delhi: Allied Publishers, 1975.

The Determinants and Consequences of Population Trends, Vol. I, New York: United Nations, 1973.

16 State and Society

The question is: What is state? Why people obey it? According to one view, the state is an organism, and men are its parts, and therefore, the state is bigger than men. State is real and supreme. The other view is that the state is a machine, an instrument, created by men, and therefore, it is not different from them. Men are real and the state is simply a device. Thus, one view is that man exists for the state, and the second view is that the state exists for man. The fact is that both are complementary to each other, and both have changed from time to time.

The existence of state is justified in terms of the goals which it aims to achieve for its citizens. The state thus exists to promote good life. It provides security, right to life, liberty and property. By obeying laws of the state, men promote their own welfare. Hegel (1977) writes that the state is the divine idea as it exists on earth. He pleads that man derives all his strength from the activities of the state. But, a state for its citizens is not simply an ideal, it is judged in terms of what it does for them. Philosophically speaking, the state is an embodiment to all virtues and perfection, but historically speaking, there are autocratic states on the one hand and liberal and democratic states on the other. There are capitalist and socialist states. The general impression about a state seeks the justification for being a coercive authority.

Nexus between State and Society

Society, state and government are closely related to each other. Society is a web of social relationships. When society and other associations are integrated into one unit, it is called state. The affairs of a state are managed by a body of persons, and this body is known as the government. State possesses a coercive authority, which is legally supreme over any individual or group living in the society. The Indian state, for example, has a territory, government, citizens, associations and organisations. The relationships between the people and various associations are determined by the authority of the state. Harold J. Laski (1956) writes: "The state, then, is a way of organising the collective life of a given society." The government is required to work to achieve the ends for which the state stands for. But, in reality, the distinction between the state and the government is of a heuristic nature. The state depends upon the government and the latter derives its strength from the former.

No doubt, the state is the basis of all legitimate power over its people. It is a power over and above the people. But no state can become so ruthless that its members threaten the existence of the state itself. However, even today, there are states which preach and practise religious and racial orthodoxy of one or other type. There are states which advocate promotion of scientific and economic development in such a way that it benefits some and harms others. The absolutist functioning, religious and racial fundamentalism, and scientific and economic hegemony have been the main causes of protests, movements and revolutions all over the world. The state becomes a class of 'haves' if monopolises economic resources and political power for its own sake or for the sake of a selected few.

The state performs several functions, but the matters such as the law, the police, the army and the navy essentially belong to the state. Bertrand Russell (1980) writes: "The essence of the state is that it is the repository of the collective force of its citizens. This force takes two forms, one internal and one external. The internal form is the law and the police; the external form is the power of waging war, as embodied in the Army and Navy. State is constituted by the combination of all the inhabitants in a certain area using their united forces in accordance with the commands of a government." No state can use force at its command against its citizens without providing convincing justification because of the fear of rebellion. Public opinion can also go against the state itself if it uses force indiscriminately against the people. The people obey the state power because it performs at least two positive functions: (1) the welfare of the whole community; and (2) the maintenance of law and order.

Evolution of State in India

The Indian state has performed at least three functions, namely, (1) collection of taxes, (2) maintenance of bureaucracy, and (3) maintenance of army and police for law and order. These functions have been accomplished by the state right from its inception. The nature of the state can be seen in terms of its historicity as: (1) classical state (having agricultural civilisation), (2) medieval state (characterised by *jagirdari* and *zamindari* systems), (3) colonial state (ruled by the British), and (4) post-independence autonomous state. A 'mix' of idealism and liberal-rationalism has been the characteristic feature of the Indian state. However, the state is the least researched subject. We have witnessed state formation movements, movements for bifurcating the existing states in the Union of India, and controversy about centre-state relations. The Indian state has not resolved some of these issues. There is a hiatus between what has been proclaimed in the Constitution and policies and what has been realised. The state plays a crucial role in structuring of equalities and inequalities. In fact, the state is the most dominant causality in determining the course of social change in India.

The statist mode of production explains the role of state in social transformation, that is, whether the state is socialist or capitalist. The statist mode of production explains dominance of the state over economy and society. The question is: What is the nature of Indian state? Is it a capitalist state? Is there peasant capitalism? Is there bureaucratic capitalism? Is it an oppressive state? Is it a welfare state? The state in India is certain different from what we see today in Pakistan and Nepal. Pakistan has witnessed generally military dictatorship and Nepal has monarchy. Both have undermined democracy and people's welfare. (Nepal has, of late, abolished the monarchy and returned to democracy). Some critics also look at the Indian state as an oppressive agency as they allege that some of the legislations are against common people and the poor. During the emergency (1975-77), several repressive measures were taken by the government. But, the fact is that barring the emergency, democracy has prevailed in India as per its Constitution. State is today the largest employment-generating agency in India. The Indian state is largely a welfare state. But, there are certain contradictions which do not fully justify its socialist and welfare stances.

The evolution of the Indian state can be seen as follows:

1. Individual ownership and cultivation of land;
2. Wage labour, poor, and very rich people;
3. Large state farms, bonded labourers and farm workers;
4. Petty peasant production, small farms and freedom to peasants;
5. Conflict between the peasant and the state on the question of revenue; and
6. Predominance of the interests of the colonial rulers in the system of production.

Various reasons are attributed to these anomalies and contradictions. One of the views is that the state has a vague mission. It does not have capacity to resolve certain conflicts. The other view is that the state is 'soft'. Social and cultural factors are the main obstacles in achieving modernisation for the Indian state. The entrenched castes and institutions do not allow radical transformation of Indian society. Another view is that the Indian state has a silicon character. It has borrowed technology, communication and management systems. The management strategem is seen as solution of its basic problems. There is structural (long-term) crisis in India, and management devices can provide only short-term solutions.

Now, the question is: What has been the nature of change in India? State in India means what is stated in the Constitution in terms of the fundamental rights, the directive principles of policies of state, weaker sections, abolition of caste system and untouchability, etc. In reality, we do not find what is stated in the Constitution. There are structures of unevenness. Uneven development of people and regions has been witnessed. Though efforts to reduce unevenness through Five-Year Plans, public sector enterprises, small-scale industries, land reforms, etc., have been made since independence, but the results are quite far away from the stated goals.

Concept of Welfare State

Welfare state has become an accepted ideology in the modern world. It generally refers to a radical transformation of feudal/laissez faire/capitalist state into a state for the welfare of all of its citizens, particularly the downtrodden. A welfare state draws relevant points of both the laissez faire and the socialist state. It creates a message of hope and inspiration for the underdeveloped nations and for the backward sections of society.

It is said that we have a welfare state in India since independence. Our Constitution guarantees fundamental rights to all the citizens. It provides the directive principles of state policy too. These directive principles indicate that our's is a welfare and socialist state. The preamble to the Constitution of India is a testimony of India being a socialist, secular, democratic and welfare state. A welfare state can be characterised in terms of the following functions:

1. It guarantees individuals and families a minimum income irrespective of market value of their work or property.
2. It narrows the extent of insecurity by enabling individuals and families to meet certain social contingencies.
3. It ensures that all citizens without distinction of status or class are offered the best available social services.

A welfare state takes the responsibility for providing means for achieving minimum standards of health, economic security and civilized living. It ensures a minimum real income for all. Sickness, old age and unemployment are eradicated to a considerable extent. Provision for education is made for all its citizens. Thus, a welfare state is not a police/capitalist state. It removes social evils and promotes welfare of the people.

India as a Welfare State

The Indian state is a welfare state because it performs certain positive functions, it upholds democratic values, and it has accepted a 'mixed economy'. However, this view is not shared by the Marxist theory of the state. According to the Marxist view, the state is a special organ in the historical evolution of mankind. It is born from the division of society into classes and would wither away with the disappearing of the classes. The state is an instrument in the hands of the 'haves', and they use it for maintaining their dominance. The state would not exist if the class domination disappears. Thus, the state is a repressive class-based institution. It is a bourgeois institution. Alternative to this 'oppressive bourgeois state' is the proletarian state. The Indian state has stood the test of a democratic and welfare state in terms of the institutions, namely, Constitution, Five-Year Plans, policies and programmes for the welfare of the weaker sections, mixed economy, adult franchise, democratic decentralisation of power, etc.

Section 31 of the Indian Constitution states that the state shall, in particular, direct its policy towards securing:

1. that the citizens, men and women equally have the right to an adequate means of livelihood;
2. that the ownership and control of the material resources of the community are so distributed as best to subserve the common good;
3. that the operation of the economic system does not result in the concentration of wealth and means of production to the common detriment;

4. that there is equal pay for equal work for both men and women;
5. that the strength and health of workers, men and women, and the tender age of children, are not abused and that citizens are not forced by economic necessity to enter a vocation unsuited to their age and strength; and
6. that childhood and youth are protected against exploitation and against moral and material abandonment.

In pursuance of these objectives the state initiated the policy of mixed economy and programmes for labour welfare, multi-purpose works, projects and cooperatives, higher agricultural production, rehabilitation of refugees, and also inducted a band of personnel to carry out these programmes.

State and Planning in India

Regarding the significance of planning, D.P. Mukerji (1958) writes: "The plan means both a change of the axis of the ideal type of man and society as well as a change of gear." Plan aims at the creation of a new society and a new man. Rationality is the key of planning. Planning seeks an adequate appreciation of new forces and their planned rational utilisation for national development. This could be achieved only by a popular, democratic, socialist and welfare state. The Indian state through planning aims at the creation of the social conditions for a new type of social order and a new type of man in place of the old order and man. The new social order, based on India's Five-Year Plans, can be outlined as follows:

1. The harmonious order.
2. A moving social order.
3. Role of technology in the social order.
4. A raised standard of living.
5. Mixed economy.
6. Equal distribution of opportunities.
7. Comprehensive development.
8. Democratic processes of decision-making.
9. A government with well-equipped administration.
10. A welfare state.

A welfare state generates community feelings, cooperative habits of action, social education and economic and social development. Welfare becomes a way of life, an interplay of non-personal interests. The psychology of building the new social order is the foremost pre-requisite. Today, we have completed nine Five-Year Plans, and the Tenth Plan is already half-way through. The First Five-Year Plan had put more emphasis on agricultural development, whereas the emphasis in the Second Five-Year Plan was on industrial development. The Third Plan envisaged a balanced growth of both agriculture and industry. In the subsequent plans, the emphasis has been put on an overall development of Indian economy, education and programmes for the welfare and uplift of the weaker sections, women, backward regions, etc. Today, planning has become a genuine instrument of economic and social change. The responsibility for formulation of a Five-Year Plan lies with the Planning Commission of India, which is headed by the Prime Minister as its chairman.

Agrarian Development in India

In 1947, when India attained independence, it was in a very bad shape – economically, socially and politically. It was then an under-developed country. Population was rapidly increasing, not commensurate with its agricultural and industrial development. About 30 per cent of India's income comes from the capitalist sector (both public and private), and the remaining from other sources, including the pre-capitalist mode of production relations. The existence of the pre-capitalist relations is a great obstacle in India's economic development. Landlords, moneylenders and *kulaks* are mainly engaged in this obstructive activity. About 65 per cent of the total workforce is engaged in agricultural and allied activities, whereas the remaining 35 per cent in industry, trade, commerce, transport, professions, administration, etc. About 10 per cent of the total workforce is engaged in all types of industry. It is clear that India is not highly industrialised. Little industrialisation, low agricultural output, low level of national per capita income, sluggish economic progress and unemployment are continuing in India since independence.

However, India has made considerable progress in the economic field by encouraging green revolution and industrial growth over the last sixty years. Fertilisers, seeds, technological devices, steel and cement plants, nationalisation of banks, credit facilities, subsidies and loans, opening of the Indian market, computerisation and substantial export-import trade are testimony of India's economic progress. However, it has not been able to ensure desired results by way of 'distributive justice'.

Before the British rule in India there was already a complex system of land tenures. The British recognised some elements of the earlier systems of land tenure, and also created new types of landholders and tenants. A class of zamindars was created to work as intermediaries between the British rulers and actual tillers of the land. The zamindars could be dispossessed by the Raj if they were found failing in the fulfilment of their duties and obligation. The state's right to land was thus protected. The zamindari system created by the British produced a new class which normally supported the Raj. In some parts of India, the mahalwari and rayatwari systems were also introduced.

The land tenure systems, which existed in colonial India, do not exist today anymore. They were abolished in 1950s by the provincial governments. However, legislation on land reforms has not taken into account the vast variability of land tenure systems. The expected 'equalisation' of the landed and the tenant-cultivator has not come about. The zamindars and the rayats were able to consolidate their position due to faulty legislations and their delayed implementation. Despite such obstacles, land reforms have brought about considerable social change in the countryside. Both social and economic change and a new form of consciousness are the net gains of the land reforms. The land reforms consisted of (1) the abolition of intermediaries, (2) fixing of ceiling on landholdings, and (3) reorganisation of agriculture through the consolidation of landholdings and modernisation of agricultural practices and production. The principal agricultural castes have been benefited immensely by the abolition of landlordism in the 1950s and green revolution in the 1960s and 1970s. The small and marginal peasants and landless agricultural workers have, however, not been benefited to a considerable extent.

A number of state-sponsored programmes through various agencies made provisions for better seeds, fertilisers, irrigation facilities, technical know-how, soil conservation, marketing facilities, etc. As a result of the land reforms, about 20 million tenants-at-will were benefited. However, atrocities on the landless labourers persist even today in many parts of the country. Agrarian movements against low wages, exploitation and forced evictions by the landlords have brought about some relief to the rural poor. The green revolution has brought about 'mixed' results – both positive and negative. One view is that the rich have become richer. The other view is that green revolution has helped medium and small farmers also in states like Haryana.

Industrial Development in India

A large number of industries have been established in the post-independence India in private, public and joint sectors. There are a lot of industrial resources and raw materials available in India. Bhilai, Bokaro, Rourkela, Ranchi, Jamshedpur, Renukoot, etc., emerged as major centres during the first one and a half decades of independence. However, later on, industrialisation at medium and small scale was taken up in all the states. The main sectors of industrialisation today are electronics, transport and telecommunication. Compared to advanced countries, there is very little industrialisation in India. About 10 per cent of the total workers are employed in the organised industrial sector. Both private and public sectors have grown side by side since independence. In 1948, it was decided to reserve right of control with the state over coal, steel, aviation, petroleum industries, etc. All other industries were open to private enterprises. In 1956, a resolution was passed under which private capital was allowed to enter into the reserved sectors of industry. A number of top-ranking industrialists were members of the Central Advisory Council and Development Council. The state enterprises and public sector undertakings ran into heavy losses, and this put a question mark on the capabilities of the Indian State and its approaches in managing its own establishment. A debate started on private-public sector partnership and divide. The debated tilted in favour of the private sector. Many of the government enterprises were handed over to private entrepreneurs and industrialists. Privatisation has entered in a selected way in offices and transport sector, including roads, railways and airways. 'Contractualism' is the new slogan today.

Large-scale industries started in the first fifteen years of planning in India. Rate of industrial growth was fluctuating between 2 to 12 per cent. However, we have observed a steady industrial progress after 1967. The enduring factors which have contributed to the growth are vast natural resources, economic surplus, large labour force, high urban concentration, concentration of surplus within a small social group, availability of trained personnel, a stable political structure, powerful means of state economic control, etc. Currently, the growth rate is around 8 per cent. Today, India is one of the top developing countries compared to the countries of Africa and South America. However, production of luxury goods, control of monopolies, sluggish rate of agricultural development, etc., have come as obstacles in industrial development. Despite these factors, investments in private sector have been increasing. Collaborations with industrially advanced countries like the USA, UK, Russia, France, Germany, Italy, Japan, etc., are a clear testimony of India's industrial progress. A boost has been given to the development of small-scale industries too during various plans. India has today a global market. India and China are considered as the fast developing countries.

Role of Public Sector in Development

The First Five-Year Plan clearly envisaged two points: (1) to concentrate on private investment rather than on public investment; and (2) to promote agriculture. Agriculture, irrigation and community development projects received priority in the First Plan. Industry was the last priority. More investment in the industrial field was envisaged in the Second Plan. Emphasis on the socialist stance also demanded public investments in the industrial sector. State capitalism made a sort of beginning around 1956. However, the state accorded fourth priority to the investment in the field of industry. In the Third Plan industrial development received first priority, and the expenditure on agriculture, irrigation and community development received second priority. Transport and communications remained at the third place. Thus, the Third Plan made a real headway in regard to the state-sponsored industrialisation. The subsequent plans, despite some very basic changes in the political situation, have given top priority to industrial, technological and scientific development.

Today, the public sector investments do not occupy an important place in India's economy. Though all major banks and insurance companies were nationalised in 1969 with a view to help the poor to realise country's socialistic goals as stated in the Constitution, but during the past one and a half decades disinvestment in public sector has come down drastically. Private sector has entered into key sectors of our economy.

The privy purses of the princes were also abolished long ago in 1969. The state established a number of consultancy agencies, undertakings and enterprises in the subsequent years in the public sector. General insurance companies, Life Insurance Corporation of India, Steel Authority of India, Engineers India Limited, etc., are only a few examples of the scores of such establishments at the Centre and in the states. Nationalisation of transport was effected. Forest produces were taken over by the state governments. Railways, postal services and telephones were already under the control of the Central government. Several inputs like coal, power, river water were taken in the public sector. Even education was controlled by the state with a view to make it easily available to the common man. Today, sectors like insurance, transport, power, telecommunications and education have been made open to the private sector. For example, maintenance of some highways has been handed over to private bidders. Management of electricity has also been handed over to private agencies. New colleges and universities are coming up in the private sector.

Today, Tatas, Birlas, Ambanis, etc., are no doubt in a dominating position in India. There are also grave complaints against the functioning and utility of the public sector enterprises and establishments. However, the public sector played an important role in Indian economy in the post-independence period, particularly by way of nationalisation of banks and establishment of heavy industries. The public sector definitely set the path of industrialisation and gave hope for self-reliance in regard to technical know-how during the first few decades after independence. Due to the public sector investments, India made a noticeable progress in steel, metallurgy, mining, heavy engineering, and electrical industries. The measure of public investment policy was rapid and self-sustained economic development with 'distributive justice'.

The state in the capacity of an agent of social transformation through public expenditure on development is required to function as owner of resources and establishments, as a banker for investing finances through public sector corporations and undertakings, and as manager of the public sector establishments. The state combines all the three roles in one in terms of its responsibility and accountability. This triple alliance of owner, banker and manager facilitates coordination and proper communication in executing the public sector plans and proposals. But, the state is not a concrete private individual like an industrialist. It is an institution, an abstraction. Public sector bureaucracy, manpower and the local situation, where the investment is made, are some of the important variables which affect the functioning of the public sector. Intervention by political parties and trade unions at times becomes a bottleneck. However, the public sector has become a fact of India's economic life. The poor feel that they could get their due only through the public sector. People have accorded an acceptance to the state-sponsored economic programmes. The private sector has come up because of weak management of the public sector enterprises by the departments of the government and public sector undertakings.

Social Reforms and the Indian State

India has adopted the democratic socialist path for its development and progress. The Constitution of India, which came into being on 26 January 1950, guarantees fundamental rights to all the citizens of India, ensuring equality, freedom and justice. Besides the fundamental rights, the Constitution also outlines directive principles for state policy with a view to give a socialistic direction to social and economic change in India. Today, there is 'rule of law', all citizens are equal and subject to the jurisdiction of the same authority. People do not enjoy privileges based on their birth, language, religion and ethnic origin. The weaker sections have been provided special facilities for their upliftment. Women are equal with men. All the citizens enjoy the right to vote and contest elections. Privy purses of the ex-princes were abolished in the late sixties. Panchayati Raj was introduced in 1959, and prior to this the Community Development Programmes were started in 1952. Today, Panchayati Raj Institutions (PRIs) enjoy statutory status like the state legislatures and parliament.

Even the British Raj enacted social legislations, particularly to discourage child marriages, *sati*, infanticide, and to encourage widow remarriages, etc. The Government of India passed the Hindu Marriage Act in 1955 and the Hindu Succession Act in 1956. Legislation was also passed to discourage child labour. There is now stringent legislation against the institution of dowry. According to the Constitution of India, untouchability is an offence. There is also legislation to ensure fair wages to wage earners.

Despite these and several other positive developments, the poor continue to remain victims of exploitation and suppression by the rich. Dowry continues to remain as a serious social evil. Dowry deaths have increased in the recent years. The upper caste/class landowners continue to exploit the lower caste/class people and commit atrocities on them. Social consciousness is still lacking among the people. The incidence of *sati* in Deorala village of Sikar district in Rajasthan is an eye-opener for the state and the educated people of India. Religion, ethnicity and caste ties are openly appropriated in elections to the village panchayats, state assemblies and parliament. Communalism erupts from time to time in an ugly form shaking the very foundation of the Indian state. Communal riots in Gujarat in 2002 are a glaring example of communal bloodshed. Regionalism also surfaces along with linguism and communalism.

Conclusion

We have discussed the concept and functions of the state in general and the evolution of the state vis-a-vis society in contemporary India in particular. The mode of state-sponsored activities and development explains its role in social transformation. The Indian state is basically a welfare democratic state in terms of its Five-Year Plans, social legislations, allocation of resources and priorities, public sector investments, and policies and programmes for the upliftment of the weaker sections. There are several anomalies and contradictions in the professed policies and their implementation.

Exercises

1. Define state. Discuss its basic functions.
2. Describe the evolution of state in India.
3. Explain the nature and functioning of the state in India.
4. What is a welfare state? Is India a welfare state?
5. Discuss the relationship between the state and planning in India?
6. What are the main features of agrarian change in India since independence?
7. What is the role of public sector in India's industrial development?
8. Analyse the nature of social legislations in India.

Select References

Betielheim, Charles, *India Independent*, London: Mac Gibbon & Kee Limited, 1968.

Desai, A.R., *State and Society in India: Essays in Dissent*, Bombay: Popular Prakashan, 1975.

Hegel, G.W.F., *The Philosophy of Mind*, New York: Harper Colophon, 1967.

—, *The Philosophy of Right*, Oxford: Clarendon Press. 1977.

Kothari, Rajni, *Politics in India*, New Delhi: Orient Longman Ltd., 1970.

Laski, Harold J., *The State: In Theory and Practice*, London: George Allen and Unwin Ltd., 1956.

Mukerji, D.P., *Diversities*, New Delhi: People's Publishing House, 1958.

Russell, Bertrand, *Principles of Social Reconstruction*, London: Unwin Paperbacks, 1980.

Wayper, C.L., *Political Thought*, Bombay: B.I. Publications, 1974.

17 Concepts and Processes of Social Change

The concept of social change is a very broad one. It consists of a constellation of processes of change in human society in terms of place, time and context. Since it is so broad, it is bound to be somewhat imprecise, tentative and value-neutral. Besides the concept of social change, in this chapter, we will also discuss the concepts of evolution, revolution, progress, development, social movements and processes. We will analyse the processes and patterns of social change and mobility in Indian society. Special attention will be paid to the views of Mahatma Gandhi and to his efforts to bring about a non-violent social revolution in Indian society. Gunnar Myrdal's rationalist approach to the understanding of socio-economic development will also be discussed.

The major approaches for studying social change in India are: (1) evolutionary; (2) cultural; and (3) structural. A discussion of these approaches facilitates understanding of the basic structural and cultural hinderances to social change as envisaged in plans and policies. A study of the resources, distributive processes, institutional devices, educational system, land relations, wages and levels of living in terms of time, people and context is necessary for a comprehensive understanding of social change. Along with structural and cultural changes traditional modes of social relations also persist. We will discuss this as a mix of tradition and modernity in Indian society.

Concept of Social Change

Broadly speaking, there are two types of processes: (1) which sustain the social system; and (2) which bring about change *in* the system and change *of* the system. The first processes may be termed as conformity, status quo and continuity. The latter may be called as processes of cultural and structural change. Social change is universal. Its pattern and factors may vary from time to time and from place to place. Change can be seen in terms of the elements of time and history in relation to a given society or social phenomena. MacIver and Page (1967) write in this regard: "Society exists only in time-sequence. It is a being not a process, and changing equilibrium of present relationship." Social change is distinct from cultural or civilisational change. In social change the emphasis is on social relationships.

A social structure is a nexus of relationships. It is sustained by those members who participate in social relationships. Social change means change in social structure. Change in social values, institutions, property relations, economic pursuits, personnel and role distribution may be cited as examples of social change in modern society. Social change is always relative in terms of time, space and economy. In fact, one can compare patterns of change on the basis of these three elements. Resistance to social change is also quite a common feature as change disturbs the ongoing social order and relations. Resistance is registered particularly by those who are adversely affected by processes of social change.

Kingsley Davis (1967) has listed several questions with regard to the understanding of social change. What is the direction of social change? What is the rate of social change? What is the source of social change? What is the cause of social change? Is the cause of social change overwhelmingly deterministic in nature? Can social change be regulated to the desired direction?

All the classical theories of society have grappled with these questions related to social change. Peter L. Berger and Brigitte Berger (1976) state that "the experience of social change is at the very core of sociology as a discipline. Sociology developed as an intellectual response to catalytic social change". The French Revolution, the Civil War in America, the Industrial Revolution in Britain, and the Indian Freedom Movement are examples of rapid transformations of society.

Sociology and the Study of Social Change

Sociology as a discipline would focus on change in society, its social groupings, institutions and behaviour patterns. Two tendencies can be ascertained in situations of upheaval and transformation: (1) to contain the change within certain limits; and (2) to channelise change in a desired direction. The first has been labelled as a conservative perspective, whereas the second is called a progressive or radical view. Berger and Berger (ibid) observe that "in either case, social change presents itself as a problem in a double sense. Social change is an intellectual problem, in that it is a challenge to understanding; social change is also a political problem, in that it demands practical actions". Thus, social change is both an ideology and praxis. There is a need to strike a balance between the two. Max Weber (1970) treats the two as distinct from each other, whereas Karl Marx (1970) believes in the unity of theory and practice.

Auguste Comte (1877), who is known as the father of sociology, predicted the direction that change would take in future. The idea of progress is basic to his evolutionary perspective. He makes a reference to laws of history. The three stages of evolution of society are theological, metaphysical and scientific. In Comte's view, sociology can be understood as a kind of religion of progress, with the sociologist playing the role of priest. Comte's emphasis is on scientific reason and progress. Herbert Spencer (1961) was another evolutionary-positivist thinker who applied the Darwinian view about the dynamics of evolution to society and changes therein. He writes: "As in the biological sphere, social change too is dominated by the conflicts and adaptations that result in natural selection. The purpose of evolution, biological or social, is the survival of the fittest." Karl Marx (1970) explains social change in terms of the class relationships. Both Spencer and Marx emphasise that conflict and struggle are the forces of history. However, Marx refers to the concept of 'false consciousness' – the consciousness of the people who are unaware of their real social position in society (in relations of production). Marx also predicts the future of society with a more specific emphasis. He visualises the emergence of a capitalist society, class struggle between the bourgeoisie and the proletariat, and the overthrow of the capitalist system.

Social Change as a Process

In academic parlance, the term 'change' is considered natural. It implies that the object to which it is applied becomes different with time. According to this view, social change suggests no law, no theory, no direction, and no continuity. The idea of continuity is introduced when we refer to social change as a process. A process means a continuous change taking place in a definite manner through the operation of forces present from the very beginning within a situation. Examples of process are communication, socialisation, accommodation, integration, disintegration, competition and conflict.

To study a process, we observe a series of transitions between one state of being and another. The quality of the two stages of the process may not be the same. Nor the same direction is followed. A process may be up or down, forward or backward, towards progression or regression. Thus, a process means movement from one stage to another with a definite direction. Processes are both system-sustaining and system-transforming. A given social system is regenerated through some processes of social change, whereas some other processes may bring about situations of malfunctioning and breakdown. Social processes are a part of social structure and we come across these frequently in system-sustaining and system-changing exercises.

Evolution

Both continuity and direction of change are present in evolution. Evolution is more than 'growth'. Growth explains the quantitative aspect of change but does not specify its direction. Evolution involves something more intrinsic, a change not merely in size but in structure also. The concept of evolution is basic to the views of Comte, Marx, Spencer, Weber, Durkheim and Hobhouse. The notion of social evolution has been taken by most of these classical thinkers from the theories of biological evolution. Spencer draws an analogy between society and organism, and between social and organic growth. Biological evolution is unilinear in nature, hence explains change from a simple stage to a complex one. It is a process of progressive differentiation with increased capabilities, efficiency, and adaptation to the environment. Evolution is an irreversible process. Its direction cannot be reversed to the simple from the complex one.

In the nineteenth century, the human history, as we have pointed out earlier, was seen in evolutionary terms. However, in the beginning of the twentieth century, the theory of cultural evolution was effectively exploded. In recent decades, after a wave of positivism, evolutionalism has flourished again. Multilinear evolutionalism takes into account ramifications of society and culture. Technological innovations have been countered with cultural strains. Cultural uniqueness do not support the idea of universal unilinear evolution advocated by Spencer, Tylor and Morgan in the nineteenth century. Social evolution is essentially multilinear. Social evolution can take many directions. It is also reversible, unlike biological evolution. External factors affect social evolution more than biological evolution.

Social Evolution and Social Structure

Social evolution is an important concept of social change. It explains form and direction of change in a very definite way. Change in Indian society can be gauged in terms of its evolution from the pre-Mughal period to the Mughal, to the British, and now to the post-independence period. In this way, we can see the evolution of laws, technological devices, political institutions, economic infrastructure and values and norms. Social division of labour, based on age, sex, caste, race and occupation, is an example of social evolution. Specialisation itself is a result of social and technological evolution. The mode of production in agriculture and industry is another example of social evolution. Several social and economic institutions have emerged due to advancement in agriculture and industry.

Thus, social evolution is viewed as a phenomenon, in relation to a specific culture. Cultures are distinct entities dividing humanity into different cultural areas, such as tribal, rural and urban. Cultural differences can also be seen in terms of ethnic, linguistic and religious variations. These are, in fact, different modes (cultural) of adaptation. Cultural variation refers to differential adaptation by a culture to its physical environment. The multilinearity of social evolution, however, does not mean that there has not been continuous growth of human knowledge. There has been steady improvement of technology and organisational devices for the management of economic life. The idea of evolution, in terms of slavery, feudalism and capitalism; traditional, transitional and modern societies; stages of economic growth (Rostov), the traditional, the take-off, maturity and high mass consumption; and from tradition to modernity, treats evolution as a unilinear process of change. Even the classical thinkers had the notion of change from tradition to modernity, that is, from mechanical solidarity to organic solidarity (Emile Durkheim), from status to contract (Henry Maine), from community to association (F. Tonnies), etc.

Ronald Fletcher (1969) considers the discipline of sociology evolutionary and developmental in nature. He writes: "Evolution refers essentially to the determinate process of the emergence, continuity, and change of forms in nature and society, which involves the accommodation of their own distinctive (and distinctly transmitted) characteristics to the conditions of their environments." A theory of evolution is a theory concerning the causal factors and interconnections involved in this patterning process. It refers to the origin of the distinguishable forms (species) found in the world, their continuity within their own particular ecological settings, and their internal changes or their proliferation into varieties of new forms within the contexts of new environmental conditions. W.F. Wertheim (1974) believes that the emancipation principle is basic to evolution. The struggle of the underprivileged to achieve at least parity with those possessing exclusive skills and their resulting emancipation from the fetters of domination and ignorance may also produce an advance in general evolution, not only in the sense of levels but also of members.

Revolution

Revolution is an extreme form of change. Since it is not gradual, it is different from evolution. Revolution is also different from concepts such as revolt, rebellion, mutiny, uprising and insurrection. The latter do not have lasting impact upon society. Revolution is different from a revolt or uprising in its magnitude as well as multitude. Revolution is also characterised by irresistibility and irrevocability because a revolution being simply an episodic disturbance highlights this point as follows: "I would suggest that the basic criterion is that a revolution always aims at an overthrow of the existing social order and of the prevalent power structure, whereas all other types of disorder, however, they may be called, lack this aspiration to fundamental change and simply aim to deal a blow at those in authority, or even to depose or physically eliminate them."

It is difficult to make an accurate estimation of the aspirations of the people and their leaders in a given revolutionary situation. Difficulty also arises in measuring the amount of basic change, brought out by revolutionary upheaval. It is also necessary to assess both subjective and objective criteria in a revolution. The subjective ones may be more concerned with the leaders of the revolution, hence, short-lived. Revolts are more guided by subjective considerations. The objective criteria include the magnitude and multitude of basic change, giving a sense of satisfaction to the leaders and the participants in a revolution. However, a sharp line of demarcation between subjective and objective criteria cannot be drawn as both delineate change of the existing social order.

Revolution refers to the actual tendency towards a fundamental change of the existing social order. The English Civil War checked royal absolutism, and promoted the commercially minded big landlords who destroyed peasant society during the eighteenth and early nineteenth centuries. The French Revolution broke the power of the landed elite and provided an alternative way of creating democratic institutions. The American Civil War also broke the power of the landed elite and paved the way for democratic institutions. Thus, revolutions envisage fundamental and enduring changes with the elan of human emancipation.

Revolution and Human Emancipation

Revolution aims at emancipation of man from social, cultural, political and economic bondage. The movements, which aim at restoration or reinforcement of the traditional social order, can be named as counter-revolutions. However, revolutions have also claimed restoration of the old social order as their objective. This certainly does not bring about a basic transformation of the prevalent social order in terms of establishing a new one. Palace revolution can be termed as a counter-revolution. World history is full of such coups.

Revolution really means modernisation and not restoration. Modernisation in the fields of science, technology, industry and agriculture in the nineteenth century created revolutionary situations in Europe. It generated several revolutionary emancipation movements. Thus, the term 'revolution' has positive connotations. However, it may also happen that at times when revolutionary movements aim at revivalism, counter-revolutions (even being reactionary) may be deemed as progressive. Several reform movements in India in the nineteenth century were counter-revolutionary as they aimed at the restoration of traditional values including the study of the Vedas. But, in the then existing situation, these were considered as restorative and new efforts towards change.

Emancipation is not a prime concern of the counter-revolutions. The basic objective of a revolutionary movement is to overthrow a rigid hierarchical system in regard to distribution of economic opportunities, power and privileges. This is not possible through counter-revolution. A revolution is, basically, not a social but a political phenomenon affecting the status quo in terms of power. A counter-revolution does not generally open a perspective to large social groups. It fortifies the political power of social groups that were already very influential within the established political order. Thus, a counter-revolution does not bring about fundamental change. However, the change it creates can be called a structural change.

Gandhi and Social Revolution

Can we envisage a revolution without violence? We have expressions such as 'industrial revolution', 'demographic revolution' 'electronic revolution' or 'computer revolution'. These are only metaphorical expressions. However, they refer to rapid transformation of society in these specific fields. In Czechoslovakia, in 1948, the Meiji Restoration of 1868 in Japan, and the Cultural Revolution in modern China are examples of revolutions in which there was little bloodshed.

Mahatma Gandhi fought against British rule in India, rejecting violence as a matter of principle. He had mass support in carrying out the Civil Disobedience Movement. The question, however, remains whether Gandhi wanted a gradual change or a quick fundamental change in Indian society. It seems, he preferred slow change with the use of non-violent methods. However, he was certainly interested in basic change in Indian society, ensuring emancipation from exploitation and suppression. Gandhi thought of himself as a true revolutionary.

Gandhi had mass support which is unparalleled in the contemporary world. The methods used by Gandhi, such as non-cooperation, civil disobedience and fast unto death, were revolutionary in nature. His purpose was to overthrow the existing social and political order. However, despite the ultimate success achieved by Gandhi in compelling the British rulers to leave India, the Gandhian movement cannot strictly be called revolutionary as it would imply that it achieved a complete overhaul of the social order. The big businessmen and landlords were not affected immediately and directly. The princes, jagirdars and zamindars were allowed to retain property and land under the new legislation, and were paid privy purses (in the case of princes up to 1969) and compensation for relinquishing their estates and jagirs.

Some people have termed this change a 'bourgeois revolution'. A revolution also needs a second revolution to see that the changes envisaged are effected and institutionalised in due course of time. Gandhi did not adopt a legalistic approach, nor his efforts resulted in a true social revolution affecting the propertied class. Gandhi and his followers believed that the landed classes would themselves give up their property in the interest of the poor of the Indian society. Thus, violence is not an indispensable element of revolution, but through non-violent means a fundamental change can be realised only under very specific conditions. Acharya Vinoba Bhave and Jai Prakash Narain followed the Gandhian principle and practice of social change. Bhave carried out the Bhoodan and Gramdan movements, collected land as *dan* and distributed it among the poor. Narain kept himself away from politics except during the last phase of his life. He did not accept any position of power. He gave the idea of 'total revolution' in the 1970s.

Revolution and Social Change

Revolutions produce fundamental changes in social life. Changes in the political structure are foremost as there is an increased participation of the people in political activities. People have more opportunity to reach positions of status and prestige, which was denied to them in the pre-revolutionary regime. In the economic field too, emancipation of the masses from the old strings is expected as a result of revolutionary change. Agrarian reforms in India after independence, particularly in 1950s and early 1960s, attacked the monolithic control of the landlords over agricultural land. The green revolution in some parts of India is also due to effective land reforms.

Finally, revolution produces a sense of human dignity and a transformed mentality among the depressed sections of society. We may note such a psychological change in India among peasants, tenants, landless labourers, SCs, STs and women. They feel more free and emancipated today than in the pre-independence days.

Progress

The idea of progress is rooted in the tradition of social evolution. It, in fact, includes the attributes of rationality, technological advancement, control over forces of nature and resolution of conflict between social groups. Comte (1877) and Spencer (1961) equated the notion of evolution with the idea of social progress. Industrial revolution has contributed a lot to social progress.

Progress refers to a desirable change, to a realisation of the cherished values. When we speak of progress, we imply not merely direction, but direction towards some final goal, some ideal, predetermined destination. When social change occurs in the desired way, it is called progress. Progress is a relative notion as it involves comparison of the present with the past state of affairs. However, evaluation of change is made on a certain common scale. Thus, only relative comparisons can give a fair idea of progress. The criteria of evaluation may be economic and technical achievements, cultural attributes, mental growth, etc. The easiest criteria are those of technical advancement. These include, for example, money economy and a technological system. However, there is a close relationship between technological and cultural or social development. The total amount of energy production in a given society cannot be the sole basis of evaluation of progress. Such a view assumes that cultural progress is secondary to technological change. Change or progress in one area is, in fact, related to and dependent upon the other area. Change is a complex phenomenon.

The evolutionists, like Lewis Morgan and Herbert Spencer, consider every successive stage of human development as progress. Morgan (1984) considers the accumulation of inventions in the realm of technology as the determinant of social progress. Spencer (1961) stresses the growing complexity of organisation, a more elaborate division of labour, and an increase in the size of a society as the main criteria of progress. However, in social terms, progress cannot simply be treated as a phenomenon "from simple to complex". Increasing complexity does not necessarily result in technical progress and higher efficiency. Complexity of caste, joint family and Hinduism have not been conducive to technological progress and social development. On the other hand, urbanisation and industrialisation have reduced the complexities of caste, family and religion by attacking their rigidities.

Criteria of Progress

A rigid division of labour is not necessarily a sign of progress as it may become a hindrance to progress. It reduces adaptability to different tasks and new technical devices because of narrow and extreme specialisation. In a competitive society, progress can be achieved by increased flexibility. The element of ideology is implicit in the notion of progress. We cannot accept the superorganic nature of culture because it implies that technological advance is secondary to cultural forces. It is also not easy to accept supremacy of technological change because cultural change becomes subservient to it. Industrial progress may be noted in a specific society over a period of time. Because there are other accompanying adverse effects of such a progress in the form of slums, exploitation, dehumanisation and exploitation of women and children. Industrial unrest has become a serious problem caused by faulty industrialisation.

One dimension of progress is that once positive gain is achieved, it continues to last. The centres of political power, technological know-how and cultural excellence become stable. This is a unilinear gradualist view, not supported by available historical evidence. Jan Romein (1974) mentions the 'skipping' phenomenon in human history as a general trend. There is evidence of shifting centres of human civilisation or political power. We know about the rise and fall of empires, civilisations, cities and centres of learning. Cyclical change is a widely accepted phenomenon. However, one must also reckon with the fact that a general worldwide trend towards progress has been noticed during the past seventy years and more.

Regression in a country, context or an aspect affects its counterparts elsewhere. Thus, Romein (ibid) puts forward two universally acceptable criteria of progress: (1) technological proficiency, and (2) organisation expediency. Romein adds a third criterion also, that is, evolution is a discontinuous process. Human evolution is, therefore, characterised by the skipping of phases and discontinuity. Romein talks of the 'dialectics of progress', that human history progresses in leaps and bounds. A society, which has achieved a high degree of perfection in a given direction, is not likely to have quick and rapid change again due to complacency and vested interests. Adjustment and stabilisation oppose fundamental change. However, fundamental change would occur where a sense of being underprivileged has become intense and the urge for emancipation has become very strong. In such a situation, resistance to change is weak. Backwardness may act as an advantage in bringing about progress where a rapid advance in wages may act as a brake. This is what Romein calls the 'dialectics of progress'.

Romein's logic does not perhaps apply to the Indian situation. In general, India is considerably behind the countries of Europe, Japan, China and America in the scientific, technological and industrial fields. Within India, backward states, regions and districts have not shown much progress. The better off states and regions have achieved more than the weak ones. The same applies to groups, families and individuals. There is hardly any 'skipping' and 'discontinuity' as observed by Romein. What we find today are substantial cumulative inequalities and concentration of wealth and power in a few hands.

Development

Like the idea of progress, the concept of development refers to a change in the desired direction. The notion of development is a recent phenomenon, whereas the idea of progress dates back to the era of enlightenment and industrial revolution. Development is contextual and relative in nature, whereas progress is considered general and based on rationalistic considerations. Yogendra Singh (1974) refers to development as a strategy of planned social change in a direction which is considered desirable by the members of a society. He writes: "The notion of development may, therefore, differ from society to society based on its socio-cultural background and political and geographical situation." According to Singh, "development is a composite concept". The development of a society includes progress in various fields, including trade, agriculture, industry, education, health, etc. It also includes the welfare of weaker sections, women and children, sick, unemployed, old people and minorities. Various policies and programmes aim at the development of rural and urban people, SCs and SCs, women, agricultural labourers and industrial workers. Thus, development is a value-loaded concept, specific to the socio-cultural and economic needs of a given society, region and people.

L.T. Hobhouse and his associates (1915) added the element of quantification to change. Four criteria of such a change (development) are increases in scale, efficiency, mutuality and freedom. These criteria are basically applicable to the notion of biological evolution. The criterion of scale is thus basic to development, hence development is unilinear. The criterion of social differentiation has also been attributed to development. Development in this way refers to a fuller growth or evolution of a social phenomenon. Man's control over his environment is one such example of development. Besides these general connotations of the idea of development, there are two specific criteria: (1) evolution of society from the primitive or agricultural stage to industrial society; and (2) economic changes. These aspects imply a growth of knowledge and man's increased control over his environment. In this sense, social development is synonymous with social progress.

Myrdal's Views on Development

Gunnar Myrdal, in his study *Asian Drama* (1968), observes that quest for rationality is the basis of development in economic and social fields. Myrdal (1968) means by development – what he calls the 'modernisation ideals'. He writes: "Development means improvement of the host of undesirable conditions in the social system that have perpetuated a state of underdevelopment." Development can be brought about through planning, which is a rationally coordinated system of policy measures.

India has a social system consisting of a great number of conditions that are causally interrelated, where a change in one will cause change in others. Such an interdependence of different parts of the system and conceiving of the system as a totality based on such relationships are the central points of Myrdal's perspective. The change in one condition which brings about a change in other conditions is known as 'circular causation'. Another implication of such an explanation of change is the idea of a 'vicious circle'. Vicious circles are found in the context of poverty, illiteracy, malnutrition, bad health, unemployment, etc. For example, if unemployment is not controlled, all other problems would remain. A proper equilibrium is needed to get out of the vicious circles in various social and economic fields.

Myrdal classifies the conditions of development into six broad categories: (1) output and income; (2) conditions of production; (3) levels of living; (4) attitudes towards life and work; (5) institutions; and (6) policies. The first three refer to economic factors. Categories four and five represent the non-economic ones. Category six is a mixture of the first three and the latter two. The interdependence of these categories does not imply the precedence of any one category over the others.

Myrdal is a strong advocate of the institutional approach to social change and development. His emphasis is on the understanding of the people's desire for development or of the articulate ones from amongst them. The desire for development includes changes in institutions, attitudes towards life and work (for example, the theory of 'karma'), levels of living, conditions of production, productivity and income. In a way, all these conditions are social. An upward change in any one of these conditions implies, according to Myrdal, an upward movement of other conditions, and hence of the whole system. However, a change may take place in other conditions independently, or it could affect the one which has already affected them. Thus, the independent value of change as well as the ability of change in one condition to effect change in other conditions are basic to the conception of causal interdependence in development.

Development has acquired currency in India as a very significant concept of change in a desired direction. Community Development Programmes were launched in 1952 for achieving an all-round development of the countryside. The concept of rural development has become popular at the governmental level because of various schemes, including the Integrated Rural Development Programme (IRDP). We hear a lot about the role of women in development. The development of women, weaker sections, economy, polity, and cultural institutions congenial to national integration has been receiving priority from the Government of India. There are policies and programmes for the development of industry and agriculture. Besides economic development, new political and social institutions responsive to economic progress have also been promoted. Development is, in fact, a composite phenomenon as it covers all aspects of human life.

Social Movements

Society in India has been highly stratified in terms of caste, class, ethnicity, religion, language, region, etc. Social and economic inequalities are deep-seated. Rigidity of norms in regard to intergroup relations, marriage, religious and ritual observances still exists despite six decades of independence. The history of India is full of social movements launched against the structural and cultural barriers which prevented people from moving up or in their desired directions. Social movements generally aim at achieving an egalitarian social structure. However, there are also counter-social movements, which resist such efforts and do whatever is possible to maintain the status quo.

Social movements have an elaborate ideology, which has the aim of re-making socio-economic and political arrangements. The programmes of social movements are based on the aim of restructuring of society. We may define a social movement as a collective effort to transform some established sets of social relations. Movements are never a continuous phenomenon as they are directed against some very specific unbearable aspects or functioning of society under the direction of a significant segment of the population.

At times, social movements may be reformative, and at other times, they may be religious or revolutionary in the same society or region. There may be a phase (even a long one) when no significant movements take place in a given society. However, a movement brings into sharp focus some basic issues which need a change or re-channelling. In fact, a movement requires two things: (1) a minimum degree of organisation, and (2) a commitment to change.

At a given point of time social and cultural forces are used by an organisation to achieve some desired goals. These goals may include socio-cultural reforms, which, for example, are not permitted by upper castes and dominant socio-economic groups. Movements could be against the exploiters, landlords, industrialists, foreigners and upper castes. They could be launched by the exploited tenants, industrial workers, natives and lower castes displaced persons, respectively. In India, movements by women, students, SCs, STs and the peasantry have acquired a special significance in the post-independence period as these classes were deprived of certain basic rights in the British period, and have remained substantially non-beneficiaries of the gains of development. The Constitution of India and subsequent legislative measures have given them some hopes for their upliftment. Today, they have aspirations which urge them to equate themselves with the privileged sections of Indian society.

Yogendra Singh (1978) writes: "Social movement is a process of collective mobilisation of people in a society in an organised manner under an individual or collective leadership in order to realise an ideologically defined social purpose". According to Singh, social movements are characterised by a specific goal which has a collective significance, ideological interpretation of the collective goal, a rank of committed workers and a strong leadership. Social movements have a life cycle of their own – origin, maturity and culmination.

Movements also transform themselves by changing from one goal to another. For example, in Jharkhand, an organisation named as the Unnati Samaj was formed in 1912 to undertake socio-cultural reforms among the tribes of Bihar. In 1938, the Unnati Samaj transformed itself from a socio-cultural entity to a semi-political organisation and renamed itself as the Adivasi Maha Sabha. The same organisation further transformed itself into a full-fledged political organisation in 1950 and rechristened itself as the Jharkhand Party, with the goal of forming a separate state for the adivasis (tribals) of the Jharkhand region.

Classification of Social Movements

There are innumerable movements, and therefore it is difficult to provide a precise classification of social movements. The most well-known categories of social movements are: (1) reformative; (2) religious; (3) sectarian; (4) sectional; (5) secular; (6) political; and (7) revolutionary. The reformative movements include, for example, the Arya Samaj, the Brahmo Samaj and the Prarthana Samaj movements. The religious movements include the SNDP movement in the South and the Akali movement in the Punjab. The sectarian movements include, for example, the Lingayat movement in Karnataka or the Sri Vaishanava movement in the north-east. Sectional movements include the movements organised by students, women, backward classes, SCs and STs and those launched by the minority groups, lower castes and other specific categories of people.

When the emphasis in a social movement is on the change of socio-economic and political conditions of the entire society or a part of it, it can be called a secular movement. Secular social movements would involve participation of several classes and categories of people. Political or ideological movements are generally launched by specific political groups and parties.

However, struggles for freedom against colonialism and foreign rule have involved all the major political groups and parties. The war of independence in America, the French Revolution and the Chinese revolution are some of the examples of revolution. All of them had the common goal of independence.

Considerations in the Study of Social Movements

How does one study social movements? T.K. Oommen (1977) suggests that "an adequate framework for the study of social movements should take into account the historicity, the elements of present social structure and the future vision of the society in which they originate and operate". Thus, a social movement involves the past, the present and the envisioned future. Besides Oommen (1977), P.N. Mukherji (1997) also observes that a study of social movements implies a study of social structure as movements originate from the contradictions, which, in turn, emanate from social structure, and social movements tend to bring about change in the social structure.

Thus, social movements are not accidental or superficially manipulated devices of social change. Political parties and groups are generally involved in organising a movement, mobilising people, and articulating the goals of a given social movement. Movements, by definition, are forces against the status quo. Oommen states that all social movements centre around three factors: (1) locality, (2) issues, and (3) social categories. Place, problems and the people, who suffer from the problems, are taken into account while making a mention of these factors.

We have recently witnessed state formation and autonomy movements launched by regional parties and organisations. A study of these movements in relation to culture, language, religion, ethnic composition, economic development and aspirations of the people in the various regions and states could reveal the nature of the congruity or lack of it between national goals and regional and local situation. The formation of the states of Jharkhand, Chhatisgarh and Uttranchal evidences fulfilment of the aspirations of the people in Bihar, Madhya Pradesh and Uttar Pradesh, respectively.

Some Major Processes of Social Change in India

We have, in a general way, discussed the concepts of social change, evolution, revolution, progress, development and social movements. We have cited examples from our experience of Indian society to illustrate a particular point of view. Now, we would give a wholesome treatment to the processes of social change in India. Yogendra Singh's book *Modernization of Indian Tradition* (1973) and his essay on the concepts and theories of social changes (1974) are adequate sources to get acquainted with the major processes of social change in India. Singh classifies approaches to social change as follows: (1) evolutionary approaches; (2) cultural approaches: sanskritisation, westernisation, little and great traditions and multiple traditions; and (3) structural approaches: differentiation and mobility analysis; and (4) dialectical-historical approach. The classification is purely heuristic and represents the dominant theoretical and conceptual orientations.

Evolutionary Approaches

The evolutionary approaches analyse the stages through which the institutions like caste, family, marriage and kinship and village community moved in India. The British enthnographers in particular emphasized the study of caste in terms of its racial composition and origin. Caste was also compared with analogous institutions elsewhere in terms of racial, occupational, ethnic and other socio-cultural criteria. The origin of caste was speculated to be based on the descriptions in myths, epics, history and oral traditions. Sir Henry Maine's study of the Indian village community and Baden-Powell's study of land tenure systems were also influenced by the evolutionary-comparative perspective. The Indian village was compared with its western counterpart to ascertain its growth. For example, the evolutionary view is explicit when it was stated that communal ownership was transformed into joint sharing and single landlord ownership.

The assumption that social institutions in India were at a lower level of evolution than in the west was opposed by several scholars.

The studies of social change based on the evolutionary-comparative perspective were followed by a functional approach to social structure and change. The studies conducted with the functionalist method were based on empirical investigations of micro social structures. These studies, in fact, lacked historical focus. Emphasis in the functional approach is on the study of interdependence of different parts of society assuming that one part is dependent upon another part(s), and such a relationship is positive and functional for the entire system.

Cultural Approaches

Sanskritisation

M.N. Srinivas (1966) explains the process of social change in India through the two concepts of 'sanskritisation' and 'westernisation'. Srinivas defines sanskritisation "as the process by which a low caste or tribe or other group takes over the customs, rituals, beliefs, ideology and style of life of a high and, in particular, a 'twice-born' (*dwija*) caste". Thus, the lower caste people imitate the life-ways of the upper castes with a view to improve their status within the framework of caste. Yogendra Singh, while commenting on the concept of sanskritisation, states that it has two connotations: (1) historical, and (2) contextual. In the historical context, sanskritisation has been a process of social mobility throughout the history of Indian society. In the contextual context, it is a process of change in a relative sense. The magnitude of the process varies from region to region or even from village to village, depending upon the factors internal to the context and also upon the factors external to it. The processes of 'de-sanskritisation' and 'tribalisation' due to local factors have been noted in some parts. Certainly, the process of sanskritisation is to some extent the resuit of the socio-economic and political deprivations of some sections of Indian society. It also points to the privileged position of those caste groups which become referents for sanskritisation. One can say that sanskritisation amounts to be an attack on the 'dominant castes'. Srinivas defines 'dominant castes' in terms of economic, ritual and social status of the people at village level. The numerical strength of a caste group and its political power may, at times, add to caste dominance. Some caste groups are also dominant at sub-regional and regional levels. However, the dominant castes have changed their strategies of perpetuating their dominance in the local context. Today, the dominant castes have been adopting those ways and means, which are beyond an easy access of the lower caste groups.

The concept of sanskritisation suffers from several limitations. It explains only socio-cultural mobility and that too in a very limited way. The lower caste people are generally able to adopt the cultural practices of the upper castes, and these practices no longer remain a source of strength and status for the upper castes. Srinivas initially thought of sanskritisation in terms of 'Brahmanisation', but later on it was brought out in several studies that the lower castes imitated the life-ways of several groups who were not necessarily Brahmanas. In fact, sanskritisation depends upon resource availability, mobilisation and accessibility at the level of the lower castes. The sanskritising castes may even face a threat or challenge from the dominant castes. Sanskritisation has also been found in economic and political arenas. The fact is that even cultural mobility of a lower caste becomes a source of power for it. Yogendra Singh (ibid) also hints that sanskritisation may result in strains on the social system. Srinivas thinks of 'positional changes' as a result of the process of sanskritisation. Positional changes are within the caste system and not of the system. Caste does not change, changes take place within the caste system. Horizontal changes are, in fact, positional changes. Slight improvements, by using channels of social mobility, have occurred quite often in the post-independence period.

Westernisation

Westernisation refers to changes brought about as a consequence of the contact with western culture, particularly with the British. According to Srinivas (1966), various upper castes adopted the cultural styles of the British. Besides cultural imitation, many people have absorbed western science, technology, education, ideology and values. The values of humanitarianism and rationalism are basic to the concept of westernisation. Srinivas does not find these two values in the concept of 'modernisation', hence his preference for the concept of westernisation. However, the point that the 150 years of British rule in India inculcated the values of humanitarianism and rationalism is not historically substantiated. In fact, the British did everything to perpetuate their rule in India, including giving communal awards, communal electorates, ruining India's economy, and putting one caste or group against other through its policy of "divide and rule".

Srinivas (ibid.) refers to three levels of westernisation: (1) primary, (2) secondary, and (3) tertiary. The primary level refers to those people who came directly into contact with the British; the secondary level includes those who were directly benefited from the people who were at the primary level; and at the tertiary level are the people who were remotely benefited by the process of westernisation.

Westernisation created new status cleavages and distinctions and did not do away with the existing ones. Both sanskritisation and westernisation are processes of cultural change. Srinivas analyses them as if these two could encompass the totality of social change. Basic structural changes in agriculture, industry and polity, and the changing relations between the rich and the poor, the landlord and the tenant, the dominant and the weak have remained outside the purview of Srinivas' culturological perspective.

Little and Great and Multiple Traditions

Robert Redfield (1956) considers the social organisation of tradition as the basis of analysis of social and cultural changes. The civilisation of India is primary or indigenous in nature. It has not been much affected by heterogenetic factors of social change. The primary civilisation of India is divided into (1) the little tradition, and (2) the great tradition. While the little tradition refers to the folk or unlettered peasants, the great tradition includes the elite or the reflective few. There is constant interaction between the little and the great traditions. Logically, there is a constant flow of ideas and transaction of social relations between the folk and the elite.

The unity of India's primary civilisation is maintained by the interaction between these two traditions through the processes of universalisation and parochialisation. McKim Marriott (1955), the proponent of this view; writes: "Universalisation refers to the spread of the elements of the little traditions which may also become a part of the sanskritic or great tradition. Parochialisation refers to the filtering down of the elements of the great tradition to the unlettered folk." These processes of spread – upward and downward – explain the nature of interaction between the little and the great traditions.

Marriott's approach is also narrow in scope as it takes into account only cultural phenomena and their cognitive dimension. It is an effort to understand structure through culture. The little tradition is equated with the folk (the little people) and the great tradition is of the elite, the literate (the sanskritic people). Such an implication is quite dangerous as it means dehumanisation of the unlettered folk and glorification of those who have access to the sanskritic tradition and literature. Besides this dangerous implication, a dichotomy at the cultural level does not automatically correspond to a dichotomy between the people at social and structural level. The nature of interaction between the privileged and the suppressed is not as simple as we notice between the great and the little traditions.

S.C. Dube (1990) is of the view that a dichotomy of the traditions is not adequate to explain the complex nature of India's structure of traditions. He refers to a hierarchy of traditions. Dube is also critical of the concepts of sanskritisation and dominant caste. In fact, corporate mobility envisaged by the concept of sanskritisation seems to be unrealistic to Dube. While criticising the dichotomy of traditions, he mentions a six-fold classification of traditions in India. These are: (1) the classical tradition, (2) the emergent national tradition, (3) the regional tradition, (4) the local tradition, (5) the western tradition, and (6) the local sub-cultural traditions of social groups. Yogendra Singh (1973) observes that this classification is also ad hoc like the concept of sanskritisation. It is heuristic. Dube also emphasizes on culture rather than structure.

Structural Approaches

Structural analysis identifies independent causal variables to understand social change. The units of study are not ideas, norms and values, but the focus is on roles and statuses, and groups and categories of people. The hierarchy of groups, asymmetry of social relations, uneven distribution of societal goods, etc., compel the formulation of new rules and regulations, emergence of new structures and transformation of the existing ones. Structural analysis of social change takes into consideration concrete elements as focal points of study. Before independence, the princes, jagirdars and zamindars controlled land and other resources. With the abolition of these systems of governance and land tenure, some structural changes have occurred. The traditional asymmetry no more exists. The tenants own land, and the ex-landlords are seen toiling with their ex-tenants. Structural changes are also due to green revolution, means of transport, adult franchise, development programmes and decentralisation of power at the local level.

Structural differentiation and social mobility have occurred in regard to family, caste, power structure and landownership. Norms, obligations, roles, functions and statuses have changed considerably in the structural units. Group mobility has become negligible. Families and individuals, independent of their castes, have moved up in economic and political fields. They have acquired dominance and power. Factionalism within caste and village has become a fact of life. Occupational mobility and migration are pronounced. Education has also contributed to these developments. Family is today functionally joint to a large extent, but structurally it is nuclear. Caste is becoming increasingly an interest group of the articulate few from among the members of a caste. In the countryside, intermediate peasant castes have gained strength economically and politically. They are holding positions of power and influence in panchayats and legislatures. Conflict between the upper and the intermediate castes (backward castes) has suddenly increased after independence, particularly in Bihar, Uttar Pradesh and Karnataka. Conflict between the dominant peasant castes and SCs has also increased in several states due to structural change in their respective positions.

Dialectical-Historical Approach

Karl Marx and Friedrich Engels are the main architects of the dialectical-historical approach. The four phases of social change in there scheme are: the Asiatic, the ancient, the feudal and the modern bourgeoisie as modes of production. Initially, Karl Marx thought of India as a static, historical and primeval social formation. But, it was wrong to think of India as fixed and stationary. Marx revised his view later on. According to Yogendra Singh (1973), Marx mentioned five stages in social differentiation: (1) the tribal community with undivided land and agriculture in common; (2) disintegration of the tribal community and its transformation into family communities with loosening of common property; (3) shares fixed by inheritance rights or the degree of kinship, thus creating inequality (tribal wars further increased this inequality); (4) transformation of inequality based on kinship into inequality based on possession as expressed by actual cultivation; and (5) a system of periodic distribution of communal land.

Studies of social change in India with the Marxist perspective have analysed caste and politics, modes of production, class relations, and access to resources and opportunities. D.P. Mukerji (1958) applied the Marxist approach with certain modifications to the study of social change. In analysing the emergence of the new class structure he found the role of the Indian tradition immensely useful. The Indian tradition is both a resilient and an adaptive cultural force. Tradition is a conserving force; it brings about adjustment by easing tension and conflict.

A.R. Desai (1966), while analysing the social background of nationalism in India, finds the Marxist approach quite appropriate and fruitful. Class-based inequalities and contradictions, according to Desai, determine the nature of social change and development. The emergence of nationalism in India is the product of the material conditions created by British colonialism.

The essence of the Marxist and the neo-Marxist views on social change is evolutionary change in human society with class and class contradictions as focal points of observation. Domination and subjugation, rich and poor, powerful and weak people (groups, societies and nations) are the main dichotomies in Marxian studies. The capitalistic world has produced social relations in this form.

Louis Dumont (1970), while advocating the cognitive-historical approach, emphasizes on change as adaptive or transformative process in the traditional ideo-structure. Cultural or ideational change is a precondition to bring about change in social structure. Another approach to social change has been suggested by Gunnar Myrdal (1968). Myrdal's institutional approach highlights the non-economic factors as obstacles in economic development. He observes that the attitudes towards life, work and institutions must be changed to ensure economic development in the desired direction.

Today, the studies of social change need to make a sharp turn towards the understanding of some very basic aspects of society, namely, nature of resources, distributive processes, creation of new infrastructures and institutional mechanisms, educational system, polity, state, land relations, mechanisms of exploitation, wages and levels of living. With a comparative focus considering time, people and context, it is necessary to know at what levels social change and mobility are taking place. Bourgeoisification and proletarianisation as processes of structural change, downward and upward mobility, migration and education need to be studied on a priority basis. A study of these aspects is more important than that of pollution-purity, commensality and connubiality.

Yogendra Singh (1973) has attempted an 'integrated approach' to analyse social change in India. His emphasis is on the sources of change, cultural structure (little and great traditions) and social structure (micro-structure and macro-structure). Singh analyses heterogenetic changes at the level of cultural structure. Islamisation and primary westernisation (little tradition) and secondary Islamic impact and secondary westernisation or modernisation (great tradition) are discussed at the cultural level. At the level of social structure, role differentiation, new legitimation at the micro level, and political innovations, new structures of elite, bureaucracy and industry at the macro level are important aspects.

At the level of cultural structure, sanskritisation or traditionalisation (little tradition) and cultural renaissance (great tradition) are referred to as orthogenetic changes. At the level of social structure, pattern, recurrence, compulsive migration or population shift at the micro level, and elite circulation, succession of kings, rise and fall of cities and trade centres at the macrolevel are the main aspects of structural studies. Singh explains causation of social change within and without the social system or the tradition. His integrated view strives at a balance between the sources of changes, cultural and social structures and within them between micro and macro levels of actual social change.

Before we close up, a reference to a nebulous and ad hoc concept of 'globalisation' may be made. Globalisation implies literally a boundaryless world, allowing free movement of people, goods and services. Such a situation of the world market has become possible after disintegration the USSR and the East Europe and liberalisation of Communism in China. The developed countries, particularly the USA, have assumed leadership of the globalisation movement by forging change in the Communist countries including Russia and China. Now, America is invading markets of these countries, particularly China and India, and outsourcing their trained manpower for the American market and industry. Such a process affected the indigenous production, consumption patterns and markets. It has created a new middle class of consumers with high salaries and perks. At the moment, only a small section of our society is associated with this process.

Conclusion

Conformity and change are universal phenomena. Change *in* the system and change *of* the system are also universally observed, but change of the system is a rare occurrence. However, change in the system is continuous and existent in almost all societies at all times. Change is a broad concept. It includes both progression and regression. Evolution, revolution, development, progress and social movements all can be called as the concepts of social change. A study of social change takes into consideration causes and consequences, their nature and differential impact on various sections of society.

We have discussed various approaches to understand structural and cultural change. Our analysis shows that cultural change has been over-emphasized, and several areas in which structural change has occurred, have been left out. A study of continuity of traditional forms of social inequality, emergence of new inequalities, and the interaction between the two could explain the nature of resources and their distributive mechanisms in Indian society.

Exercises

1. Define social change. Distinguish it from the concept of social process.
2. Discuss the concept of evolution. Differentiate between unilinear and multilinear evolution.
3. Name some prominent advocates of the evolutionary approach in social sciences.
4. Attempt a definition of the notion of revolution. Give concrete examples of revolution and counter-revolution from the contemporary world.
5. Was the Gandhian movement revolutionary?
6. In what way are evolution and revolution both processes of man's emancipation from bondage and exploitation?
7. Write a note on the notion of 'progress'. Is it a value-loaded concept?
8. What are Jan Romein's criteria of progress? Explain his concepts of 'skipping' and 'dialectics of progress'.
9. "Development is a composite concept." Discuss.

10. Bring out the relationship between social structure and development.
11. What is Gunnar Myrdal's perspective of development?
12. What are the main attributes of a social movement? How is a social movement different from social change?
13. Give a suitable classification of social movements. Draw illustrations from the recent movements launched in India.
14. Write an essay on the major approaches to the study of social change in India.
15. Explain the following:
    (i) Sanskritisation
    (ii) Westernisation
    (iii) Dominant caste
    (iv) Modernisation
    (v) Little and great traditions
    (vi) Universalisation and parochialisation
16. Write notes on the contributions of the following to the study of social change:
    (i) M.N. Srinivas
    (ii) S.C. Dube
    (iii) Yogendra Singh
    (iv) A.R. Desai

Select References

Berger, Peter L. and Berger Brigitte, *Sociology: A Biographical Approach*, Penguin Books, 1976.

Bottomore, T.B., *Sociology*, London: George Allen and Unwin Ltd., 1964.

Comte, August, *A System of Positive Polity*, J.H. Bridges & F. Harrison (Trans.), London: Longmans, Green, 1877.

Davis, Kingsley, *Human Society*, New York: The Macmillan Co., 1967.

Desai, A.R., *Social Background of Indian Nationalism*, Bombay: Popular Prakashan, 1966.

Dube, S.C., *Tradition and Development*, Delhi: Vikas Publishing House, 1990.

Dumont, Louis, *Homo Hierarchicus*, London: Paladin Granda Pub. Ltd., 1970.

Fletcher, Ronald, 1969, "Frederic Le Play", in Timothy Raison (ed.), *The Founding Fathers of Social Science*, Penguin Books.

Hobhouse, L.T., Wheeler, G.C. and Ginsberg, M., *The Material Culture and Social Institutions of the Simpler Peoples*, London: Chapman & Hall, 1915.

MacIver, R.M. and Page, C.H., *Society*, London: The Macmillan Co., 1967.

Maine, Henry, 1890, *Village Communities in the East and the West*, London: J. Murray.

Marriott, McKim (ed.), *Village India*, Chicago: Chicago University Press, 1955.

Marx, Karl, *Capital*, Vol. I., London: Lawrence & Wishart,1970.

Moore, Wilbert R., *Social Change*, New Delhi: The Prentice-Hall of India Ltd., 1965.

Morgan Lowis, H., See Lucy Mair, *An Introduction to Social Anthropology*, Delhi: Oxford University Press, for various classical references, including that of Lewis H. Morgan, 1984.

Mukerji, D.P., *Diversities*, New Delhi: Peoples Publishing House, 1958.

Mukherjee, Ram Krishna, "Realities of Agrarian Relations in India", *Economic and Political Weekly*, Vol. XVI, No. 4, 1981.

Mukherji, P.N., "Social Movement and Social Change: Towards a Conceptual Clarification and Theoretical Framework", *Sociological Bulletin*, Vol. 26, No. 1, 1977.

Myrdal, Gunnar, *Asian Drama*, 3 Vols., Penguin Books, 1968.

Oommen, T.K., "Sociological Issues in the Analysis of Social Movements in Independent India", *Sociological Bulletin*, Vol. 26, No. 1, 1977.

Redfield, Robert, *Little Community, Peasant Society and Culture*, Chicago: The University of Chicago Press, 1956.

See W.F. Wertheim, *Evolution and Revolution*, Penguin Books, for a detailed discussion on different viewpoints, including that of Jan Romein, 1974.

Sharma, K.L., "Jharkhand Movement in Bihar", *Economic and Political Weekly*, Vol. XL, Nos. 1 & 2, 1976.

Singh, Yogendra, *Modernization of Indian Tradition*, Faridabad: Thomson Press (India) Ltd., 1973.

—, "Concepts and Theories of Social Change", in *A Survey of Research in Sociology and Social Anthropology*, Vol. I, Bombay: Popular Prakashan, 1974.

—, *Social Change* (mimeographed), New Delhi: NCERT, 1978.

Spencer, Herbert, *The Study of Sociology*, Ann Arbor: The University of Chicago Press, 1961.

Srinivas, M.N., *Social Change in Modern India*, Berkeley: California University Press, 1966.

Tonnies, F., *Fundamental Concepts of Sociology*, New York: American Book Co., 1940.

Weber, Max, *The Protestant Ethic and the Spirit of Capitalism*, New York: Scribner's, 1958.

Wertheim, W.F., *Evolution and Revolution*, Penguin Books, 1974.

18 Factors of Social Change

Social change occurs in the structure and culture of a society through internal and external factors. The structure of society refers to infrastructural facilities, their distribution among people, and people's access to them. The culture of society consists of tradition, religion, and norms of living and behaving with each other. Since the structure and culture of a society are static, social change is an inevitable process.

It has been stated in the earlier chapter that the direction of social change can be upward or downward, linear, multilinear or cyclical. Social change can occur in the form of progression or regression. Thus, social change refers to shifts in the structure and culture of a given society. Generally, social change is value-neutral, but sometimes it occurs in the form of ideological expressions of a conservative or a radical nature. Change is also cumulative, particularly in the field of science and technology. Besides being cumulative and evolutionary, change is also a cyclical and curve-like phenomenon.

Since tradition and modernity co-exist, continuity and change are empirical facets of social life. Tradition and continuity co-exist because all societies need a certain amount of stability and social checks. Modernity and change are required to attain new levels of knowledge and technical know-how to meet the changing demands and challenges. It is these conditions which call for social change. Social tensions and conflicts are also sources of social change. Social conflicts are caused by differential values and interests of the old and the young, the educated and the illiterate, the townsmen and the rural folk.

Factors of Social Change

There is no single cause of social conflict and change. The following factors have, however, been mentioned: (1) demographic, (2) technological, (3) economic, (4) cultural, (5) legal and administrative, and (6) political.

Demographic Factors

Gunnar Myrdal (1968) observes that in Europe the changes have taken the form of a 'demographic transition' from high to low rates of both births and deaths, without a very wide gap developing between the two. In the case of Japan, due to late start of change, a gap developed between the two. In South Asia, the trend has been towards a gradually widening gap culminating into a 'demographic explosion'. In India, economic development has not kept pace with the population growth. Improvement in per capita income and standards of living in India will be possible only with a check on the fast growing population. India is not in a position to invest in improvements of its economy because of the high cost of feeding its people. There is a frightening rate of population growth.

Overpopulation results in the problems of unemployment and underemployment, poverty, housing shortage, illiteracy, poor health and crowding of towns and cities as there is an increase in migration from rural to urban areas. Malthusian theory does not apply to the Indian situation because the death rate has come down considerably due to improvement in health conditions. However, there has been much less change in the birth rate.

Technological Factors

Technology brings about significant changes in human society. The Industrial Revolution was a product of new advances in science and technology. Thorstein Veblen (1994) worked out his theory of leisure and the leisure class on the basis of new strides in scientific fields. The class which extracts the maximum surplus due to advancement in the technological field spends conspicuously on consumption items with a view to achieve social recognition. W.F. Obgurn (1964) has propounded the theory of 'cultural lag' to explain the lack of correspondence between technological advancement and social change. Technology changes faster than culture, hence, culture lags behind. However, one view is that such a hiatus does not exist in India. Culture changes faster in India than technology, because the latter is not coming up faster than culture.

Industrialisation and the green revolution are two major processes of change in Indian economy. Along with these changes, we also notice changes in transportation and communication, electrification and irrigation which have changed the village scene to a large extent. New classes and modes of social relations have emerged in the countryside. Industrial townships have brought about a new pattern of class relations. Towns like Jamshedpur, Bhilai, Rourkela, Bokaro, Bhiwandi, and Dharuheda are examples of the process of industrialisation in post-independence India. The cities such as Noida, Gurgaon, Bangalore, Hyderabad and Pune have become centres of computer and software technology. Thousands of engineers and technocrats are working in these cities.

India's industrial development has been slow, particularly in the pre-independence period. The British imposed heavy taxes on traditional Indian goods. The British ruined India's traditional trades and crafts through its commercial policy. Restrictions were imposed upon Indians exporting to the West, while favours were granted to British exporters, who flooded the Indian markets. Even today, only a little more than 10 per cent of the total workforce is engaged in industry. A little more than 6 per cent of the national income comes from the industrial sector. Despite this gloomy picture, India does not lack in industrial resources. A very substantial percentage of the urban population is employed in industry. Iron ore deposits, deposits of limonite, manganese, chromium, gold, gypsum, mica, bauxite, ilmenite and non-ferrous metals are available in substantial quantities. There is encouraging potential for hydroelectric power, engineering, chemical and steel industries. India has made a mark in computer engineering and electronics and information technology. The Indian engineers and managers hold high positions in America and other developed countries.

The industrial development of India began with the introduction of railways in the middle of the nineteenth century. The main railway centres became hubs of industrial development. After 1860, British industrial supremacy was challenged by Germany, America and Japan, and this challenge also encouraged the industrial development of India. Using cheap labour, they managed to defeat foreign competition while bringing in high profits. The British also began to invest by establishing some new industries in India. Charles Bettelheim (1968) observes that "throughout the nineteenth century, a mercantile, moneylending bourgeoisie was taking shape in Indian society, its roots already formed in numerous existing trade centres of varying prosperity".

It is evident that Indian commercial and moneylending capital was partially transformed into industrial capital largely due to change in the British policy. Industrialisation took new strides in the twentieth century. New industries came up in place of the traditional ones. Industrial output increased and the industrial labour force increased manifold. Today, the Indian industrial proletariat is employed mainly in big industrial enterprises. However, big industries are concentrated in a few towns located in some states.

The edifice of modernity has been constructed in India on social, ecological and regional disparities right from the beginning of the British Raj. It was a hierarchical society, and continues to be so in many ways with some transformations in legal, administrative, social and economic fields. Noticeable changes in agriculture took place earlier due to road, railway and canal construction. Today, besides these factors, the green revolution which includes the use of chemical fertilisers, high-yielding seeds, new techniques of irrigating fields, and also the use of tractors and other mechanical devices, has brought about significant changes in India's rural economy.

The British appointed a zamindar with the specific right to get commission on the land revenue he collected for the Raj. The zamindar not only collected land revenue but he also collected charges, fees and a variety of taxes from the people in his 'Mahal' (area of jurisdiction). A new form of local power structure emerged with these zamindars at the top. Below the zamindars were the *raiyats* (proprietory cultivators), who were given the right to cultivate land as permanent tenants and had direct access to the British revenue officials. Sharecroppers, tenants-at-will, agricultural labourers and kamins (servants) were other categories of people who belonged to various caste groups.

Priests and moneylenders were other influential classes, besides the zamindars. Different caste and occupational groups were dependent upon each other through the 'jajmani' system (an arrangement of fulfilling duties and obligations assigned to each caste group). Changes have taken place in India's social, economic and political structure due to legal and administrative reforms, education, industrialisation, green revolution and scientific and technological advancements. Family, caste, village and city have been greatly affected by these changes.

Economic Factors

Karl Marx (1970) is the chief architect of the economic theory of social change. According to him, the mode of production determines social, cultural, religious and political aspects of social life. Marx speaks of change in terms of thesis, antithesis and synthesis as stages of social formation corresponding with feudalism, capitalism and socialism, respectively. Capitalism has emerged because of the contradictions emanating from feudalism. Socialism would emerge from capitalism as a result of class struggle. There are two classes in the capitalistic system, viz., the bourgeoisie and the proletariat. The latter are wage-earners and the former are extractors of surplus. Capitalism might come under severe strain when wage-earners would challenge its hegemony. A revolutionary change alone is the solution for the ills of capitalism.

Intellectuals, leaders and academics have been influenced by the essence of Marxism. The quintessence of the Marxist approach is that material conditions are basic to Indian society, and change in these conditions would automatically bring about corresponding change in other spheres of life. There are two implications of this view: (1) industry and agriculture are interrelated; and (2) agricultural production in India is capitalistic in its form as well as content. In view of these assumptions, what one needs is a scrutiny as to whether there has been structural change in terms of shifting of economic power from one group or class to another; and whether technological devices have further consolidated the traditional inequalities (based on caste, status and landownership) or reduced them considerably.

There are instances of structural change, particularly during the early years of our independence. The jagirdars and zamindars lost their landholdings as a result of the abolition of these systems of land tenure. The tenants were benefited by these reforms, because proprietory rights were granted to them to own the landholdings which were earlier owned by their masters. This change refers to an obverse structural process of change. In the case of landlords, it can be called as proletarianisation, and in the context of tenants it can be referred as bourgeoisiefication. F.G. Bailey (1957) has noted a similar process of change in Orissa. With the abolition of landlordism, the toddy-tappers, who used to supply liquor to their landlords, began selling all their produce in the open market. In a short spell of time, their economic condition improved immensely, and conversely that of the landlords deteriorated. The landlords sold their lands to the toddy-tappers, who had gained substantial purchasing power from the sale of their traditional produce in the open market. This change also marked the end of exploitation of the poor and a beginning of social and economic equality.

In India, one finds a heterogeneity of socio-economic structure and an array of social tensions and conflicts. India is a developing country in which the pre-capitalist social categories co-exist with the capitalist ones. Marx basically thought of the problems of an industrial society, whereas India even today remains pre-eminently an agrarian economy with primeval social formation. India is a highly complex and differentiated society. Differentiation of the peasantry itself provides a very complex picture. The mode of production in agriculture is, to a large extent, semi-feudal, semi-colonial, semi-capitalistic and also non-capitalistic or traditional. Variations are found along with caste and regional ramifications. Family labour is still a stark reality of agriculture in India.

The state, as a welfare agency, has played a significant role in India's economic development. The abolition of traditional systems of land tenure such as zamindari and jagirdari, ceiling on landholdings, promotion of credit cooperative societies and other programmes of economic upliftment are positive indications of the state's policies and programmes. The effects of these policies and programmes and of the green revolution can be seen in the form of a new level of social transformation.

A new form of unevenness has also emerged due to socio-economic development. Caste has transformed itself to adapt to the demands of the new situations. Family cannot remain structurally joint, since family members often do not live at the same place. Family has acquired a 'functional jointness' by helping its members while they remain at different and distant places. The constraints today are such that members of a family cannot generally find jobs at the same place. Thus, change in India is more in the form of transformation rather than replacement. It is more accretive than cumulative.

Cultural Factors

The cultural structure of India includes sanskritic and local traditions. Tradition has been taken as a focal point of study by several scholars, including Robert Redfield, Milton Singer, McKim Marriott, Yogendra Singh, etc. The main argument is that a change in ideas, norms, values, rituals and religious observances is a precondition to bring about basic changes in economic and social relations. Max Weber (1958) finds that the protestant work ethic imbedded in certain elements promotes economic development. On the contrary, Hinduism, because of its emphasis on asceticism, discourages capitalistic economic development. However, recent studies of caste and family have shown that there is nothing negative and regressive in the Hindu ethic to retard or obstruct economic development.

Milton Singer (1972), in his study of entrepreneurs of Madras, shows that caste and joint family have positively contributed to business and entrepreneurship. He finds Gunnar Myrdal's idea of 'obstacles' created by institutional factors in the modernisation of India immaterial due to the resilience of caste, family and Hinduism. Caste has made inroads into politics, elections and government jobs. Members of a family help each other in economic and other pursuits. This has helped them manage their economic and business enterprises better.

M.N. Srinivas (1966) has emphasised on the significance of cultural and caste mobility as a source of social change in India. A caste group can elevate its position by emulating the ideas and practices of a superior caste group or of some of its members. In this process of change the sanskritising castes also discard those traditional callings and practices which have kept them in lower positions for centuries. Education, salaried jobs and migration to towns have also helped the lower caste groups in status elevation. It is also a fact that such efforts were met with protests from the dominant castes as they were taken as a threat to their traditional hegemony. Conflicts between the upper and the lower castes have occurred whenever the lower castes defied their traditional obligations towards the upper caste jajmans and landlords. Besides resistance to these efforts of the lower castes, the upper castes have found alternative bases of social status through westernisation of their lifestyles, higher education, lucrative jobs, migration to cities and entrenchment into politics. The net result is the continuity of social and economic hiatus between various caste and class groups. Cultural mobility, however, has latent potentiality for social change besides creating a psychological awakening among the depressed sections of Indian society.

Legal and Administrative Factors

Law has played an immense role in bringing about social change in Indian society. Indian society is complex and heterogeneous and law can ensure homogeneity and assimilation of divergent sections. Law can bring about radical changes, particularly favouring the lower sections. It can be an instrument of change in political and economic institutions and also in mitigating social evils and reforming the educational system. Knowledge of law can make a man rational and humane by exposing the irrationalities of dogmas and superstitions. Law can attack the age-old dysfunctional institutions. It can bring about rural social transformation, discipline and scientific and rational attitudes.

However, law alone cannot do much without corresponding changes in the structure of society and moral fibre of the people. Public opinion is a stronger means of change. Values cannot be changed by law alone. Law remains an ineffective means of change and control if it affects the poor only and leaves the rich out of its orbit.

Yogendra Singh (1976; 1989) refers to three functions of law: (1) as an indicator of change, (2) as an initiator of change, and (3) as an integrator of change. Law performs an integrative or assimilative function. In India, the legal system is a historical product. It has colonial and feudal roots. Law was elite-sponsored and served the elite strata and the urban middle classes.

The Constitution of India is the monumental instrument of the modern legal system. It incorporates the principles of equality, social justice, freedom and secularism. The Constitution recognises cultural pluralism as a positive phenomenon. However, caste-based inequalities and economic and social backwardness of the people still exist. Despite these positive elements, the Constitution is full of contradictions. For example, it guarantees fundamental rights, but does not include in the fundamental rights the right to work. Thus, what is necessary for the poorer sections of society has not been included in the fundamental rights of the people.

Generally speaking, some lacunae have been found in legislations. In fact, the legal system depends upon the political system for its legitimation. Legislations were formulated for bringing about land reforms in the 1950s, but they were implemented half-heartedly in most of the states of India. Caste and untouchability are illegal, but, in practice, both persist openly or in camera. Provision for seeking divorce exists, but very few women come forward to seek divorce against their cruel husbands. A stringent anti-dowry law exists, but dowry continues to grow in its ugliest form without any check.

A number of legislations related to egalitarian measures have remained ineffective because of inbuilt flaws and indifferences of the law implementors. Despite these limitations, law remains an integrative and corrective measure in Indian society. Efforts are being made to check the problems of black money, tax evasion, and corruption by having stringent laws.

Political Factors

The right to vote in elections, from village panchayat to parliament, has created a great deal of social and political awakening since independence. Both men and women have participated in general elections and elections for village panchayats and municipal bodies. As a result of these elections, one finds administrative and political linkages between the village, block, district, state and centre. These linkages are also found in regard to political parties and their leadership. Political parties have not only been working for winning elections, they have also taken up issues of national interest and ideological nature.

Sometimes one feels that everything is patterned on party lines in towns and villages. Castes, communities, specific issues and problems are looked at from the point of view of a given political party. Factions and cleavages are formed on party lines. Ideological divides are also found within political parties, and these are linked with social divisions based on castes and sub-castes and classes, and religious or ethnic groupings.

Politicisation of castes and other social entities has led to social mobilisation in elections. The numerically preponderant caste groups have often been able to acquire positions of power by forging unity at the time of elections. The principal peasant castes in various states have been very effective in elections despite their social and educational backwardness to the upper castes. At times, the traditionally entrenched castes are at the receiving end in the game of power politics.

The Indian voter has reacted very strongly on crucial issues connected with elections. The elections of 1967, 1971, 1977, 1980, and 1984 for Lok Sabha are noteworthy in this context. In the 1967 elections, the Congress Party lost in more than half of the states. In the 1971 elections, which were held after the formation of Bangladesh, the Congress came to power with an overwhelming majority. The Congress again lost badly in the 1977 elections, which were hold after lifting of the national emergency. Emergency was imposed in June 1975. Since the Janata Party failed to deliver the goods, which had come to power in 1977, the Congress came out as the victorious party in the 1980 elections. The elections of 1984 were held after the assassination of Prime Minister Indira Gandhi. The electorate disapproved of strongly such a crime and elected the Congress Party to power, breaking all earlier records of victory with more than three-fourth strength in Lok Sabha. The Lok Sabha elections of November 1989 and June 1991 were significantly different from all the earlier elections. Both the times the Congress emerged as the single largest party. In 1989, the Congress decided not to form the government. The Janata Dal formed the government with the support of the left parties, the Bhartiya Janata Party and some other smaller parties. The 1991 elections witnessed a large-scale violence in some parts of the country. Rajiv Gandhi, the President of the Congress Party and the former Prime Minister of India, was assassinated while proceeding to address an election meeting at Sriperumbudur in Tamil Nadu on May 21, 1991. The Congress Party, though not enjoying an absolute majority in the Lok Sabha, formed the government. The 1996 elections for Lok Sabha resulted into a hung parliament. The National Democratic Alliance (NDA) comprising of nearly two dozen political parties with the BJP in the driving seat formed the government. In the elections held in 2004, the Congress emerged as the single largest party. The Congress formed the government under the banner of the United Progressive Alliance (UPA), a formation of several political parties like the NDA. This brief survey speaks of the prudence of the Indian electorate and the success of democracy in India.

Analysis

The sources of change are both internal and external. Change takes place both at micro as well as macro levels. The internal factors are legislations, reform movements and education. Contradictions within the existing system also bring about change. The external factors include cultural contact, attack by foreign powers, transfer of scientific and technological devices from other countries, international trade and commerce, etc. Macro changes would include legislation, innovation, etc., whereas new roles, migration, etc., are contextual or micro changes. Change in one sphere affects other spheres of social life. Therefore, it is necessary to take an integrated view which can account for various sources as well as factors of social change.

To discern social change we have to look at village life, caste, family, urban life, and socio-cultural norms and values. Jajmani is no more a system of functional interdependence between different caste groups.

Elections have created politicisation and factionalism among the villagers. Village life has changed a great deal due to the impact of wider economy and polity. Today, caste is not simply confined to norms of commensal relations or rules of marriage and interaction based on pollution and purity. Caste has become an interest group and an instrument of social and cultural mobility.

To a large extent family in India is not structurally joint but it continues to be joint functionally. Industrialisation, urbanisation and modern education have strengthened functional jointness because people have more resources and find it easy to help each other on important social occasions and in crisis situations. All the members of a family cannot live together as they do not work at the same place, hence family ceases to be structurally joint.

Urban population increased by 11 per cent from 1951 to 2001. The pace of urbanisation has fastened in the past two and half decades. Now, nearly 30 per cent people live in towns and cities. Cities and towns have become centres of higher education and learning attracting more young people from villages, initially for education and subsequently for seeking white-collar jobs.

Other factors causing the exodus from villages are poverty, unemployment and lack of proper health care. Since towns and cities have monopolised economic resources and medical facilities, there is overburdening of cities due to migration from villages. The numbers of the middle classes, particularly the salaries groups, have shown a phenomenal rise in the post-independence period. Nearly 30 million people belong to India's middle classes.

Traditional values and norms have certainly been loosening their hold due to these changes. Notions of pollution purity and untouchability today do not pervade equally into all aspects of our social life. These norms are observed loosely on some occasions. However, rules regarding marriage, particularly hypergamy, caste endogamy and clan exogamy are observed to a large extent.

Thus, social change in India is really a complex phenomenon as it has varied forms and manifestations. Scarlett Epstein's (1962) comparative study of two villages (one dry and other irrigated) in Karnataka reports that economic development does not necessarily result in social change, hence it may not necessarily lead to economic development. The irrigated village had more economic development and less social change. The unirrigated village had more of social change and less of economic development. The former did not witness much migration, education, politicisation and diversification, whereas the latter had a lot of diversification, differentiation, migration, education and politicisation because the people had to move out of the village to seek employment. The irrigated village provided economic security to the people, hence not much social change occurred there. However, this does not imply that economic development and social change are independent of each other. This study simply explains the complexity of social change in India.

Conclusion

Social change in India can be explained in terms of co-existence of tradition and modernity and continuity and change. Factors of social change are demographic, technological, economic, cultural, legal and political. The problem of overpopulation has hindered economic development. Industrialisation has suffered from lack of proper direction because of the harm done to industrial growth by the British Raj. Cultural changes are faster than economic changes. The two have been at times independent of each other. Law and judiciary have played a significant role in providing protection to the weaker sections of society and in delegitimising the traditionally privileged groups who enjoyed economic and political power. The traditionally underprivileged people have moved up since independence.

Exercises

1. Bring out the relationship between overpopulation and underdevelopment.
2. Explain the main reasons for India's slow pace of industrialisation.
3. Discuss the relationship between economic development and social changes. Substantiate your answer by drawing facts from some empirical studies.
4. Tradition and modernity co-exist in India. Explain.
5. Analyse the role of tradition in social change.
6. "Law is an agent of social change". Explain this statement with suitable examples.
7. Write notes on the following:
   (i) Politicisation
   (ii) External and internal factors of social change
   (iii) The state and social change

Select References

Bailey, F.G., *Caste and the Economic Frontier*, Manchester: Manchester University Press, 1957.

Bettelheim, Charles, *India Independent*, London: MacGibbon and Kee Ltd., 1968.

Marx, Karl, *Capital*, Vol. I., London: Lawrence and Wishart, 1970.

Myrdal, Gunnar, *Asian Drama: An Inquiry into the Poverty of Nations*, Vol. I, Penguin Books, 1968.

Ogburn, W.F., 1964, *Social Change*, New York: Viking.

Scorlett, T. Epstein, 1962, *Economic Development and Social Change in South India*, Manchester: Manchester University Press.

Sharma, K.L., *The Changing Rural Stratifications System*, New Delhi: Orient Longman, 1974.

Singer, Milton, 1972, *When a Great Tradition Modernises*.

Singh, Yogendra, *Modernization of Indian Tradition*, New Delhi: Thomson Press (India) Ltd., 1973.

—, "Legal System, Legitimation and Social Change", in S.D. Pillai (ed.), *Aspects of Changing India*, Bombay: Popular Prakashan, 1976.

—, Essays on Modernization in India, Delhi: Manohar, 1978.

—, "Law and Social Change in India: A Sociological Perspective", in J.S. Gandhi (ed.), *Law and Social Change*, Jaipur: Rawat Publications, 1989.

Srinivas, M.N., *Social Change in Modern India*, Berkeley: California University Press, 1966.

Veblen, Thorstein, *The Theory of the Leisure Class*, New York: Penguin Books, 1994.

Weber, Max, *The Protestant Ethic and the Spirit of Capitalism*, New York: Scribner's, 1958.

19 National Integration

National integration is dependent upon structural, cultural and ideological congruity and harmony among different sections of Indian society. The values and norms stated in the Constitution of India through proclamations about democracy, secularism and socialism provide basis for national integration. Equality demands equal opportunity for all sections of society and more so for the depressed groups of people. Absence of discrimination based on ascriptive criteria such as caste, parentage and heritage, and normative considerations like pollution-purity, are the cultural prerequisites of national integration. Ideological differences are natural in Indian society because of its structural and cultural complexities, but a certain level of consensus about 'national goals' is also basic for keeping people together as a nation.

There are some positive attributes of national integration. Besides fostering a sense of emotional oneness, national integration provides strength to the people to fight against evil forces. Socio-cultural and economic disparities and inequalities tend to reduce in a situation of national unity and solidarity. Fissiparous and divisive forces become inactive when national unity is intense and comprehensive. National integration is a positive notion, and therefore, can accelerate the pace of development and social change. In this chapter, we will discuss the concept of national integration, and communalism, nationalism, regionalism, political consolidation and minorities in relation to national integration. An analysis of the 'official view' of national integration and the hurdles in its realisation shows that the 'identity crisis' is the main obstacle in national integration. Structural inequalities tend to create an identity crisis among minorities. Besides cultural and ideological integration, structural integration is needed equally or even more.

Definition of National Integration

India is characterised by a plurality of people divided on the basis of religion, region, language, caste and class. It has a hierarchical social order comprising groups and individuals with unequal status. Consequent upon the multiplicity of status groups with differential access to resources and opportunities for employment and education, we find a multitude of problems. The Constitution of India makes a reference to the 'integrity' of the nation. But, the question is: Can national integration be fostered without removing or minimising socio-cultural and economic inequalities? We know that no perfect egalitarian social order can be achieved, as no absolutely homogeneous people can be found in reality. However, despite differences among people, a certain level of unity, harmony and cohesion among different sections of society can be achieved by ensuring certain minimum institutional mechanisms and infrastructural facilities for the less advantaged and the weaker sections. But this does not mean that national disintegration is the only cause of economic inequalities and disparities. The problem of national integration is also found among the societies which have less economic disparities.

Thus, national integration is a composite concept. It has several dimensions, namely, social, cultural, economic, political and religious. It also depends upon the contextual standing of a particular group in the national, regional or local setting. The problem of the integration of Muslims is different from that of other minorities in India, because they are the largest minority group. Pakistan was formed because of the 'communal award' granted by the British. The Muslims are generally poor and 'backward' compared to the Hindus.

What is national integration? Is it desirable to have national integration by advocating 'common values' which do not bring about egalitarian relations? An extreme view is that integration can be maintained by keeping society static. Thus, lack of change or conflict can also be viewed as a state of integration. However, stagnation, immobility or a lack of change and conflict are not indicative of integration. They are, on the other hand, symptomatic of disintegration. Development, change and mobility go along with integration. What is achieved by having integration is more important than keeping society regimented or static.

Our view is that integration should be considered as a positive concept. The state should function as an agency for carrying out programme of socio-economic change to harmonise relations between different antagonistic or hostile groups. Obviously, national integration cannot be achieved simply by spreading the ideology of religious co-existence and harmony. However, it is also a fact that when people belonging to various religions live in the same society, they are bound to have some problems even if they have economic parity to a large extent. In a tribal society where economic inequalities are not pronounced, religion and magical practices work as the unifying forces. Religion plays an integrative role, but it has to be seen also in terms of an overall phenomenon in a nation-state.

Communalism, Nationalism and National Integration

Apparently, communalism and national integration do not co-exist. The policy of communal award, which we have discussed earlier in Chapter 4, was introduced by the British to divide Muslims and Hindus so that they remained a divided house against the Raj. The British instigated the Muslims to make a demand for a separate state for Muslims. The Raj was able to create cleavages between the two communities by exaggerating linguistic, regional, cultural and historical differences. Alienation and hostility between Hindus and Muslims were created by the British rulers.

To begin with, the British did not treat the Muslims at par with the Hindus, and subsequently the Raj made the Muslims aware of their econcmic backwardness and the ascendancy of the Hindus in various fields. British education also touched only a small minority of the Muslims. Thus, the British rule sowed the seeds of the unequal development of the two communities, hence disintegration. Communal representation in legislatures under various legal reforms further strengthened alienation of the Muslims from the Hindus and increased hostility.

We have, in an earlier chapter, mentioned about the formation of the Muslim League in 1906, and the Lucknow Pact in 1916, which accentuated communal disharmony. The formation of Pakistan in 1947, under the leadership of Mohammad Ali Jinnah, after large-scale communal bloodshed, was not the end of the communal problem. Even after 1947, Hindus and Muslims in India have been at loggerheads from time to time even on the slightest provocation from either side. Ahmedabad, Bhiwandi, Ranchi, Aligarh, Meerut, Surat and several other towns have witnessed situations of communal disharmony in the recent years. Entire Gujarat was engulfed in communal violence after the Godhara incidence in 2002. In the aftermath of assassination of Indira Gandhi in 1984, riots against Sikhs were a worst black spot in post-independent India.

One obvious implication of the term 'national integration' is that people belonging to a society share ideas and aspirations, emotional bonds and values. In the context of the newly independent nations, Gunnar Myrdal (1968) writes: "People must have a conception of the nation as a whole and attach positive valuations to this idea *(nationalism)* before they can feel that national independence and national consolidation are goals worth striving for and that all the other 'modernization ideals' can only be realised in the setting of an independent and consolidated nation-state". Thus, for Myrdal, national integration is the equivalent of nationalism, that is, a feeling of nation against colonialism, and after achieving independence a feeling against communalism, linguism, regionalism and other disintegrative forces.

Myrdal looks at national integration basically as a political phenomenon, but he relates it to planning for development and realisation of the 'modernization ideals' (change for betterment of India). He writes: "Nationalism, therefore, is commonly seen as a force for good by all those in the intellectual elite who are bent on planning policies aimed at development. To them, fostering nationalism will provide the means of breaking down inhibitions and obstacles."

Regionalism versus Nationalism

Is national integration in India a means for achieving desired goals of social change? Is it found with same intensity among the elite and the educated on the one hand, and the masses and the illiterate on the other? Can there be the same level and extent of national cohesiveness and integration among different strata of Indian society? Is religious tolerance the most effective mechanism of emotional unity among the people of India? Does political integration precede national or economic integration?

It is not easy to find satisfactory answers to these questions. However, an attempt may be made by giving an account of the problems of disintegration and processes of integration since independence. Immediately after independence in 1947, India's major problem was of consolidating and strengthening the state against the vestiges of colonialism, feudalism and social and cultural orthodoxy, which dominated the social situation. The problem was of making the state stable and effective after it had witnessed disorder and bloodshed. All this was to be done through democratic means in the new situation. National integration demands unity, and condemns all internal, spatial, religious and caste and creed loyalties, and parochial considerations. To achieve economic development, considerations of this sort must not find any place in Indian society.

The Nadars in Tamil Nadu agitated against the privileged Brahmanas. This had both communal and economic dimensions, but it had a positive approach, hence no disintegration was involved. South Indians demonstrate against North Indians or vice versa because of assumed cultural divide. When the Hindi protagonists agitate against the use of English and other languages or when the Tamilians demonstrate against the use of Hindi, we certainly witness the passions of communalism and a threat to the nation.

Several insurgency movements have taken place in India. Boundary disputes between different states have lent strength to regional forces. Many states have demanded autonomy in regard to 'subjects', which if taken out of the purview of the central government could perhaps endanger national unity and harmony. Loyalties of caste, religion and language dominate in elections in India, and to that extent undermine both democracy and national integration.

The problem of national integration in India refers to the fact that different states, people, castes and communities with varied backgrounds are made to work together with some common emotional bond and frame of reference. This creates a situation of uneasiness among the interacting partners. It is a stupendous task because India has a long history of continuity of its specific traditions, religious and cultural attitudes and encapsulated ideas and values. Differences between different areas, ethnic and caste groups, occupational groups and people of different generations have been permeated as reality of our social life.

The question is: Can national integration be achieved through rationalism, planning and coordination of national policies for development? Can the emotions of the people be geared towards these values? There is no denial of the fact that national unity and consolidation have been aimed at the country's progress in social and economic spheres right from 1947. The constitutional provisions for harmony and amity, establishment of the Planning Commission, the National Development Council or even the National Integration Council and such other bodies are evidence of the desire for achieving national unity and harmony.

Political Consolidation and National Integration

Political consolidation was considered as a positive step towards economic development and national integration. The government initiated various measures, including the enactment of welfare legislations. The practice of untouchability was made an offence. Landlordism was abolished in most of the states by 1960. The weaker sections were granted special provisions for their upliftment under the Constitution of India. The privy purses of the princes were taken away in 1969. The minority communities were protected against excesses.

Thus, national integration was understood not simply in terms of avoidance or resolution of conflict, but it was thought of as a process of development and egalitarianism. The first few years after independence were a period of national consolidation and unification. Both political and socio-economic measures were taken to neutralise cleavages among different sections. Territorial reorganisation of states on the basis of language, as recommended by the States Reorganisation Commission in 1955, was one such political move, though it did not satisfy many groups and communities.

The adivasis of the Chhotanagpur and the Santhal Parganas in Bihar and of the adjoining areas of West Bengal, Orissa and Madhya Pradesh demanded the formation of a separate state of Jharkhand. They were denied this as they did not form a linguistic entity like other states as suggested by the Commission. However, ultimately, Jharkhand was separated from Bihar as a new state. The same was done in Madhya Pradesh by creating Chhatisgarh as a new state. Agitation in Andhra Pradesh for the formation of a separate Telangana state continued for several years. In the Lok Sabha elections of 2003, the Congress Party had assured the people that it would work towards the creation of Telangana as a separate state. Punjab was divided into the present Punjab and Haryana in 1966. The old Bombay state was divided into the states of Maharashtra and Gujarat in 1960. Thus, national integration was attempted in the early years through the constitutional, territorial and developmental frameworks.

Regionalism and linguism have emerged in a pronounced form as national problems in post-independent India. Caste and community-based segmentation is a perennial phenomenon in Indian society. Both undermine democratic processes of change and development. Elections have been vitiated by considerations of caste and religion. The old and the new values have come into conflict with each other. The old are so strong that the new are unable to replace it. The old forces have absorbed the new ones, and hence prevented their full and fair play in the post-independent India. Secularism has not been successful as a process of change to overcome the forces of tradition.

Political consolidation is only a strategy for striving at national integration. National integration is more than political consolidation. It is a state of accommodation among different groups – ethnic, caste, linguistic, etc. It is a state of affairs in which the 'communal identity' goes along with the 'national identity'. Pluralism with cohesiveness is certainly an indication of national integration. Political consolidation was a strategy in the early years after 1947, and now economic development and distributive justice are mechanisms of ensuring harmony among various socio-cultural and economic groups in India.

The problems of the minorities, the SCs, the STs, the OBCs, the poor, the unemployed youth, women and rural people are all linked with national integration. Various sections of Indian society have agitated from time to time to seek solutions to their problems, and have, at times, threatened unity and integrity of India.

Minorities and National Integration

National integration in India is generally seen in terms of the problems and aspirations of the minority groups. What do we mean by the word 'minority'? There is no an agreed definition of the phenomenon of minority. The Hindus are a 'majority' in India, as they constitute 82.72 per cent of the total population. Though, in certain states, the Hindus are numerically less than other communities, but they are not treated as a 'minority'. Muslims, Sikhs and

Christians are majority communities in the states of Jammu & Kashmir, Punjab and Nagaland, respectively. The SCs are enumerated as Hindus, but do not share the Hindu identity in a real sense of the term.

Since Hindu society is highly stratified and fragmented, it is difficult to designate precisely a caste or community as a 'majority' or a 'minority'. The Parsis and the Jains are very small minorities, but they enjoy certain economic and social privileges which even caste Hindus, the SCs and the STs, and the Muslims do not. Thus, "minority" in a true sense cannot simply be defined in terms of numbers. Further, different communities are differentiated socially, politically and economically. It is these differences which are the cause of conflict and violence in the village community. A dalit or a Muslim is oppressed not because of his community affiliation alone, but also because he is at the bottom of the social, political and economic hierarchies.

The pluralist perspective on national integration has emanated from both the West and India. There are scarce resources, and people compete for gaining access to these resources. In this process of competition, we encounter resistance, acrimony, conflict, etc. Groups are formed on the basis of their religious, linguistic and regional identities, and the people belonging to particular primordial groups exploit their ties to get maximum share of the scarce resources of society.

Such a situation also poses the problem of dichotomy between 'tradition' and 'modernity'. Tradition, however, tends to traditionalise the modern forces by absorption and resilience. Modernity is absorbed in the structure of the tradition, but such an assimilation does not really lead to integration of the old and the new. This does not result in a process of distributive justice or egalitarianism. It may ultimately lead to a social formation with more concentration of economic, social and political power in the hands of the traditional elite. Castes have become interest groups, factions, and at times mechanisms of social and political mobilisation. However, the benefit of all this goes to dominant individuals and families of specific castes.

The Central government has constituted commissions for the SCs and STs and the OBCs with a view to ensure their upliftment and welfare. There was no commission or committee to look into the largest minority community, namely, Muslims, to have a thorough understanding of their problems and possible solutions for their progress and well-being. The Manmohan Singh government appointed a committee in March 2005 under the Chairmanship of Rajinder Sachar, a retired Chief Justice of the Delhi High Court. The committee submitted its report of the Prime Minister Manmohan Singh on November 17, 2006. Though non 'reservation' has been recommended by the committee as it is in the case of SCs, STs and OBCs, however, recommendations have been made for devising appropriate programmes to address backwardness among Muslims. As per the committee's view, "Muslims are relatively poor, more illiterate, with lower access to education, lower representation in public and private sector jobs, and lower access to bank credit for self-employment" than other religious communities (*Hindustan Times*, 18 November 2006). In urban areas, most Muslims live in slums. Muslims need equal opportunity to get rid of their social and educational backwardness. According to the *Times of India* of 18 November 2006, the Sachar Committee recommends setting up of Equal Opportunities Commission, promotion of Urdu language, increase in UGC grants to community-run colleges and schools, training of teachers, reform of *madrassas* and their affiliation to higher education boards in states, increased flow of credit, bringing all districts where Muslims are over 25 per cent of the population under the purview of the 15 point programme for minorities (as suggested in the report), and enhanced participation of Muslims in governance.

Certainly, the report of the Sachar Committee would embolden the Muslim Community in general, and the 'underdog' from amongst them in particular. In due course of time the Muslim community may demand 'reservation' on the pattern of SCs, STs and OBCs. Many political parties have appreciated the report, however, the Bhartiya Janata Party (BJP) considers the report as "a launching pad for religion-based reservations" in the country. But, the fact remains that Muslims in India are far behind than Hindus and other communities in social and educational domains. No society or state can remain immune for a long time towards the pathos of a large community such as Muslims in India.

The Official View

The official or the governmental view of national integration is that religion can bring about harmony and unity. Religion can foster 'common values' by 'tension-management' and by operating as a mechanism of social control. Means of mass communication like the press, radio, films and television can be used to promote national integration through the propagation of religious tolerance and harmony. Emphasis on moral education is being given in schools to inculcate moral and spiritual values among children.

The question is: Can religion solve the problems of national integration or does it aggravate national disintegration? Is it possible to use religion for national integration in a country like India where people of different religions, faiths and denominations live together? A particular religion can be a vehicle of fostering brotherhood among its believers. But, in a situation of multiple religions, it is not easy to formulate common values for people of all religions. Further, people having faith in the same religion are divided on the basis of caste, kinship and economic gradations. It is difficult to make people follow a uniform pattern of religiosity when they are unevenly placed in their own society. It is difficult to foster common values among people belonging to different religions.

The processes of change such as Hinduisation by tribal groups, sanskritisation by lower caste groups, and westernisation by the upper and upper middle castes make it further difficult to acknowledge religion as an effective integrative mechanism. Conversion to Christianity and Islam and neo-Buddhist movement, the movement for the formation of Khalistan and other regionalistic movements do not allow emergence of a common ideology acceptable to all the religions and faiths in India.

In a multi-religious, multi-caste and multi-lingual society like India, the philosophy of 'pluralism' and co-existence is basic to national integration because the majority community's religion or way of life tends to overshadow other religions. In a plural society, hierarchisation based on religion, ethnicity or language would promote disintegration. What we need is an inculcation of the value of tolerance, equity and national patriotism and is possible when the state does not explicitly or implicitly promote one religion or group at the cost of another.

Hurdles to National Integration

The problem of national integration has its roots partly in the partition of India in 1947, and partly in the identity crisis being faced by some communities. A number of communities have aspirations to find a place of honour and equal status vis-a-vis other communities. A feeling of smallness, inferiority and repression creeps into the minds of members of such communities. Their relatively poor economic condition and backwardness reinforces the feeling of being 'second grade' citizens. On the other hand, some communities may have a feeling of being powerful and dominant on several counts, namely, numerical strength, economic standing, education, political power, etc. Because of such notions, communal feelings flare up on the slightest issues that a Hindu has hurt the feelings of Muslims, or a Muslim has hurt the sentiments of the Hindus. Communal incidents occur due to such illusory notions of community sentiments.

There are some structural factors which have threatened national unity. The very diversity impairs national unity. Linguistic diversity in terms of national and regional languages and dialects divide the country into areas, sub-areas and sub-sub-areas. Hostility to English is expressed by some political and cultural groups because it is an alien language and symbolises the continuity of imperialism and colonialism, and because it has become a means of securing lucrative jobs and high positions for a selected few. Hindi is opposed in South India because it is a language of the North Indian people. The apparent fear is that accepting Hindi as a national language would amount to suppression of the Dravidian and other languages. This may also mean acceptance of the cultural hegemony of the Hindi-speaking North Indians in the country.

According to the 1961 census, there are 574 Indo-Aryan, 153 Dravidian, 65 Austroasiatic, and 226 Tibeto-Chinese languages in India. Language became a very sensitive issue in the 1950s because it was made basis of the reorganisation of states in India. It remains a sensitive issue because it is a medium of instruction, a source of identity, and a means of expressing one's ideas.

Various regional political groups and parties, like the Akali Dal, the Telugu Desam, the DMK, and the advocacy of Shiv Sena have demanded regional autonomy. The demand for autonomy has been reflected in the supremacy of regional cultures over the national culture. Demands for formation of new states on the basis of such cultural and ethnic identities have come up from time to time.

The issue of minorities is also very important in the context of national integration. We have stated earlier that it is difficult to arrive at an agreed definition of the term 'minorities'. The Marwaris in Assam, Bengal and Bihar are a minority, but they control trade and business in these states. They are treated as 'outsiders' and 'exploiters' in these areas by the local people. "Sons of the Soil" movements have been reported in Assam, West Bengal, Orissa and Karnataka. A couple of years ago, Marwaris were killed and looted in Bolangir, a district of Orissa, by the protagonists of the "Sons of the Soil" movement. One of the serious implications of such a movement is that people cannot move freely from one state to another.

The crux of the problem of minorities is to identify minorities not only in terms of numbers and ethnic background, but also on the basis of the actual socio-economic position of the people and their political and cultural aspirations. After identifying groups and individuals belonging to minorities based on these criteria, the principle of distributive justice needs to be implemented to reduce inequalities and discriminations.

Conclusion

The problem of national integration is very complex. The concept of national integration is a composite one. Political integration is only one facet of the problem. Underlying this is a need for economic, social and cultural integration. There is an urgent need to tackle the problem of ethnic groups and minorities. We have suggested a need for redefining the concept of minorities with a view to ensure better understanding and implementation of the principle of distributive justice.

Exercises

1. Explain the concept of national integration.
2. What are the minimum prerequisites for national integration?
3. Is national integration a composite concept?
4. Analyse the nature of communalism in India. How far are economic inequalities the root cause of this malady?
5. In what way is national integration different from nationalism?
6. Bring out the correlation between national integration, development and social change.
7. Why has 'regionalism' sprung up in India in recent years?
8. What is political consolidation? How is it different from national integration?
9. Write an essay on the problem of minorities in India.
10. Do you think that the problem of national integration persists of minorities have not been solved to their satisfaction?

Select References

Desai, A.R., *Social Background of Indian Nationalism*, Bombay, Popular Book Depot, 1959.

—, "National Integration and Religion", *Sociological Bulletin*, Vol. XII, No. 1, 1963.

Doshi, S.L., "A Sociological Analysis of Political Unification among the. Scheduled Tribes of Rajasthan", *Sociological Bulletin*, Vol. 27, No. 2, 1978.

Myrdal, Gunnar, *Asian Drama*, Vol. I, Penguin Books, 1968.

Shakir, Moin, "On National Integration", *Social Scientist*, 107, April 1982.

Index